The Latino Question

The Latino Question

Politics, Labouring Classes and the Next Left

Armando Ibarra, Alfredo Carlos
and Rodolfo D. Torres

Foreword by
Christine Neumann-Ortiz

First published 2018 by Pluto Press
345 Archway Road, London N6 5AA

www.plutobooks.com

British Library Cataloguing in Publication Data
A catalogue record for this book is available from the British Library

ISBN   978 0 7453 3525 4   Hardback
ISBN   978 0 7453 3524 7   Paperback
ISBN   978 1 7868 0038 1   PDF eBook
ISBN   978 1 7868 0040 4   Kindle eBook
ISBN   978 1 7868 0039 8   EPUB eBook

This book is printed on paper suitable for recycling and made from fully
managed and sustained forest sources. Logging, pulping and manufacturing
processes are expected to conform to the environmental standards of the
country of origin.

Typeset by Stanford DTP Services, Northampton, England

Simultaneously printed in the United Kingdom and United States of America

Contents

List of Figures and Tables

FIGURES

TABLES

Acknowledgments

We have many people to thank, and we want to acknowledge them and hope that those we have overlooked will forgive us.

First and foremost, we would like to thank our families for all their sacrifices, inspiration, support, and wisdom that set the foundation for the accomplishment of this labor. *Muchísimas gracias*. Each of you has had a fundamental role in shaping our thoughts and scholarship.

We are humbled and grateful to the study participants who shared with us personal and familial worker narratives. Their testimonials illuminate a reawakening of working-class consciousness that forms the essence of this work. We simply would not have been able to speak on the Latino question in the way we envisioned without their collective knowledge.

We wish to express our sincere appreciation to Victor Valle for allowing portions of original chapters written with Rodolfo D. Torres to be included in this book. *Gracias, camarada* Victor, your work and thoughts are woven into and rearticulated in chapters 6 and 7.

Several of our colleagues deserve particular mention. We have learned much from our conversations with Gilbert G. González, Eddie Bonilla, Antonia Darder, Rudy Acuña, Romina Robles Ruvalcaba, Mario Barrera, Carolina Sarmiento, Revel Sims, David Nack, Michael Childers, Rosalba Laredo Jiménez, Raul A. Fernandez, Karma Chávez, Ralph Armbruster-Sandoval, Erin Evans, Aaron Roussell, Analicia Mejia, Benjamin Marquez, Zaragosa Vargas, Mariana Pacheco, Ramon Ortiz, Frank D. Bean, Susan Brown and Daniel Malacara.

We would like to thank our university departments. These are the places and spaces where we exchange our intellectual labor for wages that connect us to the broader laboring classes. They are the School for Workers at the University of Wisconsin-Extension, the Chican@ and Latin@ Studies program at the University of Wisconsin at Madison, the Department of Political Science and the Department of Chicano and Latino Studies at California State University at Long Beach, and the Department of Urban Planning and Public Policy and Department of Chicano/Latino Studies at the University of California at Irvine, where this project has its intellectual roots and where the three authors met and were inspired and provoked to produce this volume.

We would like to recognize and thank all the rank-and-file social justice movement participants, such as Christine Neumann-Ortiz, Mario Garcia Sierra, Jesus Salas, Robert Nothoff, Biviana Lagunas, Petra Guerra, Jorge Rodriguez, Esmeralda Rodriguez, and Mario Ramirez, who are on the front lines organizing, leading, and participating in collective actions at the intersection of working-class movements. You carry on your shoulders the heavy generational weight of class struggle that aims to change our society into one that dignifies and respects the working class by achieving economic democracy.

We received enthusiastic and unwavering support from the University of Wisconsin's School for Workers. We wish to express our utmost respect for the School, which for more than ninety years has carried out its mission 'to empower working people and labor organizations at the job site, in the national economy, and in the global economic system through a comprehensive program of lifelong adult learning opportunities.'*

We are very grateful to David Shulman, commissioning editor at Pluto Press, for his openness to our ideas, patience, and support, and also at Pluto, design manager and head of marketing Melanie Patrick. We are also grateful to Sarah Grey, a radical thinker and professional copyeditor who helped us find our collective voice.

We offer our deepest respect for working-class people laboring in the United States and abroad. Your pride, sincerity, hard work, and perseverance in the face of adversity are exemplary and are an inspiration to all Americans.

Finally, Ibarra and Carlos hold a deep respect and appreciation for Torres for keeping true to his scholarship, fostering intellectual spaces for heterodox political economy, and mentoring generations of scholars and activists.

Para mi compañera y querida esposa, Veronica D. Ibarra, mis hijos, Sofia Magdalena, Amalia Blanca, y Armando Diego, mis padres, Maria de los Angeles y Armando Ibarra, que con cariño y ejemplo me enseñaron las

* School for Workers, University of Wisconsin, 'Education for Workplace Democracy', n.d., https://schoolforworkers.uwex.edu/about-us/mission.

virtudes que forman mi persona: Trabajo, Conciencia de Clase, Amor, Dignidad, Respeto, Derecho y Valor Civil.

Armando Ibarra Salazar

Para mi Hija, my little June bug Amelie Carlos-Martinez, your smile gives me strength and purpose, mis padres Eva Carlos Marquez y Alfredo Carlos Ramirez, gracias por todos sus sacrificios y enseñansas y mas que nada su apoyo y amor, mis hermanas y familia: Lourdes Carlos, Gabriela Carlos, Veronica Carlos. Tia Belen, you are deeply missed, thank you for helping to raise me, may you rest in power. Y para todos los que se esforzaron para que yo me adelantara con valores de justicia, respeto y dignidad.

Alfredo Carlos

To my son Jacob and my wife, Patricia Speier-Torres, I thank you for your love and support. Dedicó este libro a Jacob David Torres y su generación de activistas por la justicia social en esta era de creciente incertidumbre. I would also like to personally thank Richard Martinez, Deyanira Nevarez Martinez, and their two lovely sons for providing a source of distraction from the pettiness of academic life.

Rodolfo D. Torres

Foreword

Christine Neumann-Ortiz

Executive Director of Voces de la Frontera

It is my honour to be invited to write this foreword to *The Latino Question: Politics, Labouring Classes and the Next Left* which centres the discussion of the meaning, impact and future of Latinx* organizing in the context of US and global labour movement history.

This, in and of itself, is an important contribution because the Latinx rights movement in the United States is often perceived solely as a civil rights struggle, limited by national borders and policy solutions. This historical perspective obscures the role of US imperialism in Latin America and elsewhere in contributing to forced migration and race and class relations in the United States. As someone who has the privilege to be part of the contemporary Latinx and immigrant rights struggle, I appreciate the authors' nuanced understanding of the social struggle as inherently confronting not just a political system, but the economic system that underpins it.

As an organiser I have personally witnessed the impact of Latinx organising over the past two decades. This is most apparent in the historic statewide general strikes in Wisconsin and nationally known as 'A Day Without Latinxs and Immigrants'. In Wisconsin it has been a critical arsenal in our fight to successfully defeat aggressive efforts by anti-immigrant forces to pass laws that criminalise immigrant workers, legalise racial profiling and break up families. These historic actions have at times been ignored, overlooked or characterised as mass 'protests' and 'rallies' without acknowledging the sacrifices and economic power of workers striving to achieve our collective demands. While Voces de la Frontera has indeed organised some of the largest marches in the state's history on May Day since 2006, the 'Day Without Latinxs and Immigrants' is a unique call to action that is understood to mean 'no school, no work, no purchases' and only used at critical moments in our struggle.

* See Introduction, note 4.

At a time when there is an emboldening of the far right under the Trump administration and unprecedented income inequality, there is a practical need to treat class not as just one more 'ism' but as central to unifying collective action among workers of different racial and ethnic backgrounds to beat back the forces of hate and achieve significant breakthroughs. This analysis, put forward by the authors, has informed Voces de la Frontera's strategies to secure important political and electoral victories despite facing sometimes seemingly insurmountable political barriers in the most gerrymandered state in the nation.

Indeed, the modern immigrant rights movement was born in 2006 with a national strike against Jim Sensenbrenner's HR 4437 that would have turned immigrants into aggravated felons and criminalised anyone who knew of someone's status and did not turn them over for deportation. Through an emerging national network of immigrant rights organisations, a call to action was made for a general strike to stop this draconian bill from being signed into law. In March 2006, Milwaukee was the third city after Washington DC and Chicago to turn out in a general strike involving tens of thousands that then continued to cascade in large and small cities throughout the country for weeks, involving millions of workers.

In the wake of the strikes, the HR 4437 bill was defeated, and the national conversation shifted from mass deportation and criminalisation to the need for national immigration reform with a path to citizenship. I have often commented that US citizens owe a debt of gratitude to the immigrant workers who risked their livelihoods in beating back this law not just for themselves, but protecting civil liberties and constitutional rights for US citizens who would have also been criminalised for not turning over friends or family to immigration authorities and outlawed our own organisation.

The strategy of the general strike is a community-wide response, involving small business owners who close their shops, parents taking their kids out of school, students organising in their schools, and workers walking off their jobs across all industries. In the wake of the March 2006 national strike, Voces continued to use this strategy on 1 May 2006 and again on 1 May 2007 in Wisconsin to support demands for national immigration reform.

The most recent victories have been at the state and local level in 2016 and 2017 in Wisconsin, where tens of thousands of workers deployed the general strike strategy to organise yet another Day Without Latinxs

and Immigrants. This mobilisation defeated two state anti-sanctuary
bills, blocked 287g from being implemented in Milwaukee County and
contributed to the forced resignation of ex-Milwaukee County Sheriff
Clarke, a darling of the right wing.

Nationally, since 2006, there have been two national strikes led by
the Latinx and immigrant rights movement, the first in February 2017
that was spontaneously self-organised by workers and small business
owners through social media—inspired by Wisconsin's example in our
resistance to the 287g program—and later that year on 1 May 2017,
following a nationally coordinated effort led by Voces, Fair Immigration Reform Movement (FIRM) and the National Day Labor Organizing
Network (NDLON).

As Fabio Francisco Ortega, a dairy worker at the time of the 2016
Wisconsin strike, reflected, 'Immigrant workers know the importance
of their economic contribution as workers, it is just that up to that point
they did not have a way to express it because they needed organiza-
tional support.' This is particularly true in an industry that is so heavily
dependent on immigrant labour, as 80 percent of Wisconsin's milk is
produced by immigrants, largely undocumented. Yet these strikes have
had an impact across all industries—construction, service, manufacturing, tourism and others.

These strikes have not occurred in isolation but have simultaneously
organised strategic alliances unique to the struggle. In Milwaukee, the
strike strategy brought in the voices of those who had been victimised
by Sheriff Clarke, creating an alliance with the Black and Muslim communities to challenge the politics of surveillance, profiling and mass
incarceration. At the state level, our alliance has lifted the voices of
small- and medium-sized dairy farm owners who have similarly suffered
the consequences of free trade policies under the North American Free
Trade Agreement as small farmers from Mexico who migrated to the US
due to competition from large agribusiness.

As a worker centre, Voces has always understood that the immigrant
rights struggle is fundamentally a workers' struggle. The additional
barriers Latinx workers face due to discrimination or legal status or
perceived legal status only compounds that inequality. The struggle for a
living wage, access to affordable health coverage, the right to organise on
the job free of retaliation, all of these are as essential to Latinx workers
who are disproportionately part of the working poor and are of equal
necessity as immigration rights. Latinx immigrant workers are among

the most militant sections of the US labour movement. Their leadership is not generally recognised because it largely functions outside organised labour. Yet, they are increasingly exercising their power as workers.

The community-wide strike is unique as a labour struggle because at the heart of the immigrant rights movement are workers fighting for the right to work legally and not be threatened by the separation of their families. The power of the movement is that it is community-wide— workers, small business owners and their families in collective action, involving larger circles of participation including teachers, counsellors, unions, friends, and others. It mobilises immigrant workers at the point of production, leverages their economic power in pursuit of political objectives.

The role of immigrant youth in the campaign to win the Dream Act in the wake of Trump's repeal of Deferred Action for Childhood Arrivals (DACA) emerged from this labour struggle. Many youths remember marching as young children in the 2006 marches and the pride they felt in doing so. They represent the next generation of young workers fighting for their right to work legally, support their families and pursue their education. The struggle has had international reach through social media and news and links workers across borders through family ties.

The best history books are not just for academia but relevant to the most urgent issues confronting our society and generation. *The Latino Question: Politics, Labouring Classes and the Next Left* is a critical contribution to that conversation.

Introduction

I try to stay away from terms that rely on ethnicity. I use terms that represent what people do for a living—*occupation* is a more meaningful term.

—Ernesto Galarza, 1982[1]

This remarkable quotation locates two central overlapping themes we address in this book: to highlight the 'race and ethnic relations' problematic[2] and to assert the analytical utility of production and class relations as central to our explanatory task in the interrogation of Latino cultural political economy.[3] Our book articulates an alternative Latino politics (see endnote for a discussion of this label[4])—that is, a critique of political economy embedded in voices of Mexican American men and women and their children, their practices, and their actions.

Over the past five decades, Latinos in the United States have emerged as strategic actors in the processes of socioeconomic and spatial transformation. This so-called Latinisation of the United States comes at a time of increasing social polarisation and class inequalities with wide and deep divisions. These forces assert themselves economically, demographically, and politically, in schools, workplaces, and the everyday life of Latino/a populations. Yet, when we scratch the surface of urban centres like Los Angeles, San Francisco, Chicago, New York, and Atlanta—cities portrayed as having a rich mosaic of multinational cultures—a grittier truth emerges. Behind the huge, shimmering urban economy, we discover a hidden economic trap that limits the genuine social progress of poor, working-class, and the fragile first generation of middle-class Mexican Americans.

Considering this reality, *The Latino Question* offers a critical assessment of political and economic trends of Latino populations in the United States, as exemplified by the conditions faced by Mexican Americans, who constitute over 60 percent of the Latino population in this country. Moreover, weaving together categories of radical political economy devised by Karl Marx and Antonio F. Gramsci, along with poignant personal stories and vignettes of Latino workers, will speak to what Mike Davis so rightly calls 'magical urbanism' to refer to how Latinos are reinventing the US cultural political economy.[5] The book also seeks to show how Latino labouring classes (including the fragile middle class) struggle to go beyond the limits imposed on them by the logic of capitalism.

We also intend to demonstrate that the 'Latino question' can only be fully understood within the context of the US political economy and the new international division of labour. By deciphering both the historical and contemporary Latino question under capitalism, we can advance a more critical and long-term dialogue on concepts, agendas, and theoretical challenges in understanding Latino politics in the United States. Without question, the United States is the wealthiest country in the world, yet it is the nation-state with the greatest economic inequality between the rich and the poor, and with the most disproportionate wealth distribution of all the 'developed' nations of the world. To overlook this economic reality in the analysis of Latina/o populations is to ignore the most compelling social phenomenon in US society today: the increasing income gap between rich and poor.

BACKGROUND

The current Latino/a population is a result of the dynamics of the political economy of the contemporary neoliberal capitalist state.[6] Today, Latinos number nearly 57 million and comprise 17.3 percent of the total US population, up from 3.5 percent in 1960. If these trends continue, it is projected that, by 2060, the 'Hispanic' share of the US population will reach 28.6 percent and number approximately 120 million. Again, the demographic group that self-identifies as being of Mexican origin now holds the dubious distinction of being the largest 'ethnic' minority group in the United States[7]—leading to the so-called 'browning of America'.

California has the largest share of US Latinos. The *Los Angeles Times* reported that 'as of July 1, 2014, about 14.99 million Latinos live in California, edging out the 14.92 million whites', making it the first state in the nation to have a minority as a majority in its demographic composition.[8] This shift has caused the onset of one of the most dramatic cultural and demographic transformations in the state's recent history. Conflicts have intensified between social and economic justice movement organisations and the state, and those who directly and indirectly benefit from the status quo, as a direct result of this demographic shift. The issues at the epicentre of these conflicts are rooted in the age-old questions of 'American' identity, racialised working communities, class, citizenship, and inclusion.[9]

Anthropologist Leo R. Chávez describes this fixation on 'browning' as the perceived 'Latino Threat' narrative to the future of white America: 'Although race continues in importance, the crisis over citizenship in today's world has moved to a different register, one complicated by globalisation—a term that refers to how the world and its people are increasingly becoming integrated into one giant capitalist system'.[10]

While Chávez argues that the ideological roots of this perceived threat lie in the cultural and political processes of racialisation within the slippery soil of contemporary globalisation, which he describes as 'one giant capitalist system', we are considerably more explicit in our argument that this 'threat narrative' is a purposeful product of capitalism (production relations) that services capitalist class interests. This narrative is diffused through legal structures and culturally accepted norms of ethnic and racial discrimination and perpetuated by the neoliberal state through oppressive structures that employ different forms of violence. *The Latino Question* furthers this articulation by offering a thorough political economy critique of migration, power, and social relations that is informed by the academic literature on the subject and—as important—by workers' voices.

The 'browning' of California is not unique; this demographic trans-formation is occurring not only in the traditional Southwest, but also in the Midwest, South, and Northeast.[11] In fact, this shift, along with the conflict it has brought, is occurring across the country, in urban and rural areas whose local populations once believed they were immune to internal and international Latino migration and settlement.[12] States such as Wisconsin are now witnessing similar transformations as the Southwest did decades ago. In June 2014, a *Wisconsin Journal-Sentinel* headline proclaimed, 'Hispanics Now Make Up Wisconsin's Largest Minority Group,' signalling that Latinos had surpassed African Americans as the largest minority group in less than twenty years.[13]

Chapters 3 through 6 are informed by interviews with Latino/a workers and offers four case studies that use 'grounded theory'[14] to offer 'thick descriptions'[15] of the lives of this working-class subgroup within the current neoliberal capitalist context. Here we are informed by the work of Marxist political theorist Alex Callinicos, who has said, 'Any study of politics which detaches the apparatuses of state power from "real foundations" in the forces and relations of production' is analytically limited.[16]

One of our research sites is Wisconsin, where the bulk of 'browning' is rooted in Mexican labour migration and settlement patterns within the context of US foreign policy toward Mexico and other Latin American countries.[17] The contemporary Mexican pioneers follow employment trails to urban and rural areas, where they work in agriculture and the service and manufacturing industries. They have settled in cities like Milwaukee, Green Bay, and Racine and rural towns like Fond du Lac and Gibraltar, where they have established coethnic barrios that are becoming vibrant working-class communities that grow daily with new arrivals. It is a story not so different than that of the German, Polish, and Italian working-class labour migrants who faced similar racial and cultural barriers rooted in xenophobic attitudes and policies at the turn of the twentieth century. The societal challenges these workers faced were addressed—though not solved—by a militant working class rooted in social-movement unionism.[18]

Social scientists agree that this shift is being shaped by two demographic variables. The first is the steady flow of immigration from Latin America (primarily Mexican labour migrants and their families). The second is the high fertility rate within that community. Latinas have the highest fertility rates of all major ethnic and racial groups counted by the US Census. Between 2000 and 2010, 4.2 million immigrants came from Mexico to the United States, while an additional 7.2 million Mexican American babies were born in the country.[19] This is why demographers point out that even if immigration from Latin America were to cease today, a demographic shift would make Latinos the second-largest group in the United States by 2050.[20] That shift, we argue, is nothing more than capitalism replenishing the ranks of the working poor.

There is little doubt that the primer to this demographic shift is the economic restructuring that has occurred in the last century and has transformed the social and economic landscape. Newcomers, US-born Latinos, and Mexican Americans of several generations are closely intertwined with the very forces that are causing the ongoing economic restructuring and reshaping of once-familiar local, regional, national, and global socioeconomic arrangements. For nearly a century, these changes have created the conditions for mass labour migration and skyrocketing inequality, and this increase is not going away any time soon.[21]

More important than the sheer numbers is the fact that Latina/o families are a growing sector of the US working class. Equally significant, they are increasingly concentrated in the very industries that have been most influenced by the economic restructuring of the United States. Latino/as are trapped in low-wage jobs in an economy that is producing far too few of the living-wage jobs needed for the increasing number of workers entering the labour market to sustain a robust and democratic economy.

THE LATINO QUESTION IN LATINO POLITICS

During the presidential election of 2016, Democratic and Republican strategists talked about 'Latinos' and their potential political power in terms of the so-called 'sleeping giant' myth.[22] This tired metaphor is used by political pundits, news media outlets, and scholars to describe a mythical and monolithic voting bloc with the power to swing and the potential to determine a national election outcome. The public context for the 'sleeping giant' narrative is akin to a horse race in which the announcer gets louder and louder about the long-shot runner prior to and during the race, only to lament its loss and applaud its valiant effort. What is seriously missing in the description of this population(s) is not only its ethnic diversity, but its class dimensions and divisions. The most salient aspect of the 'Latino' population is the growing class divisions within it. Thus, it's becoming more difficult in these changing political and economic times to speak of 'Latinos' as a block or as a singular class formation.

Well-intentioned academics and pundits willingly participate in a social process that essentially racialises diverse and distinct communities into a predefined, homogenised 'Latino' population category. They usually report on basic demographic characteristics and civic and economic participation. What is not thoroughly discussed is that Latinos are a vastly heterogeneous population with divergent economic histories, diverse cultures and languages, multiple ethnicities, and numerous nationalities; more important to our analysis, Latinos disproportionately represent the working-but-poor class. These analysts also tacitly fail to mention that the category itself is predominantly made up of Mexicans, who make up more than two-thirds of 'Latinos'. Puerto Ricans are the second-largest subgroup making up around 9 percent, followed by Cubans, Salvadorans, Guatemalans, and other Central and South

Americans.[23] The homogenisation of these different groups into 'Latino' is packaged tightly into a marketable discourse about a 'sleeping giant' to simplify their experiences into a narrative that fits neatly into the way media cover political contests.

As obscure and vague as this identifier is, it does have a crystallising effect on this population, placing the 'Latino' into the ranked US racial and ethnic taxonomy produced by the political economy of our neoliberal democracy.[24] Galarza describes how this process manifested itself in the Mexican and Mexican American community in a speech he gave to the California Council for Social Studies Annual Conference in 1969 entitled 'Minorities: The Mirror of Society.' Galarza argued that the Mexican American position is that of a racialised minority where the majority has created a myth of difference and value between minority ethnic and racial groups and the majority white population. The perceived differences are used by the economic and political elite (owners of capital, who are predominantly white and male) to determine access to public and private decision-making processes that ultimately determine a minority group's ability (power) to access resources that determine long-term cultural, political, and economic mobility and vitality:[25]

> Mexican Americans are members of more than one minority. As members of industrial and service economic organizations they belong to the trade-unionist minority. Mexican Americans are mostly Roman Catholics, which makes them members of a religious minority. Overwhelmingly they are poor and thus are bracketed with 20,000,000 or more blacks and some 30,000,000 so called 'Anglos' who are also poor. And if we try to put the best face on the matter we can say that in the last presidential election much of the Mexican Americans voted for Democratic candidates. For this presidential term, they will be a minority in national politics.

To describe such a human grouping as a compact, homogenised minority is to use a convenient but loose term. The common characteristics of a skin colour and language are obvious enough. But beneath them lie the deep needs of personal productiveness and of family nourishment. If the word *minority*, then, is to help rather than hinder our discourse, it must mean a group classified arbitrarily by colour or by selected cultural traits whose members suffer acute and chronic denial of opportunities for personal growth and social identification.

Poverty is the result of such denial. It too becomes an inherited trait, like skin colour and speech. Add to this odd combination of poverty, colour, and racialised stereotypes—Tonto, a man's body with a child's mind, siestas by the cactus—and you have the package. By this process the individual and the family—the vital, human elements of the minority—are framed in the popular mainstream cultural narrative.

Thus, framing Latinos as a 'sleeping giant,' political or otherwise, and speaking of 'the Latino vote' as a monolithic political interest lends itself to false assumptions similar to those bound up with the Latino label itself and is plagued by the problem of powerlessness described by Galarza. This is the primary reason we explicitly question the analytical utility of the term *Latino* that is used by the academy and public policy officials to categorise diverse populations into a homogenised minority group. We agree with Oboler's statement that a label such as Latino and or Hispanic 'obscures rather than clarifies the varied social and political experiences in US society of more than 23 million [in 1995; 55 to 57 million in 2017] citizens, residents, refugees, and immigrants'.[26]

People's lived realities are shaped by the material conditions produced within the spaces they occupy. Forcing a label and presumed behaviour onto a working population based on assumptions derived under the false pretences that there are a universal hemispheric language, culture, and history and specific political and economic ideologies is inaccurate and factually wrong.

The same is hardly ever done with a white voting demographic. Few discussions arise of the 'white vote'; instead it is broken down and critically analysed between distinctions such as rural/urban, gender, age, class, etc. But nonetheless, during the election, we found ourselves here, discussing the 'Latino vote' as an analytical frame to try and understand if it was going to sway Republican or Democrat. Candidates from both parties even hired political consultants to try to capture the mythical Latino Voting Giant. Hillary Clinton hired the gold standard, the closest thing she could get to a Latino Nate Silver, the polling firm Latino Decisions, whose tagline is 'Everything Latino Politics'. This polling firm was to be the smoking gun for Clinton in her attempt to capture the Latino Voting Giant or, as Clinton staffers referred to it in emails, the 'Taco Bowl engagement'.

We now know that their polling was terribly off. Trump's surprise victory in the Electoral College despite losing the popular vote to Hillary Clinton by nearly 3 million (notwithstanding Trump's ridiculous and unfounded claim of voter fraud) stunned the pollsters and the Clinton campaign. How did they get it so wrong? And how did they fail to assess voter support for Bernie Sanders? Approximately 30 percent of 'Latinos' voted for Trump: that is, one-third of the supposed Giant. More importantly, the 'Latino' vote in Florida helped carry and ensure a Trump presidential victory. This reality was captured in a post-election *New York Times* article 'We're Looking at a New Divide Within the Hispanic Community': The Latino vote in Florida upended the Clinton campaign's strategy, and what we thought we knew about where politics is headed'.[27] We argue that this is not a new phenomenon but a long-running and predictable one.

How can we continue to speak about the 'Latino vote' as if 'Latino' is one unifying category? The reality is we can't and shouldn't; it is just poor social science. More importantly focusing on this very conversation obscures more pressing questions about what types of experiences unify or differentiate groups of people meaningfully. As we state above, social class divisions amongst Latinos themselves vary, and they inform the political interests of working-class Latinos. This political behaviour revealed itself as far back as the presidential primaries.

During the middle of the 2016 presidential primary season, former labour leader Dolores Huerta went on National Public Radio to debate Cornel West, a noted and highly respected African American scholar. Leading up to the Democratic National Convention, Huerta had been championing Hilary Clinton and using her historic position within the Chicana/o and Latina/o community to argue that Clinton is a better spokesperson whose policies more accurately reflect Latinos' needs. At the same time, Rosario Dawson, a prominent Latina Hollywood actor with progressive activist credentials, argued that Bernie Sanders' policies better represented and spoke to the needs of working-class and middle-class Latinos and their families within the wider context of structural inequalities and economic injustice. There you have it: a microcosm of a much larger debate about the Latino position by two prominent Latinas, pulling for two very different candidates who represented different visions for a democratic future. Hillary Clinton called for advancing a neoliberal platform, albeit with a human face, while Bernie Sanders, a self-identified democratic socialist, advanced a European style of social democracy with an agenda that included, but was not limited to, weakening the power of corporations and increasing that of working people.

Huerta campaigned for Clinton by questioning Sanders's ability to represent Latino interests. She specifically argued and attacked him, while he was still exploring a presidential run, for voting against the immigration reform bill in 2014. This critique serves as an example of the convoluted facade called 'Latino politics'. Huerta's argument—that because Sanders voted against the reform bill he is against immigration reform—oversimplifies an issue that affects immigration, immigrants, and working communities, not solely 'Latinos'. What Huerta failed to acknowledge was that Sanders' no vote was because that specific bill included a guest-worker programme that would have essentially been a Bracero Program 2.0 (see chapter 1). It would have established a legal permanent second tier in an already vulnerable and exploitable cheap-labour workforce in agriculture and other industries that could demonstrate worker shortages. A vote for this bill would have been an endorsement of institutionalising the mechanisms for a programme that the Southern Poverty Law Center recently described as 'close to slavery'.[28]

The irony, of course, is that Dolores Huerta made her mark as a labour leader and organiser of Mexican and Mexican American farmworkers, an extremely difficult feat which the United Farm Workers of America (UFW) accomplished. But the UFW, under the leadership of Huerta and Cesar E. Chavez, were successful in doing so only after the National Agriculture Workers Union, led by Ernesto Galarza, led a successful ten-year campaign to bring an end to the Bracero Program.[29] Ending the Bracero Program had been key in working toward organising farmworkers, yet Huerta now argued for immigration reform that would recreate it.

All of this is to say that 'Latino politics' is vastly undertheorised and requires much more nuance and complexity. The term *Latino*, which is meant to simplify, does so at the expense of obscuring rather than clarifying politics of specific ethnic or racial communities with growing class divisions. The nuance and complexity that we aim to discuss in this book is not tied to any of the media spectacles that occur during horse-race campaigns. In fact, it is an attempt to theorise the experience of these ethnic/racial categories when the cameras and the pollsters aren't paying attention: to make sense of the experience of labouring classes and how they seek to build political and economic power for themselves and their communities within the context of neoliberal capitalism, irrespective of political parties.[30]

'LATINISATION', CLASSES, AND INEQUALITY

This so-called Latinisation (or 'browning') of the United States comes at a time of increasing inequality of income and wealth. These macro-level political and economic forces have also been asserted within Latino communities themselves, producing internal class divisions with income growth at the top while those at the bottom have lost ground. Nevertheless, the Latino population continues to occupy an unequal position in the wider political economy.

New immigrants are entering a society that is vastly different from that entered by their predecessors. For one, the high-wage manufacturing jobs that were once the basis of a largely middle-class society have been exported overseas, having been supplanted by skilled professions in the information economy that require specialised training through years of increasingly costly education at the postsecondary level. At the lower end of the service and information economy are masses of Asian and Latina/o labourers who hold ethnically typed low-wage jobs preparing and harvesting plants and animals for consumption, cleaning, and clothing, serving, feeding, and attending to the needs of those on the other side of the widening class divide. The janitorial, clothing, agriculture, and construction industries are the principal employers of immigrant workers. In extreme instances, immigrants work under conditions comparable to slavery.[31]

Latina/os remain an important segment of the immigrant population, one whose growing presence and conditions are closely intertwined with the very forces causing the ongoing economic restructuring and reshaping of once-familiar international, national, regional, and local landscapes. For nearly a century, these global political and economic changes have continued to sustain Mexican migration to the United States.

Los Angeles's overall economic profile worsened in the 1990s. The effects of economic recession and restructuring in Southern California in the early to mid-1990s are revealed in Los Angeles's Census 2000 economic profile. The 2008 'Great Recession' severely impacted Los Angeles's overall economic profile; it was only recently (2015) that Los Angeles County recovered all the jobs it lost during the recession.

According to an analysis undertaken by the *Los Angeles Times* in 1999, nearly all job growth in the 1990s in Los Angeles County since the low point of the recession in winter 1993 was in low-income jobs.[32]

In January 2017, the Los Angeles Economic Development Corporation (LAEDC) reported fewer jobs in the medium-to-high income bracket, while 92,000 food-service and 49,000 in-home support service jobs were added, with low average salary ranges of $20,000 for food-service positions and $14,000 for in-home support services.[33]

Manufacturing, which once played a pivotal role in the region's economic stability, employs fewer than one in ten of the city's workers today, according to recent estimates by the 2015 American Community Survey (ACS). According to the LAEDC, 'manufacturing employment has been on a long-term decline for decades and is not likely to reverse anytime soon.'[34]

Meanwhile, only 58 percent of adults currently participate in the labour force, according to 2015 ACS estimates. LAEDC notes that real median household incomes declined by 0.53 percent per year from 2000 ($60,144) to 2010 ($57,054), adjusted for inflation. In 2015, real household income was 3.6 percent higher than it was in 2010, but still 6 percent below where it was in 1990.[35]

Again, in places like Los Angeles, the rich are increasingly richer and the middle class are besieged by the threat of unemployment and rising debt levels. Los Angeles's overall economic profile has worsened over the past four decades. The Pew Research Center describes it as a city where the middle class is a minority. Los Angeles is not alone; from 2000 to 2014, the share of adults living in middle-income households fell in 203 of the United States' 229 metropolitan areas.[36]

Since the Great Recession, there has been a turnaround in employment in manufacturing at the national level, but not in California.[37] Manufacturing jobs in that state remain responsible for about 11 percent of the nation's manufacturing production. Southern California has the nation's largest manufacturing base, but the cost of land, housing, and energy are major factors in the region's lack of jobs. The most significant job loss in manufacturing (which traditionally has offered middle-class, family-supporting jobs unionised at greater rates than other industries) in Southern California since 2007 have been in more labour-intensive fields such as automobile manufacturing, textiles, and apparel, where Latino/a workers were once a growing segment.

We maintain that the current socioeconomic condition of Latino/as in the United States can be traced directly to the relentless emergence of the global economy and recent economic expansion policies such as the North American Free Trade Agreement (NAFTA), which have weakened the labour position of Latino/as through the transfer of historically well-paying manufacturing jobs to Mexico and other 'cheap-labour' manufacturing centres around the world. The consequences highlight the need for scholars to link the condition of US Latinos in cities to the globalisation of the capitalist economy. Few scholars have contributed more to our understanding of the social consequences of US economic domination in Mexico than historian Gilbert G. González. Chapter 1 of this volume is informed by his original and insightful critique of empire and the history of Mexican labour in the United States.

As González and Fernandez posit, US foreign policy toward Mexico over the last century has led to widespread destruction of the social fabric of Mexico, massive internal migration northward, and migration to the United States. Pre-neoliberal migration did not result in widespread desertion and disappearance of villages, but now, under 'free trade', whole villages take flight to escape the onslaught of economic depression. The United States promised that NAFTA would 'lift all boats', but instead Mexico's economic independence has retreated while the country undergoes a process of recolonisation.[38]

González's above critique leads us to understand that Latinos must be understood with respect to their structural position in the political economy. Sociologist William Robinson argues in his work on the global economy and the US Latino population that

> much sociological writing on Latino groups has focused on demographic phenomena, language, culture and other descriptive or ascriptive traits. Other studies have stressed emerging ethnic consciousness, pan-Latino political action, and other subjective factors as casual explanations in minority group formation. These factors are all significant. However, in my view there are broad, historic 'structural linkages' among the distinct groups that constitute the material basis and provide the underlying causal explanation for Latino minority group formation. In other words, cultural and political determinations are relevant, but subsidiary, in that they only become 'operationalized' through structural determinants rooted in the US political economy and in an historic process of capital accumulation into which Latinos share a distinct mode of incorporation.[39]

In the final analysis, we hope, this work represents an intervention on a wider range of conceptual and empirically driven questions concerning the forces shaping modern society and the new patterns of labour migration and settlement, work, class structure, and social formations emerging in the contemporary period. Does the current configuration of these macroeconomic forces require a rethinking of what we mean by 'Latino politics' in a deeply unequal capitalist society?

BOOK ORGANISATION

Our aim is to provide a stimulating interdisciplinary volume about the Latino question in an era of growing US inequality. A unique feature of this book is the synthesis of original primary and secondary research throughout the volume. We have kept the personalised narratives within our research intact intentionally. We chose to do so because they allow us, as researchers, a more holistic method of analysis that, along with highlighting the working people we studied, also humanises our work, not just as researchers but as members of the working class whose lives are shaped by the same political-economic context. Also, to address the common materialist-determinist critique often levelled against Marxist scholars, we connect the human element to our discussion of systems. Economic structures, systems, and social relations are, after all, about people.

While each chapter focuses on an aspect of Latino politics, all chapters have overlapping themes, including; mass labour migration, Latino politics as class politics, a critique of market-driven politics, the extent to which so-called Latino politics is conditioned or even determined by macroeconomic trends, and the changing forms of Latino and Latina labour and work. The chapters also include vignettes and other literary techniques to strengthen the narrative and add to the overall analytical and user-friendly nature of the book.[40]

Chapter 1, 'Mexican Mass Labour Migration in a Not-So-Changing Political Economy', places Mexican migration in the context of the *longue durée* of Mexico–US political and economic relations. The chapter builds upon the empire theory of migration literature in lieu of the neutral-seeming, 'natural' 'push-pull' of markets and living conditions or social capital theories, and provides a power-driven analysis stressing hegemony and domination, in which the United States exerts control over Mexico, as a root cause of international labour migration.

Chapter 2, 'Hegemony, War of Position and Workplace Democracy', develops a Gramscian framework to analyse and question the existing nature of work and its current form of organisation. Antonio F. Gramsci was largely concerned with the praxis of developing a counterhegemony and recruiting troops to fight the cultural battle with what he referred to as 'organic intellectuals' of subaltern social groups that could be tasked with opposing and transforming the existing social order.[41] This transformation, for Gramsci, takes place in the realm of ideology as well as the material social relations of production. We question the hegemonic logic of current work relations and develop an alternative framework for building worker power and developing a counterhegemonic class consciousness rooted in democratic workplace practices and new grassroots social movements, often led by Latino workers.

Chapter 3, 'Poverty in the Valley of Plenty'; chapter 4, 'Racism, Capitalist Inequality, and the Cooperative Mode of Production'; chapter 5, 'Working but Poor in the City of Milwaukee'; and chapter 6, 'Latina/o Labour in Multicultural Los Angeles', focus on current case studies that challenge the capitalist workplace logic. Our focus here on workplaces is purposeful and strategic, considering not only that 'Latino' workers organise their daily quotidian lives around their workplaces but also that their work conditions every other aspect of their material lives, structuring the vast majority of their experiences. We look at the experiences of and try to give voice to Mexican migrant workers, workers in worker-owned cooperatives in the San Francisco Bay Area, 'working but poor' communities organising in Wisconsin, and restaurant workers in Los Angeles.

Chapter 7, 'Latino Futures?', offers a general case for grounding a twenty-first-century critical urban future in something we provisionally call 'cultural political economy.' It is a modest attempt to address the cultural turn in Latina/o studies, politics, and the social sciences and rescue class from the cultural turn. It is our view that class is about power, interests, and politics and must be addressed in terms of production relations. This allows us to implicate capitalism and market-driven politics in our attempt to understand the Latino problematic. In doing so in this chapter, we attempt to resolve lingering theoretical tensions between socioeconomic (structural) and culture-based (semiotic) approaches to our neoliberal present. Finally, it is our hope to suggest new lines in Latino urbanism and class politics that can revitalise Latina/o Studies and progressive politics to confront capital in the era of concentrated wealth and poverty in its neoliberal form. This chapter also offers our ongoing critique—a manifesto in progress—of Chicano/a studies and current 'Latino politics' discourse that fail to acknowledge how Latino/as (including working-class youth) are being produced and reproduced in the struggle against capital in this period of growing class inequality and an authoritarian state.

The Conclusion contextualises our alternative vision of Latino politics and places our position within the contemporary epoch—that is, an interrogation of the material conditions of Mexican American men and women and their children, embedded in a critique of political economy, their practices, and their actions. It juxtaposes our critique and the 2016 US presidential election to demonstrate the ongoing war of position for power between capital and democratising forces who are working toward an alternative future.

1

Mexican Mass Labour Migration in a Not-So-Changing Political Economy

Pobre de México, tan lejos de Dios y tan cerca de los Estados Unidos.
Poor Mexico, so far from God and so close to the United States.
—Porfirio Díaz, president/dictator of Mexico, 1880–1911

Academics, politicians, and pundits have widely used this quote from former Mexican president Porfirio Díaz to characterise unequal US-Mexican political-economic relations during the late nineteenth century. The statement is rooted within a historical political-economic context in which American capitalist production and exchange have dominated Mexico's economic and political structures. Relations between the two countries have changed little in the last century.

In 2016, US Latinos reached 55.3 million, making this group 17.3 percent of the total US population. When this group is disaggregated by country of origin, those of Mexican origin comprise 64 percent (34,038,599) of US Latinos, while the second-largest group is Puerto Ricans at 9.4 percent (4,970,604).[1] Mexicans and Mexican Americans as a subset of Latinos outnumber all other country-of-origin groups in forty-two of fifty US states. By 2050, the Latino population is projected to nearly triple, from 55.3 million to 132.8 million, making Latinos the second-largest group in the country at 30.2 percent. If growth rates remain constant, the Mexican-origin population will number 85 million.[2] As this population has increased and expanded geographically newfound academic interests have emerged to investigate similar questions that academics and activists probed in the early and mid-twentieth century. Why are there so many Mexicans and Mexican Americans in the United States?

In this chapter, we argue that the current demographic position of the Mexican and Mexican American population cannot be understood apart from the historical impacts of the United States' actions and its capitalist economy on this population. Our argument builds upon literature supporting the empire theory of migration (ETM) and specifically looks at how labour migration is linked to unequal economic policy between Mexico and the United States.[3]

POPULAR IMMIGRATION THEORIES

Mexicans have continually migrated and settled in the United States since the turn of the twentieth century. This population has been at the forefront of various political and academic interests for many decades.

Early research and publications on Mexican mass migration to the United States conducted by Galarza, Gamio, McWilliams, and Taylor[4] are considered foundational in the development of literatures on immigration, adaptation, and industrial labour relations studies. Central to these scholars' findings is that the political economy of production is fundamental in establishing the conditions for migration and labour integration within various industries (specifically agriculture, mining and smelting, railroad, and construction). It is within this contextual framework that we analyse the political economy of Mexican migration to the United States.

Since these initial publications, a robust and valuable interdisciplinary body of literature has developed through debates on the impulses and impacts of immigration, economic and labour integration, political and civic behaviour, and the overall processes of assimilation of immigrants. Nonetheless, there is still no 'grand unified theory' of Mexican migration; instead, scholarly debates on immigration have produced multiple bodies of literature offering valuable insights into various aspects of this phenomenon.[5] For the purposes of this chapter, we briefly discuss three theoretical constructs of immigration as they relate to Mexican migration: neoclassical economics, social capital, and empire theory.[6]

Neoclassical Economic Theory

Contemporary neoclassical economic theory proposes two explanations for immigration. The first argues that individuals make decisions based on a 'rational' assessment of their relative personal positions. In this construct, immigration is the process of individuals' rational choices as they weigh the cost of immigrating against the potential material benefit gained upon arrival in the new country. The second approach argues that the decision to migrate is not only rational and based on a calculated formula, but is also influenced by competitive market pressures.[7]

George J. Borjas, economist and prominent immigration scholar, invoked neoclassical economic methodologies to study Latin American immigration to the United States.[8] Borjas argued that econometric models utilising immigrants' origin and certain individual variables can be used to predict the size and composition of immigration, the skill level of those immigrating, and how they will fare in the United States. The assumption is that 'individuals make the migration decision by considering the values of the various alternatives, and choosing the option that best suits them given the financial and legal constraints that regulate the international migration process'.[9]

This micro-level approach has been challenged on at least two fundamental points by Piore et al.:

> First, the behavior of the actors, which it assumes, is not consistent with the way in which they actually think about the world in which they live and conceive of their own actions. . . . The second problem with standard economics is the story about the human endeavor, which I find impoverishing and ultimately morally suspect.[10]

In sum, the neoclassical theory of migration identifies individual 'rational' choice as the root cause of migration, and is critiqued as ignoring the external forces that shape the structural context of migration. In that sense, the theory is not necessarily wrong so much as narrowly focused and incomplete. People do not make migration decisions in a vacuum. What structural forces create the conditions that affect rational actors' choices? Nonetheless, this theory has continued to gain academic popularity and is increasingly applied to explain world migration patterns.

Social Capital Theory

Social capital theory argues that engaging in formal public and private organisations creates a set of norms, values, and trust in people that leads to stability in community networks and/or democratic structures.[11] Extending social capital theory to immigration, Massey, Durand, and Malone argue that Mexicans migrate to America because of high levels of transnational social capital.[12] Social capital among Mexican networks has reached a level at which immigrant social networks are so well informed and linked to the processes of migration and labour economies that movement perpetuates itself. This phenomenon has been called the 'cumulative causation' of migration. As Massey and others argue, 'the causation of migration becomes cumulative because each act of migration alters the social context within which subsequent migration decisions are made, thus increasing the likelihood of additional movement'.[13]

Some scholars question the application of social capital theory to immigration. Their major critiques are that this theory does not fully consider the impact of immigration policy, North American neoliberal practices, and US trade practices on immigration and the people involved in migration. In our view, social capital theory best describes *how* people come to migrate and how they get to their destinations, but does not speak at all to *why* they leave to begin with.

Both neoclassical economics and social capital theory ultimately fail to account for the structural factors that condition migration and the extremely difficult choices people make when embarking on a migratory journey. Leaving the place you call home and family and friends with no guarantee of seeing them again is a major, life-altering process that is not undertaken lightly, despite social capital networks. Such choices also are not made with a simple cost-benefit calculation, but rather are made only if absolutely necessary for survival and as a last resort.

EMPIRE THEORY OF MIGRATION: AN ALTERNATIVE THEORY

A polemic of migration has recently resurfaced and is gaining popularity within the academy and popular narratives. With the passage of NAFTA in 1994, scholars began to revisit the impact of US-Mexico economic relations on mass migration and consequently immigration.[14] Like scholars from the early and mid-twentieth century, contemporary proponents have argued that mass internal migration in Mexico and immigration to the United States are a consequence of the power the United States has over Mexico's economic and political structures.[15] We refer to this model of mass migration as the empire theory of migration (ETM).

ETM argues against the push-pull theories that have shaped traditional understandings of immigration because these theories have

reduced the causes to sets of conditions within the sending and the receiving countries, conditions that functioned *independently* of each other. In one country a push (supply), or too many people and too few resources, motivated people to consider a significant move; in the other country a pull (demand), usually a shortage of labour, operated to attract the disaffected. In tandem they synergistically led to transnational migration.[16]

ETM argues that there are few independent conditions that cause imbalances between sending and receiving countries. Rather, the conditions are interdependent and manifested by a process of global capital flows in which a dominant country like the United States seeks to exploit a subordinate country's natural resources, including labour.

Lenin suggested that this situation is possible only because 'numerous [dependent] countries have been drawn into international capitalist intercourse', a process that leads to the creation of an international division of labour.[17] Similarly, Fernandez and Ocampo argue that these processes are manifestations of imperialist relations between capitalist countries and countries that serve a colonial function of supplying raw materials and labour to the capitalist countries.[18] These dependent countries are those 'which, officially, are politically independent, but which are in fact enmeshed in a net of financial and diplomatic dependence'.[19] For a country like Mexico, the result is 'uneven development and wretched conditions of the masses [which] are fundamental and inevitable conditions and premises of this mode of production'.[20] These conditions in turn have a direct effect on migration patterns. Lenin contended that a 'special feature of imperialism . . . is the decline in emigration from imperialist countries, and the increase in immigration into these countries from [underdeveloped/dependent] countries where lower wages are paid'.[21]

Thus, mass internal and international migration is the direct by-product of political-economic arrangements stemming from a hegemonic conquest of a country's economic and political structures through forced economic arrangements, coupled with propaganda to justify these arrangements. Gramsci argued that hegemony and state domination help to create and maintain the particular division of labour.[22] For him, hegemony is a type of domination not only exhibited through physical or overt force but also 'used to designate a historical phase in which a given group moves beyond a position of corporate existence and defence of its economic position and aspires to a position of leadership in the political and social arena'.[23] Therefore, hegemony is a dialectical process involving discursive practices that have material impacts. For example, the United States has continually sought not simply a position of international leadership but *the* dominant position, both through having the world's largest military and through establishing itself as the moral arbiter of the global economic, political, and social systems.

This dominant position has been manifested in very particular ways regarding its neighbour to the south. Since the Mexican-American War, the United States has promoted a very specific image and discourse regarding Mexico that first was used to justify taking half the Mexican territory and then to justify maintaining that country in a subordinate economic position. González suggested that the current understanding and representations of Mexico as well as its economic relationship with the United States date back to the 1800s, when 'US capital interests sought to penetrate Mexico'.[24] William S. Rosecrans, a land speculator, promoter of Mexican railroads and the ambassador to Mexico in 1868, made this historical context clear when he stated, 'Pushing American enterprise up to, and within Mexico wherever it can profitably go . . . will give us advantages which force and money alone would hardly procure. It would give us a *peaceful conquest* of the country'.[25] This 'peaceful' conquest was reached through promoting a very specific and purposeful hegemonic discourse that consistently painted Mexico as a social problem and its people as inferior to Americans, a discourse that continues to dominate US understanding.[26] The promotion of this discourse has become a significant tool in establishing hegemonic power.

Michel Foucault argues that 'discourse serves to make possible a whole series of interventions, tactical and positive interventions of surveillance, circulation, control and so forth'.[27] Discourses generate knowledge and 'truth', giving those who speak this truth social, cultural, and even political power. This power 'produces; it produces reality; it produces domains of objects and rituals of truth'.[28] For Foucault, 'what makes power hold good, what makes it accepted, is . . . that it traverses and produces . . . forms knowledge, produces discourse'.[29] In essence, power produces discourse that justifies, legitimates and increases power. Similarly, speaking in reference to literary discourse, Edward Said noted that literature is not an autonomous cultural form but is about history and politics and supports, elaborates, and consolidates the practices of empire.[30] Television, newspapers, magazines, journals, books, advertisements, and the internet all help construct stories, creating cultures of 'us' that are differentiated from 'them'.[31] All these forms elaborate and consolidate the practices of empire in multiple overlapping discourses from which a hegemonic discourse emerges.

Hegemonic discourses are constructed and perpetuated strategically. As Dunn has pointed out, representations have very precise political consequences[32] and, according to Said, either legitimise or delegitimise power, depending on what they are and whom they are about.[33] Said affirmed that a narrative emerges that separates what is nonwhite, non-Western and non-Judeo/Christian from the acceptable Western ethos as a justification for imperialism's policies and practices, and argued that discourse is manipulated in the struggle for dominance.[34] Discourses are advanced to exert power over others; they tell a story that provides a justification for action. According to Said, there is always an intention or will to use power and therefore to perpetuate some discourses at the expense of others, and this intentionality makes such discourses dangerous and powerful. As Doty suggests, through repetition, discourses become 'regimes of truth and knowledge',[35] Although they do not actually constitute truth, they become accepted through discursive practices that circulate representations that are taken as truth.[36]

US discourse on Mexico dates to the turn of the twentieth century: 'As Mexico opened her doors to the US inspired modernization, a cohort of writers that included professional travellers, Protestant missionaries, academics, journalists, business people, diplomats, engineers, tourists descended on Mexico . . . [and] in turn began to publish accounts of their travels'. Mexicans were depicted in popular US journals and newspapers as an 'uncivilized species—dirty, unkempt, immoral, diseased, lazy, unambitious and despised for being peons'.[37] Through constant repetition, a racialised identity of the non-American, 'unkempt' Mexican was constructed, along with a US identity that was considered civilised and democratic despite its engagement in the oppression, exploitation, and economic domination of Mexico. Consequently, the hegemonic discourse provided a veil for 'imperial encounters', turning them into missions of salvation rather than conquests or, in Mexico's case, economic control.[38]

This discourse set the stage for creation of what González called a 'culture of empire', which the United States has used since the 1800s to justify its concerted effort to dominate Mexico economically and subordinate the country to US corporate interests.[39] This dialectical process of hegemony, involving both the dissemination of discourse and strategic economic policy, continues to allow the United States to justify its dominant relationship with Mexico, continuing a long history of a not-so-changing political economy between the two countries.

This 'peaceful conquest', as Rosecrans called it,[40] was anything but peaceful and led to the mass disintegration of the Mexican countryside and the collapse of the social fabric of towns and cities. Many of these places were left completely without working-age men and often women, resulting in half-populated towns with seniors caring for children, as if a plague had swept people away in their prime. One can only imagine the effect of 120 years of social dislocation on communities in Mexico and Mexican enclaves in the United States.

ETM provides a counternarrative to popular theories of migration and offers a conceptually sound theoretical alternative to explain the contemporary political economy of mass internal migration in Mexico and immigration to the United States. In the following section, we use ETM to demonstrate how the political-economic arrangements between capital—or its latest iteration, known as neoliberalisation[41]—and the two countries have created the conditions for labour migration from Mexico and settlement in the United States. ETM places the processes of capitalist production at the centre of any analysis of immigration.

THE POLITICAL ECONOMY OF MEXICAN MIGRATION TO THE UNITED STATES

The ETM is a sound alternative framework to study a generalised pattern of mass internal labour migration in Mexico and immigration to the United States. The theory's unifying argument places the United States' economic, political, and social hegemony over Mexico as the root cause of mass immigration. Below, we identify how that discourse has led to key watershed moments in Mexico–US economic relations to show that this theory based on hegemony can best be used to study the complex nature and nuances of Mexican migration and immigration to the United States.[42]

Mexico's first economic modernisation period, 1880 to 1910, took place against the backdrop of unprecedented territorial[43] and industrial growth in the United States and political and economic turmoil in Mexico. Under the Porfirian regime, foreign capital investment was allowed to flow into Mexico unfettered. The expectation was that direct private investment could more efficiently modernise major Mexican industries and lead to job creation, economic and democratic stabilisation, and Mexico's ability to trade with other industrialised nations, specifically the United States. Under Díaz, foreign finance and development of industrial sectors increased to their highest levels in the country's history. For example, US investment in Mexico surpassed $2 billion, resulting in ownership of all of the country's oil, 96 percent of agriculture, and 76 percent of all industries.[44]

However, this investment did little to spur any sort of internal growth in Mexico's own internal economy, as most of the profits were siphoned out of Mexico. Francisco Bulnes provides detailed accounts of the impact the unequal economic policy between the countries had on Mexico's sovereignty and highlighted their understanding that Mexico was operating within a context of US imperial dominance over the Western hemisphere.[45] In his estimation, the massive foreign investments that led to industrial modernisation benefited only the Mexican elite and foreign investors, not the country or most of its people. The ultimate outcome of modernisation during this period was the destruction of local industries, extraction of natural resources, implementation of coercive labour systems, and the beginning of mass siphoning of wealth out of Mexico, which eventually led to economic stagnation. This control of the Mexican economic and political structures by private foreign capital and the resulting economic stagnation set the conditions for the Mexican Revolution (1910 to 1921).

González and Fernandez detail the processes of US imperial expansion and their impact on Mexico over the past century.[46] They note that, during the Porfirian regime, peasant communities that historically subsisted on farming and participated in local economies were uprooted and used as labour in capital's construction of the railroads and modernisation of agricultural, mining, and smelting industries. They argued that uprooting communities for the purpose of labour integration became a cornerstone of capital development in Mexico that continues to this day:

> By 1910 US corporate capital had largely financed the building of 15,000 miles of track, providing a basic infrastructure that would insure the transport of raw materials northward and technology south; which led to massive investment of US capital in mining and smelting; while initiating the onset of the destruction of Mexico's agriculture rooted in local economies, the displacement of large segments of Mexico's peasant population as a consequence of the foreign inspired modernization.[47]

Step migration of uprooted communities toward cities and production centres occurred during this period. The first step was internal migration toward cities where immigrant labour served the needs of the elite and the city. Next, migrants moved north, where many were integrated into different modernised production sites. As a result, immigration grew from 1,000 to approximately 18,000 during this period. When these production sites became saturated they left many with little work, so migrants continued to move north toward the United States, using the railways as guideposts.

Roots of Contemporary Mass Labour Migration

ETM argues that the political-economic context for mass labour migration and immigration from Mexico to the United States was institutionalised during the Porfirian regime and reinstitutionalised sixty years later with the implementation of the Bracero Program (1942 to 1964). This gendered labour importation, or 'guest-worker programme', was implemented under the historically false pretext that World War II had caused labour shortages in the agricultural and railroad industries. At the programme's height in 1955, approximately 500,000 labourers were imported to the United States annually; altogether, 4.6 million Mexican men were contracted.[48] The Bracero Program was the largest state-managed labour importation system of its kind during the twentieth century.

This programme is a standard example of ongoing unequal economic relations between the countries. The Bracero Program did not allow for capitalisation of this labour force within Mexico's economic structure, but rather led to underdevelopment and the localised and national economy's dependence on bracero and unauthorised labour migrants' remittances. To date, in large part due to this programme, remittances continue to be Mexico's second-largest source of foreign currency, totalling $27.7 billion in 2012, second only to oil.[49]

The termination of the Bracero Program did not end labour migration from Mexico. On the contrary, industries across the southwestern United States have become dependent on this predictable and exploitable labour pool and continued to recruit workers actively through state mechanisms. With conditions in Mexico relatively unchanged, large numbers of former braceros (many accompanied by family members), unauthorised labour migrants and a growing coming-of-age working population began to follow the step-migration patterns of previous labour migrant generations: moving first internally to cities, then north toward the border, and finally into the United States. From 1965 to 1989, approximately 36.5 million unauthorised Mexican migrants crossed the border. Although 23.3 million eventually returned to Mexico during this period, 4.6 million unauthorised migrants 'permanently' settled in shadow communities near jobs throughout the United States.[50]

Anticipating this massive population movement, the United States entered into a new economic arrangement with Mexico's executive branch of government.[51] The stated intent was to offset the impact that the end of the Bracero Program would have on an already high unemployment problem in Mexico by instituting free trade zones (FTZ) along the border. This programme, known as the Mexico Border Industrialization Program 1965 (BIP), attracted corporate investors who built *maquiladora* assembly plants within the FTZ that promised limited government oversight or intervention, financial incentives, and a readily available, inexpensive labour pool.[52] It marked the beginning of a more intense US capitalist production agenda in Mexico rooted in the 'neoliberal orthodoxy of industrialisation through foreign direct investment'.[53]

The *maquiladoras* turned Mexico's northern border into an enclave with few links to the rest of the economy. Into the border area flowed duty-free manufacturing inputs to be assembled into final products using cheap labour, for entry into the United States or export to other countries. The northern tier of Mexico became a direct appendage of US manufacturing, replicating the examples of railroads and mining in the Mexican economy during the early 1900s.[54]

Capital investments in the maquila industry have maintained historically high returns on investment, reaching a profit ratio of almost two to one. For this reason, the numbers of assembly plants have steadily grown along the border region, and since the Maquila Decree (1980) have begun to spread into the interior of Mexico. In 1976, 448 maquilas employed 74,500 workers; in 1986, 865 maquilas employed 227,900 workers; in 1998, 3051 maquilas employed 1,035,957 workers; and by 2013, 5094 maquilas employed 2.1 million Mexicans.[55]

The maquilas in the FTZs erode labour, worker and human rights, healthcare, and safety in these industrial zones. With a priority on employment at any cost, the government has sanctioned company labour unions to disempower maquila workers, which has limited their right to participate in workplace democracy.[56] With ten- to twelve-hour shifts, workers earn roughly ten dollars a day, and the demands they can make on their employers or the state are legally and structurally limited.

Although the Mexican *maquiladora* sector has largely accomplished its goals of attracting foreign investment to Mexico and creating jobs for its workers, critics contend that these successes have come at a high price. Labour law violations are perceived to be commonplace. Issues such as substandard working conditions, debilitating health effects, and mandatory pregnancy tests are often a part of the daily life of *maquiladora* workers.[57]

The BIP also has had negative environmental and health effects on workers and surrounding communities. Toxic pollutants dumped in Mexico's waterways and communities have led to abnormal cancer clusters within maquila worker communities.[58] In addition, the BIP has done nothing to slow immigration to the United States. On the contrary, unauthorised and authorised immigration have reached unprecedented levels, numbering 454,000 in 1950, 760,00 in 1970, 2.2 million in 1980, 4.5 million in 1990, 9.4 million in 2000, and 11.7 million in 2012, and has remained steady since.[59]

The Mexican Miracle

To make the case for neoliberal trade, scholars often point to a period of positive growth and economic stabilisation known as the Mexican Miracle (1940 to 1970). However, this period of growth occurred under a context quite opposite of that required by neoliberal trade. Growth was stimulated by a domestic economic development strategy based on import-substituting industrialisation (ISI) and industry and trade protectionism. Under this strategy, many of Mexico's financial and industrial sectors experienced unprecedented economic growth. At its height in 1968, during the *sexenio* (one-term, six-year presidency) of Gustavo Díaz Ordaz (1964 to 1970), the peso was stable and the economy grew by nearly 10 percent with little inflation. A thriving middle class seemed to be taking root in many metropolitan areas. In the absence of any hint of neoliberal policies (free and open markets, deregulation, privatisation), these developments occurred because the Mexican state made a concerted effort to guide the economy and protect it from outside interference.

But by 1976, the Mexican Miracle had begun to unravel as the country moved away from ISI. That year, 'the peso had fallen from 12.5 to 22 per dollar. The foreign debt had sextupled [to US$26 billion]. Real salaries [adjusted for inflation]—the buying power of the average income—were half what they had been during the much-maligned "Stabilisation Development".[60] The presidency's policy of modernisation was carried out without a clear, coherent, strategic economic plan and rested on a single economic indicator—the price of oil in the open market.

By 1981, foreign investors owned 87 percent of the production of PEMEX, Mexico's nationalised oil industry. In February 1982, the peso fell from 22 to 70 pesos per dollar, eventually reaching 150 pesos per dollar, a direct result of a stagnated economy burdened with external debt and corrupt presidencies. Seven months later, President José Lopez Portillo was forced to declare the country unable to service the $90 billion in external debt it owed the US government and the Washington-based International Monetary Fund (IMF): Mexico was all but bankrupt and in the midst of an economic crisis.[61]

Mexico's international debt crisis crippled its internal economy and forced the country into a series of economic agreements to pay its creditors. Its agreements with the United States government and IMF used the nationalised petroleum reserves as collateral (called 'petrodollars'). Many of the petroleum products and petrodollars generated immediately after the agreement were used to pay this debt. The IMF also initiated a structural adjustment programme (SAP) for Mexico to ensure prompt debt repayment. Consequently, by the end of 1982, this agreement had crippled many public institutions that provided public and social goods such as nutrition, housing, education, and healthcare. Sectors of the Mexican economy were opened to foreign goods and capital services that previously had been nationalised. These adjustments and NAFTA, which followed in 1994, caused the displacement of millions of Mexicans.

NAFTA and the Neoliberalisation of Mexico's Economy

In 1986, Mexican officials were all but coerced into joining the General Agreement on Tariffs and Trade (GATT), now the World Trade Organisation, which institutionalised many of the 1982 SAP measures. Foreign industrial and agricultural goods and financial services were introduced in quantities not seen since the late nineteenth and early twentieth centuries. Meanwhile, the GATT measures called for decreases in internal investment on national agricultural and industrial production;

local farmers and business owners could no longer compete with foreign interests. At the same time, the US Congress passed the Immigration Reform and Control Act (IRCA), a comprehensive measure intended to curb illegal immigration by offering amnesty to current unauthorised migrants and creating sanctions to penalise any employers who hired 'illegals'.[62]

In Mexico, President Carlos Salinas de Gortari oversaw much of this process. Having done postgraduate work in economics at Harvard's John F. Kennedy School of Government, Gortari's involvement began during his days as the Secretary of Programming and Budget (1982 to 1987) and ramped into high gear during his presidency from 1988 to 1994. Under Gortari's presidency in 1992, an amendment to Article 27 of the Mexican Constitution set the stage for the destruction of the *ejido* system. The Mexican Constitution had instituted agrarian reform that expropriated lands from individuals and corporations that had amassed millions of acres prior to the Mexican Revolution; Article 27 mandated farmland to be redistributed to the peasants in the form of communal properties (*ejidos*). With Gortari's amendment, elites and international interests were allowed to purchase large territorial expanses, including some of the most fertile cooperatively owned farmland as before the revolution. Following this action, legislation was passed that eventually retracted subsidies and price supports for many Mexican products, a very conscious effort to dismantle the Mexican economy, sector by sector, for the sake of entering the global market.[63]

Meanwhile, in the United States, Operation Gatekeeper was instituted along the southwestern border in 1994 to stem the flow of unauthorised immigration from Mexico. This increased the number of border patrol agents and supplied the Immigration and Nationalization Service, now Immigration Customs and Enforcement, with high-tech military training and equipment. Also that year, NAFTA was passed, which allowed a free flow of capital between the United States, Mexico and Canada. Ironically, the first measure sought to restrict movement of people from Mexico while the latter opened the borders to free flows of capital, giving consumer goods more rights of passage than human beings.

The implementation of NAFTA was the culmination of an imperial process to formally neoliberalise Mexico's political and economic structures. González and Fernandez described NAFTA as having two purposes: to 'guarantee a free hand to US enterprises willing and able to invest in Mexico to take advantage of that country's cheaper wages' and to 'deny in various forms and degrees to other economic powers the advantage of operations in and exporting from Mexico'.[64] NAFTA continued Mexico's long history as a US economic colony, providing cheap labour, raw materials and manufactures for consumption in the United States while restricting Mexico's access to the US market. NAFTA called for the privatisation of state companies and the 'flexibilisation' of the labour market through 'restrictions on wage increases, curtailment of vacations and sick-leave time, extensions of workweek, and increased management powers'.[65] The trade agreement mainstreamed the construction of 'a series of satellites subjected to an overriding economic influence tantamount to colonization'.[66] By 1995, Mexico had suffered an economic crisis that mirrored many of the US-Mexico political-economic conditions of the nineteenth century. Mass migration at first internally into major Mexican cities and then northward toward the border and ultimately into the United States was set in motion. As a result, displaced and unemployed Mexican migrant labourers have become integrated into various labour-intensive economic sectors in Mexico and the United States.[67]

Gortari and his Institutional Revolutionary Party (PRI, Partido Revolucionario Institucional) vigorously pursued NAFTA as a mechanism for injecting foreign capital into Mexico's ailing economy.[68] Among those who have fervently proclaimed NAFTA a resounding success are former US trade secretary Jaime Serra and economist J. Enrique Espinosa, formerly on the Mexican president's Council of Economic Advisors; both have cited increased foreign direct investment as evidence.[69] However, free trade has led only to the enrichment of a few monopolistic corporations in the United States and the deterioration of the Mexican people's economic situation.[70] As Serra and Espinosa point out, foreign direct investment has increased from $3.5 billion to about $13 billion annually, but this increase does not necessarily translate into growth for the Mexican economy—largely because the money invested in Mexico is mainly in the form of loans that must be repaid, often at high interest rates.[71] Such investments aim to extract capital rather than to allow it to circulate within the local economy, which would create a multiplier effect, considered a major factor for economic growth. So, while foreign direct investment has increased, the increase is not an accurate measure for NAFTA's impact on the Mexican economy because the investment does not automatically translate into Mexican economic growth. In fact, to date, Mexico has the largest trade deficit in Latin America, a mediocre annual growth rate of 1.1 percent in gross domestic product, placing it sixteenth among thirty-two countries in Latin America in annual growth.[72] Its inflation rate was 15 percent from 1994 to 2003; overall, since the passage of NAFTA, Mexico has averaged a 10 percent annual inflation rate and a growth rate of 0.76 percent from 1994 to 2013.[73] As far as opening its markets is concerned, Mexico remains the least diversified exporter in Latin America, and with 89 percent of its exports going to the United States, it is almost completely dependent on the US market.[74] NAFTA has largely led to the deindustrialisation of Mexico's 1,100 capital-goods plants: 396 have closed and 17,000 enterprises of all kinds went bankrupt shortly after Mexico's 1994 monetary crisis.[75] González and Fernandez argued that 'NAFTA is just one of the most recent examples of US domination over Mexico and how it continues to misdevelop and tear apart the socioeconomic integrity of that society'.[76]

NAFTA's Impact on the Agricultural Sector

NAFTA's impact has been the greatest on Mexican agriculture because agricultural production was once the foundation of Mexico's national development. State investment in agriculture was reduced by 95.5 percent and credit available to the rural sector by 64.4 percent.[77] Disinvestment in Mexican agriculture has meant that agricultural enterprises are unable to compete with subsidised US commodities. The United States maintains domestic subsidies that allow it to export corn at 30 percent below the cost of production, wheat at 40 percent below, and cotton at 57 percent below—a practice known as 'asymmetrical trading' or 'dumping', deemed illegal in world commerce.[78] The outcome has been the disappearance of profitability for Mexican national agricultural producers. Five years after NAFTA, corn had lost 64 percent of its value and beans 46 percent, while at the same time prices of staple consumer goods rose 257 percent.[79] Despite these figures, the Office of the US Trade Representative in 2006 cited the growth by US$5.6 billion in Mexican agricultural exports to the United States during the previous 12 years as proof of NAFTA's success.[80] Yet producers have continued to abandon agricultural endeavours en masse, vacating 1.6 million previously cultivated hectares (3.95 million acres) in the first eight years of NAFTA.[81] Goodman related the story of Ruben Rivera:

[He] sat on a bench in a forlorn plaza, rather than working on his seven-acre farm. He used to grow tomatoes and onions, hiring 150 workers to help at harvest. Now he doesn't even bother to plant. He can buy onions in the supermarket more cheaply than he can grow them. A crop of tomatoes yields less than the taxes. He lives off the $800 sent home monthly by his three sons, who run a yard work business in Macon, [Georgia].[82]

Stories like this have become all too common. As Quintana writes, 'One of the historically great agricultural civilisations of the world [now places] its food supplies in foreign hands'.[83] Mexico now imports 95 percent of its edible oils; 40 percent of its beef, pork, and other meat products; 30 percent of its corn; and 50 percent of its rice. NAFTA has resulted in the 'complete inability of the Mexican nation to produce the food required to feed its own people'.[84]

Promise Unfulfilled

The promise that liberalising industries in Mexico would lead to opportunity for the common citizen and 'lift all boats', as US president Bill Clinton claimed, has not been fulfilled. On the contrary, neoliberalism also has had devastating social costs for Mexican society. Poverty in rural areas has risen significantly, from 37 percent in 1992 to 52.4 percent in 2002, with 86.2 percent of rural inhabitants living in poverty.[85] NAFTA has left half of Mexico's 106 million people (51 percent of the population in 2010) living in poverty, causing mass displacement of workers and forced migration.[86] Since 1994, an average of 600 peasants a day (at least 2 million people) have migrated from rural areas, many to northern cities along the US-Mexican border and others into the United States.[87] Migration means family disintegration and the destruction of the social fabric of Mexico. Many jobless displaced workers will try their luck at crossing a militarised border into the United States. Interviewing Luz Maria Vazquez, a tomato picker from Jalisco, Goodman reported that six of Vazquez's brothers and sisters are in the United States, most without papers.[88] More than 11 million Mexicans (a conservative estimate) now live in the United States without documents, 7 million of whom migrated to the United States after NAFTA, between 1994 and 2005, an estimate that continues to hold true in 2017.[89] What other choice do these people have? Even if they had access to land in Mexico, they cannot compete in the agricultural market because they lack their government's support. This situation creates internal migration toward the border where vast numbers of maquilas are in place and ready to exploit desperate labourers.

The story might have turned out differently had Mexico continued to follow the development path that led to the 'Mexican Miracle'. If Mexico had slowly lowered trade barriers—but under its own conditions and rules—it may have continued to prosper. In an issue brief for the Center for Economic Policy Research, Weisbrot et al. suggest that if Mexico's economy had

> grown at the same pace from 1980 to the present as it did in the period from 1960 to [just before] 1980, today it would have the same standard of living as Spain. . . . To have 25 years of this rotten economic performance, you'd have to conclude something is wrong. . . . It is hard to make the case that Mexico's aggregate economic performance would have been even worse without NAFTA.[90]

The spectre of NAFTA continues to haunt the Mexican working class and much of the US Mexican working community. Since the mid-twentieth century, the United States has effectively used free markets and trade (under the guise of democracy) to usurp Mexico's economic

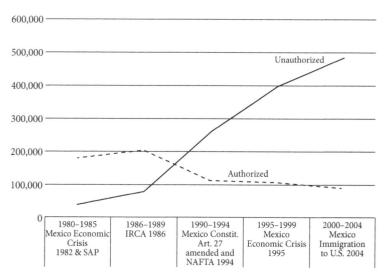

Figure 1.1 Mexican Immigration to the United States, 1980–2004

and political structures. Today, under the guise of economic and energy reforms, Article 27 of the Mexican Constitution is again under attack by the ruling elite, who have amended it once more to denationalise the energy and petroleum industry (PEMEX). To privatise the largest and last state-owned industry in Mexico completes the reversal of populist victories and sounds the final death knell for the Mexican Revolution. The 'modernisation' efforts are all but complete, without any actual modernisation in sight.

THE PEOPLE PUSH BACK

While these conditions seem bleak, empire and hegemony are never omnipresent or totalising: they are always contested. Thus, in response to US-backed and Mexican LC elite supported market-driven policies (such as the Bracero Program, BIP, NAFTA, and the recent 'energy reforms' by President Enrique Peña Nieto) there has been a large public backlash on both sides of the border. In Mexico, there have been mass demonstrations against the reforms that have put extreme public scrutiny on the Mexican president. In the United States, a historic immigrants' rights social movement has organised. This movement is demanding the end of exploitative legal and economic structures targeting immigrant communities in the United States and labour communities in Mexico.[91] The goal from both sides is to begin to change the practices of empire and curtail their effects.

This immigrants' rights social movement had been escalating, fuelled by anti-immigration policies such as militarisation of the border, surveillance of workplaces and homes, and further criminalisation of migrant labour. Intensifying the movement are the effects of NAFTA—the uprooting and displacement of millions who would otherwise not migrate and a US economy that thrives on a seemingly endless supply of foreign workers.

The first large-scale collective pushback from immigrants, workers, and labour and community activists and their supporters in the United States took place in 2006. Not a spontaneous or isolated incident, this campaign was a nationally coordinated effort to stop HR 4437, the Border Protection, Anti-Terrorism, and Illegal Immigration Control Act. In the single largest protest in US history, millions took to the streets across the country with signs that read: *Immigrants built the USA! Legalisation Now! Working is not a crime! We are workers not criminals!*

Undocumented and unafraid! No human being is illegal! Immigrant rights strengthen all worker rights! End mass detention! Stop deportations! We are ALL Americans!

Although HR 4437 passed the House of Representatives, it failed in the Senate. Many immigrants' rights leaders, activists, and liberals framed the defeat as a victory. However, the immigrant community continues to wait for comprehensive immigration reform. Even so, recent talks have focused on increased spending on the continued militarisation of the border and a new guest-worker programme that would mirror the gendered Bracero Program that created a tiered, exploitable labour system for migrants. Within this discussion, rarely is there any mention of amnesty or the fundamental human right to remain in one's home country.

Ten years later, the immigrants' rights social movement continues to challenge the established anti-immigrant orthodoxy and government authorities through sustained collective and organised public actions. The movement's ultimate goal—social change through legislation, specifically a comprehensive immigration reform law with a wide path to citizenship—has had limited success to date. The movement did successfully pressure President Barack Obama to issue, on 15 June 2012, the executive order known as the Deferred Action for Childhood Arrivals (DACA) which to date has approved 800,000 applicants.[92] DACA has since been rescinded by President Trump, leaving those with temporary relief in limbo and on a path, once again, to illegality.[93] Nonetheless, under the Obama administration, more than 2 million people were repatriated (deported), more than any other presidential administration, earning Obama the nickname 'Deporter-in-Chief'.[94]

The current use in horse-trade politics of the DACA program—much like the Immigration Reform and Control Act (IRCA) of 1986, the Bracero Program of 1942–64, and other immigration and labour policies—for 'border security' funding and as a whipsaw for current and future immigrants who do not meet the desired qualifications for status adjustment is morally corrupt and a classic divide-and-conquer strategy. Political attacks on immigrant communities, especially on the most vulnerable, are not new and have consistently been used through the manipulation of media outlets to perpetuate public discourses that promote racialised policy outcomes. The sole intent of this mass manipulation is to reinforce the 'other' frame that has been commodified and used by elite and corporate interests who thrive and profit from a legitimised second class of workers who are easily exploitable, replaceable, and deportable, and from the policing of this so-called Latino threat: the 'other'. [95]

This is standard practice in today's US political economy. Creating categories of human value by 'naturalising' difference with the use of social processes is systemic and embedded within our governance structures.

CONCLUSIONS

In this chapter, we have introduced the ETM as a way to conceptualise the complex nature of immigration from Mexico to the United States. Mexican immigration to the United States is a process involving mass movement of people as well as individual choices that can be understood only within the context of the power that foreign capital has over Mexico's economic, political, and social structures. Applying ETM, we have argued that capitalist production, free trade, and labour migration are intrinsically linked and condition the context in which migration occurs.

Therefore, migration as a process of mass movement of people can be best understood by these structural forces that make it necessary for people to leave the places they call home. They leave without a clear vision of what they will encounter on their journey or knowledge of what awaits them on the other side. Often lost in the fight for immigration reform is a discussion of people's fundamental right to stay home: to live in their countries of origin, where they grew up, know their neighbours, have their families, and have made their memories without fear of their government selling them out and forcing them to compete with subsidised US agriculture.

Viewed from this context, neoclassical economic push-pull theories of cost-benefit calculations do not quite capture the complexity of these very human, very personal decisions of survival. Likewise, social capital theories do not capture the structural conditions that force people to decide to travel to a foreign land. Both theoretical strands also make a basic assumption that, for migrants, coming to the United States is a positive logical outcome. We question this assumption because often the end result is anything but positive. Migration leads to social dislocation, the disintegration of social fabrics in Mexican communities, and, for many, lives filled with indignity and fear in the United States.

ETM places these migration processes within the context of capitalist production, free trade, and the need for labour. Free trade cannot take place without a steadily available, docile, exploitable, and cheap labour force. Such a labour force is created when masses of people are displaced from the Mexican countryside and urban centres; thus, labour migration and free trade are inextricably linked.

Coincidentally, these processes of domination do not happen without resistance. As peasants, workers, city dwellers, and intellectuals rose up in the early twentieth century against the foreign-backed Porfirian regime to incite the Mexican Revolution, today the Zapatistas and social movement organisations in Mexico have found common ground in resisting neoliberalism. In the United States, the immigrants' rights movement is beginning to make inroads that may bring social change.

The contemporary era of mass migration from Mexico to the United States harkens back to the nineteenth-century context, as its cause is grounded in unequal economic policy between the two countries. Simply put, mass labour migration is a product of the political economy of capitalist production for the sake of profit and places Mexico's role in the international division of labour squarely in the provision of labour and raw materials to the United States. The latest wave of migration is simply the most recent iteration of a process of US hegemonic dominance over Mexico, which has been ongoing since the late 1800s and will continue until working people on both sides massively challenge the current practices of empire.

2

Hegemony, War of Position and Workplace Democracy

BACKGROUND

On Wednesday, 9 April 2008, Simon Johnson, research director for the IMF, one of the two largest financial institutions in the world (the other being the World Bank) that have overseen global financial capitalist policies since the Bretton Woods agreement of 1944, stated that the American economy had spiralled into 'the largest financial shock since the Great Depression.' The statement warned of a one-in-four chance of a full-blown global recession in the following twelve months.[1] The recession, Johnson stated, had inflicted 'extensive damage on markets and institutions at the heart of the financial system.'

The crisis itself began in 2007 in the housing market, due to failed investments in derivatives based on US subprime mortgage securities.[2] Herman M. Schwartz describes what followed:

By September 2008, $1.3 trillion of equity in US financial firms had evaporated. Banks worldwide had written down $0.5 trillion just in subprime mortgage losses, and legendary and lucrative Wall Street firms such as Lehman Brothers, Bear Stearns, and Merrill Lynch had disappeared as independent entities. Global stock markets were in free fall. In the supposed bastion of neoliberal orthodoxy and free markets, US taxpayers suddenly found themselves renationalizing the housing finance giants Fannie Mae and Freddie Mac, as well as owning substantial holdings in the giant AIG insurance company, the largest commercial banks in the United States, and the one remaining independent investment bank. The Federal Reserve meanwhile was providing liquidity to all parts of the financial system against any kind of collateral, in a sharp departure from normal practices limiting lending to depository institutions and against US Treasury and agency bonds. By October 2008, the Fed and the US Treasury had committed in excess of $2.25 trillion in bailouts and liquidity, more than 16 percent of the US GDP at that time.[3]

Global financial behemoths like Wells Fargo, Bank of America, JPMorgan Chase, Citigroup, and Goldman Sachs each received tens of billions in Troubled Asset Relief Program money[4] while also raking in billions in profits in the same year. However, more important than its impact on markets and financial systems was the disastrous impact of the American economic crisis on people.

At the same time, over the past twenty years we have seen one of the largest increases in income inequality since the beginning of the industrial revolution. The Economic Policy Institute argues that in recent decades the majority of income growth in the United States has gone and continues to go to the top 10 percent of families.[5] In 1978, compensation of CEOs was thirty-five times greater than compensation of average (not the lowest-paid) workers. Since the recession, that ratio has actually increased from 185 to 1 to 303 to 1 in 2014.[6] In September 2008, toward the beginning of the what is now termed the Great Recession, the Economic Policy Institute reported that there were 9.5 million unemployed workers in the United States, up from 7.5 million in January and 6.7 million in March of 2007; there were 2.9 unemployed workers for every job opening in August 2008, up from 1.9 the year before; the median weekly wages for full-time workers fell by 1.6 percent in the previous year; and an estimated $2 trillion in pension wealth had been lost as a result of the crisis, leaving many workers unsure about their retirement status.[7]

For those companies that remained successful during the crisis, the benefits of profits are all siphoned to the very top, while average workers continue to face the perils of downsizing, layoffs, furloughs, pink slips, increased medical premiums, and stagnant wages (even though it is because of them that these corporations are successful). This was made clear when, right before the recession hit, directors and executives in 120 public companies in such sectors as banking, mortgage finance, student lending, stock brokerage, and home building cashed out a total of more than $21 billion—and fifteen of the top corporate chieftains in these companies *each* reaped more than $100 million in cash compensation and proceeds from such stock sales.[8] At the same time, in early 2009, after a $182 billion federal bailout financed with public money, AIG planned to pay out $165 million in bonuses to executives and subsequently considered whether to sue the federal government for intervening.[9] In 2008, the top-'earning' CEO raked in more than $702 million. As Washington continued to mull tax breaks and corporate tax loopholes between 2008 and 2012, oil companies consistently documented record windfall profits.[10] In the third quarter of 2012, corporate earnings were $1.75 trillion, up 18.6 percent from the previous year, bringing in a record $824 billion while total wages fell to a record low 43.5 percent of GDP.[11]

The results of this mismanagement of the American economy are as follows: poverty rates increased from 13.2 percent to 14.3 percent in 2009 alone, representing an increase of 3.7 million people for a total of 43.6 million Americans living in poverty, the highest rate in over 50 years. One-third of the poor (35 percent) are children; Blacks and Latinos were the hardest hit groups.[12] Unemployment in December of 2012 was 14 percent for Blacks and 9.6 for Latinos.[13] Unemployment skyrocketed from 6.7 million workers in March of 2007 to 7.5 million in January of 2009 and 9.5 in September 2009, then rose to 12 million by the end of 2012.[14] As of 1 November 2014 the unemployment rate stood at 5.8 percent, which should indicate a recovered economy. However, Josh Bivens suggests that the number is misleading because it doesn't factor in the kind of jobs the recovery has created, nor does it reflect what he calls 'sidelined workers'.[15]

The unemployment rate does not count those that are 'underemployed'[16] which the Economic Policy Institute currently estimated was 11 million workers in 2013. There were six unemployed workers for every available job, and a total of 27 million workers either unemployed or underemployed.[17] In October of 2013, Heidi Shierholz estimated that there were at least 5 million workers missing from these official unemployment and marginally attached figures because, in order to qualify for the latter designation, one has to have been looking for work within the past year.[18] When people who have given up looking for work over a year are factored in, along with incarcerated persons and undocumented persons (who are not reflected in any official figures), the numbers easily and quickly soar. It is important to note that these figures take account of the positive impacts of the American Recovery and Reinvestment Act of 2009, without which the situation would have been much worse.

The recession, as scholars have documented, affected Americans but especially racial minorities, of which Latinos were the hardest hit, in areas of health, education, and housing, resulting in an increase in mental health issues, food insecurity, forced housing dislocations, poor physical health, and families having to forgo college for their children. Such results in turn lead to increased risk of low earnings, crime and poor overall health. John Irons describes this process as long-term 'economic scarring'.[19] Children bear a disproportionate share of the burden. Amy Novotny argues that poor children 'could be haunted by the devastating effects of the recession for years to come . . . research shows that children who slip into poverty, even for a short time, suffer long-term setbacks'.[20] These setbacks take the form of poor readiness as well as negative educational and cognitive outcomes that result from less mental stimulation and increased stress in their living situations.[21]

All of this economic devastation leads to a situation that severely limits the life conditions of Latinas. According to the Labour Council for Latin American Advancement (LCLAA), 'Latinas are part of the largest and fastest growing minority group in the US . . . [yet] earn a meagre 60 cents for every dollar earned by a white man, representing the largest wage gap of any other group of working women'. More than one-third of Latinas also have less than a high-school education; as labourers they have the lowest employment-to-population ratio in the nation at 52.7 percent. Latinas are also more likely to work in the low-wage service industry than any other population of colour; this lack of stable financial opportunities places them in a very vulnerable economic position, with one of the highest poverty rates of women in the labour force.[22] But where did these conditions arise from? We know for sure that theories that blame individuals either because of cultural or biological deficiencies have long since been disproven.

Instead, to understand the condition of these Latinas we need to understand the unique form of the organisation of work under capitalism. The way work is currently organised is a historically unique circumstance, not natural but conditioned by the power relations of who owns and controls the means of production. We don't realise this because all of us are socialised into the current mode of organising the social relations of production: we assume that the world has always functioned this way. This nature of work has evolved over a long period of time to meet the needs of those who own over the needs of those who work. This evolution is currently resulting in a fragmented economy that is displacing workers into contract labor (the 'gig economy') at an alarming rate. If labouring classes, including Latino labouring classes, are to respond effectively to this neoliberal onslaught, then they too must look to challenge these processes in unconventional and nontraditional ways. Doing so necessitates understanding how our current social relations of production appeared and how they have been challenged historically, so that we may be creative in thinking about how to bring about alternative futures.

THE CHANGING NATURE OF LABOUR: CAPITALISM AND WORKPLACE DEMOCRACY

In the late 1700s and early 1800s, what we now call capitalism was still in its early stage, the period of manufacture in England. Manufacture was a transitional stage where the former guilds and tradespeople gathered to work on projects in one location, known as a manufactory. At this point there was no difference in how their work was done or any of the processes involved in doing their work. This was before the Industrial Revolution and before any mechanisation. However, there was an important and fundamental change in how their work was arranged.[23] They were now working in one warehouse doing skilled work cooperatively, but for someone else. This began to change as the work itself began to require less skilled tradespeople as a result of mechanisation and the deskilling of the work itself. Workers increasingly began doing solely one task. This extreme division of labour gave rise to what we now know as the factory system, which reached its pinnacle in the form of Ford's assembly line. The work was still done cooperatively, but there was less need for expert craftspeople, as workers began to focus on only one aspect of the overall job. This process of deskilling labour changed the nature and meaning of work, which was also accompanied by the ideological and cultural triumph of capitalism. This form of organising work, in which workers are seen as being as expendable and interchangeable as parts of machines, has largely remained intact. It has also been perpetuated in the United States through a racialised de-skilling of labour that used the ideology of white supremacy as a justifying mechanism to dehumanise workers of colour and relegate them historically to the bottom rungs of the workforce.

The deskilling of labour occurred alongside the displacement of masses of people from formerly commonly held lands through the Enclosure Acts.[24] Skilled craftsmen who were forced out of their trades by mechanisation and forced to work to earn a living because of displacement landed in assembly-line work. This process was not just technically and materially jarring; it was also spiritually alienating. Paul Thompson recounts how workers reacted:

> Attracted there by the money, soon they found there was nothing else. They didn't like the line, the last thing they wanted to do was to screw on wheels. They left jobs unfinished; they plagued the foremen; they threw bombs of bostic into scrap bins. The effects of such work systems on productivity, absenteeism, labor turnover and industrial conflict were of sufficient concern for the US government to set up a task force to investigate the problem.[25]

While the assembly lines have been decentralised and work is contracted and outsourced all around the world, workers are still largely organised by the idea of expendability. This process of devalued and alienated labour is taken for granted and assumed to be natural, rather than a historically specific form of organising labour that has resulted from a material change in the social relations of production by the owners. It has also been accompanied and fortified by an ideological and cultural struggle by the class of owners to legitimise that form of organisation.

CAPITALIST HEGEMONY AND A WAR OF POSITION: HUMAN NATURE, CULTURE, AND IDEOLOGY

One of the historical problems that accompany this development of capitalism and work is the tendency to see that development as natural, as if 'capitalism happened because it was inevitable and final'. Marx reminds us that 'Nature does not produce on the one side owners of money or commodities and on the other men possessing nothing but their own labour power': this sort of relation has no natural basis and is not common to all social periods.[26] Marx makes an important contribution in this regard when he states that scholars 'presuppose private property, the separation of labour, capital and land, and of wages, profit of capital and rent of land—likewise division of labour, competition, the concept of exchange value etc.'[27] In arguing against this same tendency in his time, Marx argues:

> Political Economy [by which he means classical economics; Adam Smith, Ricardo, Malthus etc.] *starts* with the *fact* of private property, but it does not explain it to us . . . [classical economics] does not

disclose the source of the division between labour and capital and between capital and land . . . it takes for granted what it is supposed to explain.[28]

It is important to note that the current relations of production and social relations resulting therein are a consequence of historical processes and not the result of 'human nature' or a 'natural' evolution or progression. It is only through a historical process that 'the advance of capitalist production develops a working class, which by education, tradition, habit, look upon the conditions of that mode of production as self-evident laws of nature'.[29] However, capitalist production originates first in the period of manufacture and commences as a spontaneous formation here and there, but only through consistent practice, expansion, and experience does it *then* become the recognised method and form of production and hence the 'normal' state of society.[30] Raul Fernandez argues:

Once the 'dice' are loaded things look different. Once the capitalist mode of production is established [and hegemonic] . . . there are haves and have-nots, owners and workers, and inequality appears as a *self-evident* law of nature, or a consequence of individual, or group, characteristics.[31]

Similarly, Gramsci argues 'there is no abstract "human nature", but that human nature is the totality of historically determined social relations'.[32]

Scholars often unknowingly partake in this construction of a myth of the *natural* evolution of capitalist society by participating in the creation of a dominant culture that appears to be natural and perpetuates itself through hegemonic control of the society's culture and ideology. For Gramsci, hegemony is an explanatory tool for cultural subordination: power based on control of consciousness through the creation of common sense and ethical leadership, producing consent rather than overt control.[33] Williams describes this process as

an order in which a certain way of life and thought is dominant, in which one concept of reality is diffused through society in all its institutional and private manifestations, informing with its spirit all taste, morality, customs, religious and political principles and all social relations, particularly in their intellectual and moral connotations.[34]

Gramsci sees this struggle over hegemony and the logic of domination as spilling over from the economic sphere and into the terrain of culture and ideology in what he attributes to Marx as the superstructure, which is the depository of dominant culture.[35] Hegemony is created, built, and fought over in the realm of culture and ideas, but also within the contexts and material conditions (structure) of a given economy or society.

Thus, the hegemony of the capitalist paradigm has been constructed not just through the structure and organisation of the economy, but it has been supported and maintained by what Gramsci outlines as the role of intellectuals in a given society. In the United States, this hegemony has been largely built by the construction of different racial classes, through the cultural development of the ideology of white supremacy that justified first the conquest of Indigenous territory and then the enslavement of African labour, followed by the conquest of Mexican territory and the resulting forced labour relations into which the first Latinos (Mexicans/Mexican Americans) were drawn. Having had their land taken from them by a whole series of processes, including but not limited to squatting, force, and lynchings as well as corrupt legality, the first Mexican Americans quickly became the labourers of the Southwest. They were thus relegated to be miners, railroad workers, agricultural fieldworkers, nannies, housekeepers, and a whole slew of other menial jobs. The hegemonic discourses of racism, American exceptionalism, Manifest Destiny, and capitalism relegated the first Latinos into a position within the social relations of production of being cheap, disposable labour. All of this, of course, was justified by an intellectual current based on scientific racism; the ideology of white supremacy developed and perpetuated for the needs of US capital.

Gramsci suggests that intellectuals are 'anyone whose function in society is primarily that of organising, administering, directing, educating or leading others' but in a given society they function on behalf of a dominant social group to organise coercion and consent of the dominant social group's way of life.[36] Intellectuals could be 'managers, engineers, technicians, politicians, prominent writers and academics, broadcasters, journalists, civil servants, officers of the armed forces, judges and magistrates. It is these people, along with priests above all who produce the ideas, values and beliefs that consolidate the . . . social formation'.[37] Those in society who have the role and function of intellectuals, then, are the ones tasked with 'maintaining and reproducing a given economic and social order (in the exercise of hegemony) on a daily basis'.[38] In the day-to-day organisation of hegemony, the 'intellectuals are the dominant group's "deputies" exercising the subaltern functions of social hegemony and political government'.[39] Marx and Engels first posited this line of reasoning when they stated:

> The ideas of the ruling class are in every epoch the ruling ideas, i.e., the class which is the ruling material force of society, is at the same time its ruling intellectual force. The class, which has the means of material production at its disposal, has control at the same time over the means of mental production, so that thereby, generally speaking, the ideas of those who lack the means of mental production are subject to it. The ruling ideas are nothing more than the ideal expression of the dominant material relationships, the dominant material relationships grasped as ideas; hence of the relationships which make the one class the ruling one, therefore, the ideas of its dominance.[40]

Intellectuals have helped to construct this dominance through the promotion of what J. Pocock refers to as a 'hegemonic language'. Pocock describes hegemonic language as verbal manipulation as:

> I impose on you, without your consent, information you cannot ignore. I have demanded your response, and I have also sought to determine it . . . and the more complex and intelligible the information imposed by this act of verbal rape—this penetration of your consciousness without your consent—the more I have tried to determine what your response shall be.[41]

The hegemonic discourse of economic capitalism and the free-market paradigm has resulted in its unquestioned acceptance as a fact of life rather than a historically specific organisational form. The assumption that Latinos are better suited for menial labour is specifically tied to this historical hegemonic discourse of racism, one that specifically suits the needs of capital. Not only has this limited the opportunities of Mexicans, Mexican Americans, and Chicanos in the workforce, it also limits our imaginations when we attempt to combat these historically produced relations of production.

The hegemonic discourses of capitalism and racism have devalued the thinking and innovation of other forms of economic organisation and class solidarity for the vast majority of society. In this respect, Baldacchino argues that 'the cooperative logic (organising workplaces as cooperatively worker-owned and -run enterprises) is subsumed by powerful indoctrinating agents which transmit and inculcate the legitimacy of top-down hierarchical and inegalitarian principles and values which fashion the social relations of capitalist production'.[42] This occurs to the extent that even to think of alternatives is regarded, at best, as naïve. As suggested by Aronowitz et al., the very idea of social change, let alone socialist futures, has all but been excluded from the public imagination; in essence, there is a complete lack of radical imagination.[43] This lack of imagination also limits our ability to transcend the politics of different racialised identities into building class consciousness and class solidarity.

None of this, however, is to say that there isn't any resistance to the racial capitalist hegemonic paradigm, only that such resistance is not taken seriously. *Hegemonic* does not mean the same thing as *omnipresent*. Gramsci was largely concerned with the praxis of developing a counterhegemony and recruiting troops to fight the cultural battle, with what he referred to as 'organic intellectuals', of subaltern social groups that could be tasked with opposing and transforming the existing social order.[44] This transformation, for Gramsci, takes place in the realm of ideology as well as the material social relations of production. He argues that, in order to oppose and transform the current situation,

> one of the most important characteristics of any group that is developing toward dominance is its struggle to assimilate and to conquer 'ideologically' the traditional intellectuals, but this assimilation and conquest is made quicker and more efficacious the more the group in question succeeds in simultaneously elaborating its own organic intellectuals.[45]

In addition, these organic intellectuals attempting to engage in intellectual and moral reform must articulate a programme of economic reform.[46] In order for the dominant hegemonic logic to be eroded, it must be replaced to some extent by an alternative logic or a counterhegemony, which must emerge from the mass organisation of workers invested in counterhegemonic education and institution building.[47] We chronicle multiple attempts to elaborate the counterhegemonic logics of Latino workers through workplace and community democracy and new social movements in the following chapters. We argue that these counterhegemonic logics are both strategic and creative within this on-going ideological war of position because of their nontraditional forms of grassroots organisation, as well as the focus and targets of their strategies.

For Gramsci, this political and economic struggle is about winning hearts and minds over a vision of how society should function. In these struggles competing parties or groups engage in different strategies in the terrain of ideology and culture to assert their dominance. Using the metaphor of war, Gramsci states:

> War of movement is a frontal assault on the state where war of position is conducted mainly on the terrain of civil society. Civil society is a site of consent, hegemony, direction . . . [it is] at once the political terrain on which the dominant class organises its hegemony and the terrain on which opposition parties and movements organise, win allies and build their social power.[48]

In a situation where a group is struggling to build hegemony against the current hegemon, Gramsci argues that 'one cannot choose the form of war one wants, unless from the start one has crushing superiority over the enemy.'[49] And since one is struggling for hegemony against a group that already has it, it makes sense that one doesn't already have the capacity to crush the hegemon. Baldacchino describes this process as follows:

> One such strategy for social change has been described as a 'war of position'—a strategy based on a power model of society but which seeks an evolutionary sequence for transforming power relations and overcoming vested interests. The concept is of military extraction. It distinguishes the frontal attacks and maneuvers characteristic of classical and heroic warfare from the trench-bogged techniques of superpower conflicts, of which the First World War (1914–18) is the most notorious example. The tactic is conditioned by the strength of the enemy. To formulate military strategy as a 'war of maneuver' when pitted against a powerful adversary is tantamount to a lethal and suicidal adventure.[50]

And so, in the absence of the capacity or ability to engage in frontal assault or war of movement (social movements or revolutions), opposing groups engage in a war of position to jockey for advantageous positions. Gramsci considers these strategies part of the same struggle:

> War of position does not entail a renunciation of revolution, only a
> change in its strategy and its form . . . the strategy must be different.
> It must involve the building of hegemony between the working class
> and its allies. It must involve ideological struggle. It must involve the
> construction of mass democratic movement.[51]

This war of position demands enormous sacrifices by infinite masses
of people. The war of position can be seen as an ideological as well
as political struggle over recruiting troops to a cause and vision. If
labouring classes in the United States are to be successful, they will
need to adapt recruitment and organising techniques of the past to meet
the realities of the present and future. This means recognising that the
changing demographics of the labouring classes look very different than
they have in the past. Latinos are currently the fastest-growing segment
of working people; within that category, workers of Mexican origin make
up the majority. This, coupled with the changing economy (toward a gig
economy), will put pressure on workers to be creative in their response.
But it is in times of shifting and changing economies that opportunities
for advancing in a war of position present themselves.

During the second period in the development of capitalism,[52] the
period of manufacture approximately from 1600 to 1775 where the bourgeoisie had not yet become hegemonic, it engaged in a war of position
with the aristocracy. Together the bourgeoisie deployed a very specific
vision and ideology of natural laws and human nature through conceptions of natural rights and the state of nature, conceptions that had
their basis on the individual and self-interest. This conception of human
nature was the ideological complement of the historical development of
the bourgeoisie and the values it prized (i.e., maximising profit), and as
such it became an enormously powerful weapon, which the bourgeoisie
used against the privileges and oppressions it sought to destroy in the
hegemony of the aristocracy.[53] This war of position allowed the bourgeoisie to develop a hegemonic discourse and an ideological programme
and culture to accompany their economic model, which then through
experience and practice became dominant as it won the war of position
against the aristocracy. But there was nothing inherent or natural about
the values purported in this vision of human nature.

Albert Hirschman shows us how the historical development of ideas
changed how capitalist forms of economic organisation actually became

dominant. In his discussion of 'interests' and 'passions' he suggests that the 'triumph of capitalism . . . owes much to the widespread refusal to take it seriously or to believe it capable of a great design or achievement.'[54] Hirschman outlines the development of this specific way of thinking as connected to only one specific epoch of social, political, and economic organisation, and that is our current epoch of capitalist development, where there is an alignment of social and political forces which consolidate capitalist development and culture, what Gramsci would call a historical bloc. Capitalism arose out of the slow legitimisation through a war of position against the aristocracy of an ideology that privileged bourgeois self-interest. Hirschman shows that the profit motive as the fundamental way of achieving self-interest was not always as accepted as it now is; it was a process that occurred over a long period and through a prolonged war of position over the ideological underpinnings of capitalist culture, a process that resulted in its normalisation. Once capitalism and its ideals of self-interest and private individual property are normalised and hegemonic, so too are the accompanying ideologies that help advance capitalist interests by justifying horrendous acts, namely, racism, the ideology of white supremacy and manifest destiny.

It is this very war of position that Gramsci and Marx seek for workers to develop in order to change the current social order that results in the mass inequality rampant in our society. It is key to understanding this on-going struggle over ideology in attempting to break out of the hegemonic language and paradigm in order to allow people to consider alternative forms of economic and social organisation, specifically democratic ones oriented around ideas of cooperation, collectivity, worker power, cross-racial solidarity, and class consciousness. Understanding the development of culture and ideas as occurring in a terrain of struggle allows for spaces of contestation to develop alternative visions that take seriously ideas and practices that are alternatives to the racial capitalist paradigm. Ultimately,

> the great task of workers all over the world is not simply to combat repression and exploitation, they must primarily achieve victory in the terrain of the superstructure, escaping ideological incorporation. It is this which, in the Gramscian tradition, essentially enables the ruling class to enjoy cultural ascendancy and, therefore, to rule by consent.[55]

CAPITAL, LABOURING CLASSES, LABOUR UNIONS,
AND THE WAR OF POSITION

One of the effects of this normalisation of capitalism is that it limits the boundaries by which workers can effectively organise for their right to a dignified life. Even though the naturalness of capitalism had set in and become the dominant economic, political, social, and cultural ideology of the United States and the world, its effects were always heavily and violently contested. Indigenous people fought fiercely to retain their territories; enslaved people fought bravely to escape their wretched treatment; Mexicans and Mexican Americans fought with honour to keep their lands; workers in the 1930s organised en masse against the exploitation inherent in the system. They formed workers' organisations: labour unions that engaged in wildcat strikes, sit-ins, factory shutdowns, picket lines meant to be impenetrable by scabs, and self-help mutual-aid societies that promoted cooperative values. The majority of the gains in work conditions, wages, and benefits were gained by engaging in a simultaneous violent war of manoeuvre where thousands were killed, many of them Mexican, in labour struggles like the Haymarket (1886), Bay View (1886), Ludlow (1914), and Everett (1916) massacres, as well as a war of position that sought to combat the ideology of profits above all else by changing what was a reasonable and acceptable workday, wage, and work-age. In the Mexican/Latino community many of the labour leaders leading these struggles were fierce and radical women like Emma Tenayuca, Luisa Moreno, and Josefina Fierro.

Emma Tenayuca was a lifelong resident of the barrio on San Antonio's West Side. At sixteen she became involved in a strike by the city's cigar workers. At seventeen she helped the garment workers to strike. At nineteen she became the head of the West Side's unemployed council and at twenty-one was elected to the National Executive Committee of the Workers' Alliance of America. This was the first time a national organisation had chosen a Mexican American woman for a top position. In January 1938, eight thousand pecan shellers walked out on strike under Tenayuca's leadership. She was arrested and released, then walked door to door to ask Mexican Americans to support the workers and not to scab. She continued fighting for labour rights for Mexican Americans, becoming affiliated with the Communist Party. She later wrote a manifesto, 'The Mexican Question in the Southwest,' connecting the role of capitalism with the experience of Mexicans in the United States.

She argued that 'the treatment accorded Mexicans is a carryover to the United States of Wall Street's imperialist exploitation of Latin America'.[56]

Luisa Moreno, as a teenager in Guatemala, organised for the admission of women to universities. She moved to New York City and worked as a seamstress in Spanish Harlem to support her family when the Depression hit in 1929; she proceeded to organise her co-workers into a garment union. In 1935 she was hired by the AFL as a professional organiser and later joined the CIO. She became a representative of UCAPAWA (the United Cannery, Agricultural, Packing Allied Workers of America) and co-organised El Congreso de Pueblos de Habla Española (the Spanish-Speaking People's Congress) in 1938.[57]

Like Tenayuca, she argued and fought for the rights of Brown people, stating in 1940, 'These people are not aliens. They have contributed their endurance, sacrifices, youth and labor to the Southwest. Indirectly, they have paid more taxes than all the stockholders of California's industrialized agriculture, the sugar companies and the large cotton interests, that operate or have operated with the labor of Mexican workers.'[58] She was deported in 1950 for her radical activity through 'Operation Wetback' an INS programme that targeted labour leaders.[59]

Moreno collaborated with Josefina Fierro, who attended the University of California at Los Angeles. Fierro had planned to study medicine, but activism took over. She left UCLA and went on to become an exceptional organiser, co-founding the Spanish-Speaking People's Congress and running its day-to-day operations. She organised protests on discrimination in schools and supported the struggle for fair wages and better working conditions for Spanish-speaking workers in the furniture, shoe manufacturing, electrical, garment, and longshoremen's unions. The Congress was formed to build a progressive national coalition between Mexican American labour and civil rights organisations. It was the first national Mexican American and Chicana/o organisation and addressed labour issues, education, health care, police violence, citizenship and naturalisation (immigration). Its main focus was on building labour power amongst Mexican Americans, with the help of the CIO.[60]

All of these struggles and many more massively advanced workers' rights and conditions but this all changed when, in 1947, the Labor-Management Relations Act (also known as Taft-Hartley) was enacted. It effectively ended labour's[61] war of manoeuvre against capital and has since also fundamentally altered how the labour movement operates and engages capital in this country, resulting in a limited and scattered war of position. In one fell swoop the law effectively de-radicalised labour unions and limited the scope in which they could act. It outlawed wildcat strikes, solidarity strikes, secondary boycotts, mass picketing, promoted the red scare, and ultimately allowed the government to control labour if it was 'in the national interest' to do so.[62] What is more surprising is that at its passing it largely had the support of the bureaucrats of the labour unions. Since that time the labour movement has ceased to be a 'movement' in the traditional sense. Smith argues that, 'by the 1950s, the labor movement had entered its long-term decline'.[63] Currently it represents only about 11.3 percent of the workforce and only 6.6 percent of the workforce in private industry, both of which are all-time lows.[64] But even at its height at the end of WWII, union membership reached only 35.5 percent of the workforce, which not coincidentally was also the era of mass communist and socialist labour organising.[65] There is also a long, sordid, racist history of labour unions not just excluding workers of colour but also figuratively throwing them under the bus. In the present context it is difficult and analytically impractical to equate 'labour' with unions, even though historically they were almost synonymous.

This is unfortunate because labour unions have traditionally been the organisations at the forefront of workers' historic war of position against capital, pressing forward on issues of economic inequality. Over the last thirty to forty years, this has ceased to be the case. Labour unions and 'labour', broadly speaking, have been on their heels in this period, losing many concessions that capital had agreed to in the past. This includes but is not limited to pensions, healthcare, wages, and other working conditions. Bureaucratic unions have been unsuccessful in their struggles to fend off these attacks. The acquiescence of the leaders of the AFL-CIO to the Taft-Hartley law essentially spelled the slow demise of the labour movement as a mass 'movement'. According to Fletcher and Gapasin:

> The US trade union movement finds itself on a global battlefield filled with land mines and littered with the remains of various social movements. It is engaged in a war for which it was entirely unprepared, having convinced itself that it had secured a permanent seat at the table of national authority because of its loyalty to the state during the Cold War and to the interests of US capitalism.[66]

Taft-Hartley essentially converted the labour movement overnight into a giant bureaucratic machine that limited its field of vision to lobbying the Democratic Party in government and limited its role in labour relations solely to negotiating collective bargaining agreements.

It has done this all while capital has become increasingly sophisticated in its ongoing war of position and war of manoeuvre with labour, labour unions, and labour relations. This can be seen in how capital has successfully promoted de-unionisation drives and outsourcing and spent millions of dollars to prevent unionisation, as in the case of Walmart, as well as successfully criminalising and policing public strikes and protests.[67] The attack on labour by capital has taken on all sorts of forms, frontal as well as ideological. Currently public employee labour unions are fending off ideological and policy attacks in right-to-work states where tea-party Republicans are blaming government bloat on unions.[68] But in the last sixty years, the AFL-CIO and its affiliated unions have generally not changed their approach to fighting these varied attacks, even though the terrain of struggle has shifted tremendously. For the most part, outside of a few unions doing interesting grassroots organising (a few examples of which we chronicle in later chapters), most have stuck to their approach, mostly unsuccessfully, of fighting for labour by negotiating collective bargaining agreements. The larger unions have also confronted membership from paternalistic trustee perspectives, where they act in what they believe to be the best interest of the workers[69] instead of building up the organising skills of their membership to fight collectively and democratically for their rights. This is coupled with and extended by implicit socialised racism of a mostly white union bureaucracy that deals with Latino/a workers and workers of colour with racial paternalism. This has resulted in dwindling union membership in the United States and inactive members with little organising skills in times of organising need.[70] Thinking of labour-capital relations as a sort of chess game, unions have lost because the government at the behest of corporations has dictated very rigidly what moves can be made on the terrain of struggle. Union officials have at best largely limited themselves to playing within that framework; at worst they have maintained capitalist order in the labour market.

In this regard, Ness and Azzellini argue that 'trade unions . . . operating through institutional frameworks of governments have held a monopoly over labour history . . . and have had no interest in promoting workers' autonomous struggles, since the mere existence of those struggles called into question the traditional union structures and roles'.[71] One of the problems that bureaucratic labour unions present is that they limit the terrain from which workers can build power, not inherently but because they have made a choice to acquiesce to capitalist relations of production, between workers and owners. Melman, quoting Lawrence B. Cohen, argues that the continuous history of trade union activities represents an approach that traditionally 'has neither sought to eliminate the employer nor to share his managerial functions. Rather it has pursued a course seeking to ameliorate the workers' position and to modify their relations *with* the employer'.[72]

Martin Carnoy and Derek Shearer agree with the limits of unions when they argue that 'the unions have never moved out from their production base to develop an overall labour political program'; instead, the labour movement has failed to extend workers' rights or decentralise and democratise union organisations.[73] Thus, traditional unions have been unwilling to go beyond collective bargaining, in part because, as Carnoy and Shearer argue,

> the growth of union bureaucracy and the decline of rank-and-file initiatives is *built* into the theory and practice of collective bargaining . . . Labour leaders have become more concerned with maintaining their own powers and privileges than with organising the unorganized, contributing to innovative trends in unionism, or promoting a program of labour reform.[74]

The result is unions serving a contradictory function under capitalism: 'on the one hand they exist to improve the conditions of work for their members; but on the other, they compromise themselves to deliver disciplined labour to capital owners and their managers'.[75] Similarly, Schuller argues that 'labor movements, where they exist, have been largely incorporated within this dominant ideology. Having accepted the rules of the game, they are constrained in both the range and style of their collective political action'.[76] Wendy Brown broadens this argument to include not just unions but the larger left when she states that 'leftists have largely forsaken analyses of the liberal state and capitalism as sites of domination and have focused instead on their implication in political and economic inequalities . . . [instead they] turn to the state for protection against the worst abuses of the market [and in doing so] they decline to consider the state as a vehicle of domination'.[77]

AN OPPORTUNITY TO CHANGE THE NATURE OF LABOUR

The failure of unions in the United States to fight these attacks on labour through creating their own sophisticated forms and thinking outside of the traditional collective bargaining agreement has out of necessity created an opportunity for nontraditional forms of labour relations in the United States. Fewer and fewer people are able to join unions, and as of the writing of this book the Supreme Court case *Janus v. American Federation of State, County, and Municipal Employees, Council 31*, which is meant to undermine the already struggling labour movement, looms. The ideas of the so-called radicals who were purged from the AFL-CIO in the fifties have made a sort of comeback. While those ideas come from a long line of history dating back to William Thompson, Thomas Spence, and Robert Owen, the United States last saw them active within the labour movement in the 1950s. Currently the ideas of property in common and self-help, heavily influenced by the peak of union activism in the 1930s during the Great Depression, the Communist Party and its focus on mutual aid organisations, and socialist internationalist, anarcho-syndicalist, and social and solidarity economy movements in Europe in the 1940s and 1950s are again raising the question of the changing role of labour in the United States. They are also challenging the role of traditional labour unions—often, but not always, to hostile receptions. These varied ideas all converge on the question of changing conceptions of property relations and, more importantly, of the social relations of production in the United States. These reconceptualise the roles of labour and capital within the larger social relations. This can be best understood through Abraham Lincoln's understanding of the two: 'Labor is prior to and independent of capital. Capital is only the fruit of labor, and could never have existed if labor had not first existed. Labor is the superior of capital, and deserves much the higher consideration.'[78] In this same respect Mikel Lezamiz, director of cooperative outreach of the Mondragon Cooperatives, suggests that capital is only a factor of production, a tool for creating jobs, and doesn't or shouldn't have privileges over and above of those of labour.[79] If labour-management relations are indeed a game of chess, then US labour must move beyond collective bargaining and begin to use and expand all of the available means and moves in order to give itself the best possible chance for success. This means changing the game and expanding the ideological terrain of struggle.

Capital has become successful at subordinating labour with help from the state as it responds to protests and strikes using repression, propaganda, and coercion. Capital has been fighting a technologically savvy war on multiple fronts, with the newest weapons like right-to-work, outsourcing, and increased mechanisation of production—and labour unions have failed to adapt. Labour should, and has begun to, engage in a war of position to change the relative position of power between labour and capital to one reflective of Lincoln's and Lezamiz's statements. We argue that Latino/a workers in various ways have always been, but are now more than ever, at the forefront of the war of position to contest the hegemonic ideology of capitalism.

Given the unsuccessful attempts of massive social transformation in the early part of the twentieth century, labour has been forced to engage in this political struggle, but it has done so without really engaging in this form of 'war of position.' Where capital has adapted to new techniques and methods of union organising, unions have not done the same. The current economic crisis has resulted in a double crisis, what Gramsci calls a 'crisis of hegemony' or a 'crisis of authority'.[80] He describes this as a historical period where social classes become detached from their traditional parties because the ruling class has failed in some major political undertaking, or because huge masses have passed from a state of political passivity to activity and put forward demands. The current crisis fits this description: most people continue to be disillusioned by both traditional parties, but people on the left are also disillusioned with historical forms of activism through unions. The crisis of hegemony really is a crisis of a lack of trust in the political process, as well as a crisis of hegemony and of the authority of those historically entrusted to fight on behalf of labour. This can be seen in the shrinking ranks of union membership, the lack of recruitment by unions in the Mexican/Chicano/Latino community and other communities of colour, the outgrowth of the Occupy movement, and the grassroots organisations of workers, which are largely a response of labouring classes completely outside of labour union structures to the current economic situation. This double crisis has resulted in the fact that labour and unions are no longer synonymous. It also provides an immensely important opportunity to reconceptualise different potentialities for all labouring classes.

Sheldon Wolin calls such a moment of rupture a 'democratic moment'. Wolin understands democracy as being one form of the political that is always episodic and rare.[81] He goes on to suggest that democracy is about how the political is experienced and asserts that it has a fugitive character.[82] Democracy, he says, is destined to be a moment, temporary, one that is rebellious and may assume revolutionary, destructive proportions or not, but a moment nonetheless[83]—one where ordinary individuals realise they are capable of creating new cultural patterns of commonality and act accordingly. This democratic moment provides an opportunity for labour to attempt to engage in a war of position, outside the rigid boundaries of the collective bargaining process or party politics, to adapt to the manoeuvring of capital over the last sixty years.

In this war of position, labour is responding in various ways, especially trying to subvert concepts of private property relations—building not only new political and social programmes but also economic programmes where workers themselves either become owners through cooperative democratic ownership or begin to challenge labour and government to democratise undemocratic local-government structures and policies, bureaucratic, paternalistic union structures, and even workplaces by demanding more participation in collective bargaining.

It is this democratisation of the economy that we seek to excavate in regard to the so-called 'Latino' experience in the United States. How do 'Latino' workers face their workplaces and the economy on a daily basis? How do workers challenge the rigidity of a capitalist economy that means to extract every ounce of labour from them before discarding them as expendable? How do they make sense of the power relations and challenge and confront them as they seek to live more dignified lives? This, we argue, is the 'Latino question': how 'Latino' populations confront the onslaught of capital outside of traditional worker and party organisations. 'Latinos' experience daily life not only as semi-limited by the capitalist economy but by also being at the forefront advancing a war of position in the struggle over the hegemonic ideology of capitalism, challenging that system through innovative grassroots community building and worker solidarity, and ultimately advancing more human notions of community building, solidarity, and democratic economies and communities.

3
Poverty in the Valley of Plenty: Mexican Families and Migrant Work in California

[The migrant] is forced to seek better conditions north of the border because of the slow but relentless pressure of the United States' agricultural, financial and oil corporate interests on the entire economic and social evolution of the Mexican Nation.

—Ernesto Galarza, 1949

Interviewer: How many Latinos work on this farm?
Farmworker: There are no 'Latinos' who work here, only Mexicans.*

—Yuba City, California

INTRODUCTION

Farmworkers in California and across the nation toil long hours, often without overtime pay; live in squalid conditions; and earn low wages that have remained virtually unchanged for decades. Moreover, farmworkers are isolated from the larger society, which often views them with suspicion as unwanted 'illegal aliens'.

This chapter offers an account of the lives and work of contemporary farmworkers in California. It is based on two years of fieldwork in California's Office of Migrant Services (OMS) farmworker labour camps, involving interviews with workers, managers, and government supervisors. This revealed that migrant farmworkers are faced with a unique context of reception that stimulates migration and hinders incorporation.[1]

Into the Valley

At the labour camp in Parlier, California, on the southernmost tip of the Central Valley, five miles east of Interstate 5, it was the start of the

---

* Translated from Spanish. All quotations marked with an asterisk have been translated from Spanish by the authors.

agriculture work season and the opening day of the migrant labour camp when we began photographing and requesting interviews. City, county, and state administrators as well as individuals from nonprofit organisations, there to inform migrant farmworkers about the services these organisations provide, were more than willing to be interviewed and praised us for taking interest in this community. Convincing migrant farmworkers to share some of the most intimate parts of their lives was more difficult. We met a worker named Ernesto from Zacatecas, Mexico, who explained that migrant families lived and laboured under a context of exploitation and institutionalised poverty. They were suspicious of outsiders, especially those who asked questions about their immigration status, family success, and migration. Ernesto introduced us to family and friends that resulted in additional interviews in Parlier.

Parlier became a central part of this study, along with many more migrant labour camps, as we visited the following two seasons to conduct field research and interviews. We interviewed forty-five migrant farmworkers in seven labour camps and conducted observations in seventeen. That data serves as an essential base for understanding contemporary international labour migration from Mexico to the United States.

A second and equally important element of this research was taking place simultaneously: we were in discussions with the OMS about family and demographic information they had collected about every head of household and migrating family member who lived at an OMS centre while migrating on the season. After several months of negotiation, OMS granted us sole access to this data. Each year, housing applicants fill out a Family Demographic Information sheet in the presence of a labour camp official. The information collected includes family members, ages, and relationships, previous jobs, and immigration status. In all, information on more than 100,000 heads of migrant farmworker households and migrating family members had been collected and was being stored in boxes at the OMS office in Sacramento.[2]

The Labour Camps

The California Department of Housing and Community (HCD) is the state agency that administers the OMS and offers startup and maintenance finance, oversight, and enforcement for migrant labour communities.[3] OMS is responsible for maintaining twenty-six migrant

Figure 3.1 California Office of Migrant Services labour camps.

Source: Office of Migrant Services (OMS), 'Migrant Families Housing Centers: 2008 Season', Sacramento: California Department of Housing and Community Development, 2008.

labour camps and distributes funds to various county and city organisa-tions that operate migrant farmworker-housing centres.[4] Many counties have established housing authorities that receive state and federal funds to operate seasonal and semi-permanent farmworker housing.[5] These programmes rely on guidance from state and federal agencies about implementing their policies.

The OMS labour camps are strategically placed in fifteen agriculture-producing counties from Kern County to Modoc County, California, near the Oregon border, and house families that follow the migratory employment routes that correspond to crop production. Each centre operates for approximately 180 days a year, and there are a total of 2,107 rental units that provide housing for approximately 12,500 registered migrant farmworkers and family members.[6] Prior to being admitted into the centre, applicants must provide proof of marriage and/or that they are living with immediate family members, of employment in agriculture, of primary residency fifty miles beyond the labour camp, and of authorised immigrant status. This proof comes in the form of previous-year tax forms (or a letter from a current employer) that shows at least 51 percent of their household income was from agriculture work and valid immigrant status documentation (usually a resident alien card, naturalised citizen certificate, temporary alien card, or proof of being born in the United States). If the housing applicant cannot provide the required documentation, they are denied OMS housing.

La Jornada

Mexican labour migrants have been part of America's landscape for well over a century and have been a major influence in many of California's economic and settlement patterns.[7] This migration stream continues, and many of the struggles, obstacles, and barriers historically associated with pooled labour[8] continue to manifest in the daily lives of contem-porary migrant-farmworker families.[9] In interviews, they spoke of the hardships their families endured because of their precarious position within agribusiness. In an examination of the dynamics that influence the daily lives of migrant farmworker families, patterns are revealed that support the overall theoretical argument that they are bound to a historical and contextual narrative linked to agriculture development and production. Rarely do consumers relate the near-perfect produce we purchase for sustenance to the hidden world of labourers.

Agribusiness has integrated people of all ethnic and racial backgrounds. Men, women, and children of Chinese, Japanese, Filipino, Caribbean, African American, and white American backgrounds, immigrants and US-born, all supply it with labour. A shift in demographic composition to a predominantly Mexican agricultural workforce began to take shape in the 1930s[10] as a direct consequence of US capital's penetration into Mexico's economic structures, institutionalised state labour-recruitment programmes, and agribusiness-industry practices.[11]

As a consequence, today over 1.3 million seasonal and migrant farmworkers and their families travel to live in migrant communities and labour in the fields and orchards of California.[12] This agricultural workforce is comprised of over 90 percent Mexican foreign-born labourers.[13] Everyone interviewed in OMS migrant labour camps for this qualitative research and the 1,369-family sample drawn from eight years of residents at OMS labour camps for the quantitative analysis was Mexican or Mexican American. According to Arturo Rodriguez, director of the OMS programme, these demographic characteristics are substantiated by state reports on migrant farmworkers who use OMS housing and have been consistent since 1966.[14] As farmworker Elias Torres, interviewed in Watsonville, California, put it:

We are all Mexicans here. One season there was a family from El Salvador, but they did not return [the following year]. I have been coming to this camp for twenty years. . . . There are many families from my hometown here.*

Table 1 Descriptors of OMS Migrant Farmworkers, qualitative interviews, 2008–2009

	Mean		Mean
Age	43.18	US Citizen	28%
Gender	44%	US Citizen family	82%
Total family	6.41	Unauthorized in family	56%
Currently employed	82%	Year 1st migrated	1980
Income	$20,836	Age at time of 1st migration	16.21
Poverty	54%	Former Bracero in family?	72%
Education – formal years	6.72	Share of life in the US	38%
Speaks English	67%	Years at labor camp	13.08
Primary residence in Mexico	46%	Share of life in labor camp	48%
Own primary residence	28%		

A brief examination of the descriptors from the interviews reveals a complex narrative that transcends spatial boundaries.[15] Compared to national data on migrant farmworkers, the economic similarities are striking. Similar demographic and economic patterns emerge in the urban service sector.[16]

The mean age of the research subjects was forty-three, which is consistent with the Family Demographic Information OMS data estimate but much older than the national estimate of thirty-three.[17] Sixty-seven percent of those interviewed reported having completed less than seven years of formal schooling; only 2 percent reported having finished high school or its equivalent. Twenty-eight percent reported being US citizens, which is slighter higher than estimates of farmworkers as a whole in California.[18]

Income trends drawn from the interviews seem to fit a national phenomenon for migrant farmworkers as well. Fifty-six percent of this population reported a combined family income of less than $23,000 annually; another 10 percent made from $26,000 to $32,000. Fifty-four percent of OMS migrant families reported having annual family incomes below the federal poverty level. The National Agricultural Workers Survey (NAWS) data show that the proportion of migrant and seasonal farmworkers with annual family incomes below the federal poverty level in the nation was 59 percent in 2000 and increased to 66 percent in 2005.[19] Over half of California farmworking families earn less than $15,000 per year.[20]

These descriptors of the study population show that when compared to non-OMS residents they are older and speak some English. They also have larger-than-average families, higher rates of US citizenship, higher rates of US citizens within the immediate family, and high rates of unauthorised migrants within the immediate family. They tend to have a generational attachment to labour migration (such as the Bracero Program), to have spent half of their life in the United States and to have spent half of that time in OMS migrant labour camps. More than half have incomes below the poverty threshold.

Poverty is central to farmworkers' narratives and consistently influences their decisions with regard to immigration and migration destinations, settlement patterns, education outcomes, composition of family work units, and political practices.

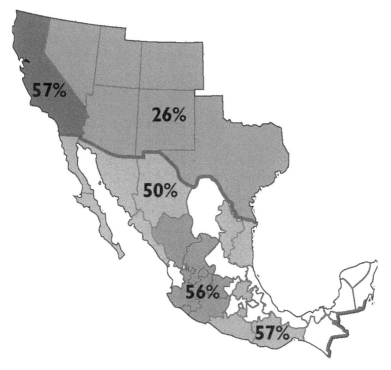

Figure 3.2   Poverty rates of migrant farmworker
families by place of permanent residence.
Source: OMS, 'Migrant Families Housing Centers'.

MIGRATION AND DESTINATION

Why do people immigrate and migrate to California on the season? There are those who see the trip as an 'adventure.' Some are first-timers and want to try their luck in agriculture. Some are recruited. Most have no alternative and follow this lifestyle for many years because they depend on it for subsistence.

Three distinct labour-migrant generations emerging from studying the interviews are used to guide the discussion on international labour migration. They are the post-Bracero generation, the Immigration and Reform Control Act (IRCA) generation, and the NAFTA generation. It is important to note that even though these categories are used to distinguish eras of first migration, their narratives indicate very little deviation in the root causes of migration and the constant challenges they have faced upon arrival in the United States.

Post-Bracero Generations

The OMS temporarily houses residents who are not immigrant pioneers or unfamiliar with employment routes. Most have been exposed to California agriculture prior to first migration and their choices associated with migrating are made within a larger context that has been set by market-driven politics, policies, and agribusiness.[21] About three-quarters of migrant farmworkers reported being part of migrant labour networks that can be traced to the Bracero Program. Having a bracero in the family heavily influenced decisions about first-time migration and choice of labour destinations. Few scholars have articulated the impacts this binational agreement has had on immigration in general and, specifically, on contemporary labour migration as well as Gilbert G. González.[22] His works have chronicled the lives of farmworker families and former braceros and demonstrates how US economic domination over Mexico has shaped the contexts of reception and integration of Mexican labour migrants in both countries. In his estimation, Mexican migrants are incorporated into the American economic order prior to their migration and choice of destination.

The post-bracero generation is a diverse population; it includes ex-braceros who experienced agriculture employment under managed migration and now migrate on the season with their families, second-generation migrant families where the father of either the husband or wife was a bracero, and third-generation families where at least one of the heads-of-household grandfather was a contracted bracero. Most of these migrant families still live in and/or are from northern and central Mexico.

Donato Perez is seventy-two years old and a veteran of the migrant lifestyle. He sits with his son Manuel underneath a shade tree with other men at the Artesi II labour camp outside of Stockton, California. Older male residents frequent this common area during early evenings to share all types of information. Such gathering spaces are found in almost every OMS labour camp. As Donato puts it, 'Here we come to gossip.'* While other migrant farmworkers have limited access to information about migration routes, communities, and government services, such information is readily distributed among those at the OMS centres.[23]

Migrant families rely on these informal communication networks for insight into their surroundings and other possible destinations where family employment is needed.[24] Heads of households make decisions they perceive to be in the best interests of their families with such information. The decisions range from which jobs to take, which require piece work or pay an hourly wage, which *contratistas* (contractors) to avoid, and what government services are available—to name a few. Also, these spaces provide a forum for older men to discuss politics and share their *stories*.

Donato recalls being contracted for the first time in 1959. He was 'recruited' informally: his father and older brother had established a working relationship with a grower in San Joaquin County who promised contracts to any of their family members. The *patron* (boss) considered them *los trabajadores buenos* (the good workers) who didn't mind the hours, pay, and housing, and wanted to return to Mexico. Donato's first job as a bracero was in the asparagus fields. He recalls spending late April, from sunrise to sunset, bent over, using a specially designed eighteen-inch knife to pierce the sandy, soggy earth and harvest the spears from the base of each plant. When the programme ended, Donato continued migrating to this region—now with his family.[25] Consequently, one son and his family still accompany Donato, his wife, and a daughter on their yearly migration from their home base in Mexico to California. Another son and his family live on site at an orchard and work for a local grower, while two more remain in Mexico. They are a transnational family with economic, political, and cultural roots in the migrant lifestyle in both the United States and Mexico.

Donato's life has been dictated by growing seasons, and he sums it up by saying, 'Because of that small plant [asparagus], I was contracted for the first time, and because of this small plant I brought my family, and because of this small plant I keep coming.'*

Post-bracero families originate from impoverished areas in Mexico where jobs are scarce and the local economies depend on the dollar. For example, the economic development of the Mexican states of Michoacán, Jalisco, and Zacatecas has stagnated because of continual outmigration and nonlocal capitalisation of labour.[26] This historic economic debasement has forced these economies to rely on remittances from the United States for survival. The stories recollected by older Mexicans with direct attachments to the Bracero Program demonstrate how crop production dictated much of labour migration during and after the programme; in interviews, they discussed low wages, hard work, oppressive heat, lack of housing, abusive bosses, lack of medical care, lack of education, lack of opportunity, and oppressive politics in both countries, and these topics are reflected in the experiences that young women and men undergo today. This continuum of issues influences almost every facet of the daily lives of migrant families.

The IRCA Migrant Workers

Many migrant farmworker families emerged out of the shadows and began to apply for OMS services after the passage of IRCA in 1986.[27] This comprehensive immigration legislation allowed unauthorised immigrants who met certain criteria to apply for status adjustment. It included a special provision for farmworkers that was a direct result of agribusiness lobbying, based on its perceived need for pooled labour. This provision created a special status-adjustment category and processes specifically for farmworkers. As a result, of the 2.7 million immigrants who adjusted their immigrant status under this legislation, more than 1.1 million were farmworkers and their families.[28]

IRCA migrants share that their initial decision to immigrate was not made in a vacuum. It came during an era when unauthorised immigrants faced a hostile and exclusionary reception in the United States. They were aware of the dangers they would face upon arrival at the border, while crossing, and inside the United States, but the need for food and shelter compelled them to leave their ancestral homes and families. They were forced to live in constant fear while providing a precious service to agribusiness and US society.

As with OMS families from the Bracero Program era, immigration occurred in steps for the IRCA-wave migrant families, and that this was gendered. The interviews show that men immigrated first, often separating from the family for an indefinite amount of time. Most worked in the United States long enough to save money for passage for a spouse and possibly a child. Families often brought working-age children and left younger ones behind. It was not rare for parents and siblings to miss the formative years of adolescents and toddlers. Parents and children articulated the pain and suffering caused by family separation.

Patricia Ayala left four children behind the first time she immigrated to the United States. She shares her narrative in the presence of her daughter and they sigh simultaneously. Patricia followed her husband to

California via Tijuana, Mexico. Her husband had immigrated to United States in 1971 *sin papeles* (without documentation) and sent for her in 1973. Now sixty-five years old, she recounts her first migration. The money they saved was not enough for the entire family to immigrate. They needed to pay for passage, food, a hotel in Tijuana, and the *coyote* (smuggler). In those days it took close to a week to travel from rural Jalisco to the border. This journey as *campesino migrantes* defined their identities; it has lasted for forty-three years and continues today. Ayala makes it a point to note that their story is no different than thousands of other migrant families across the nation.

To add to the stress of immigrating for the first time, they were forced to decide how to best separate the family. Four daughters were to stay behind, while the oldest and the infant would join them on the first immigration trip; the second eldest and the twin sisters would stay with her husband's family in the countryside; and the five-year-old would stay with Patricia's parents in town. This decision has haunted her to this day. She turns, embraces, and apologises to her daughter. It took one-and-a-half year of working in sweatshops and in the *jardines* to gather the funds necessary to unite the family in the United States. She feels it was their family's *castigo*—(punishment) for immigrating.

Patricia recounts the second time she crossed into the United States, now with her entire family. It was a rainy November evening. Victor used other peoples' documents for himself and their youngest child; the rest crossed by running through the hills. The *coyote* used a smuggling route located at the edge of Tijuana that connected to the Otay Mesa neighbourhood in San Diego. Once across, the family reunited and headed to Culver City, California, in an old station wagon. Immigration stopped them at the San Clemente inspection centre, but let them go because they had permission to reside within the United States. Patricia and Victor had a daughter who had been born in Los Angeles: immigration policy at that time allowed any US-born person to sponsor immediate family members.[29] In early 1974, the Ayalas filed a petition with the Immigration and Naturalization Services (now ICE) for status adjustment under this provision. Because of this documentation, they were not deported.

The struggle for survival did not end once they reunited, however. They lived for a while in an apartment with three other families, but soon were homeless. Patricia called an uncle who lived in a farmworker labour camp in Yuba City, who urged them to trek further north and join him. They did. They journeyed inland for ten hours and arrived at the labour camp with a total of sixty-three cents. They lived with this uncle and his family for five months until they found housing.

Eventually, the Ayalas made their way to the Coachella Valley, where farm work was available almost year-round and plenty of 'safe' communities with housing existed.[30] They migrated back and forth from the Coachella Valley to Yuba City for the next ten years, staying with the same relatives. These migratory patterns continue for the Ayalas, but since adjusting their status under IRCA, they now use OMS housing and own their three-bedroom, two-bathroom trailer home on a one-acre plot outside of Indio, California.

A collective sense of relief resonated from all of the interviewees who adjusted their immigration status under IRCA. They are all too aware of the added hardship of being part of a family with unauthorised immigrant members who are trapped and openly hunted within the United States. This anxiety also manifested when they spoke of having unauthorised children in public schools, having to seek healthcare, fearing interactions with public officials, and not being able to return to Mexico—especially in times of emergency.

Status adjustment meant that children now had the opportunity to escape the migrant farmworker lifestyle. Education became more than a set of skills to help the family: it became a reason for many to continue beyond middle and high school. It also allowed families like the Ayalas to now set down roots and become permanent members of communities in migrant labour destinations. Interestingly, most have chosen to settle near agriculture areas close to the OMS camps they once called home.

The NAFTA Generation

NAFTA is the latest in a series of comprehensive US foreign-trade policies that continue to destabilise Mexico's economy. This neoliberal trade accord between the United States, Canada, and Mexico has allowed goods and capital to flow freely between the three countries—but not people. As we argued in the previous chapter, the local economies that once sustained Mexico's countryside have been forced to compete with multinational corporations in a global market. Consequently, Mexico's countryside is no longer able to produce enough food to feed its people. Since its implementation, approximately 2 million Mexicans who would not otherwise have immigrated have been displaced and forced to seek employment in the United States.[31]

Aurelio Mendoza's father was an international labour migrant for many years, until 1984, when he saved enough money to purchase fifteen hectares (thirty acres) with irrigation. Four families farmed this land— his father and mother, two brothers and their families, and his own family. They grew corn, peppers, tomatoes, and beans and sold them at the local open-air market and to distributors. For many years they lived a good life as *campesinos* and small-business people. As a collective they were able to provide for each family and kept a savings account that they reinvested into the family farm and used for emergencies. They lived the lifestyle their parents had dreamed of for them.

Aurelio and his family immigrated to the United States for the first time in 1999 and now migrate on the season from Texas to California. He shares that the only reason they are in the United States is because of the impact of the Tratado de Libre Comercio (NAFTA) on their hometown of Piedras de Lumbre, Michoacán. Most young families have left Piedras; it has become a virtual *pueblo fantasma* (ghost town). Now most of its residents are elderly or very young. The town is dying.

Aurelio's story resonates with new and old migrant labourers. Many had achieved the dream of land ownership for farming in Mexico. But few have been able to compete in a globalised marketplace dominated by multinational corporations. They are forced to buy seeds, fertilisers, pesticides and other chemicals from the same companies that they compete with in the 'free market'.[32] 'Al vender nuestro producto, no nos queda nada' (after selling our product, there is nothing left), Aurelio says. As a result, they have slowly been marginalised from local markets and pushed off their lands.

Aurelio states:

There is no [local] commerce in the ranch or nearby town . . . even the agriculture is foreign . . . to plant we must buy American seeds and chemicals [fertilisers and pesticides] and compete in the same markets as them . . . [and the result] is that those that stay behind await the remittances. *

Migrant farmworkers' narratives make it clear that few would willingly submit to such hardship if the conditions in their local economies had not deteriorated. They would rather live and labour within their *ranchos y pueblos* than have to migrate to provide for their families.

Migrant farm workers—ex-Bracero
and spouse

Migrant farm worker (IRCA)—awaiting
housing

Migrant farm workers—evening gathering

Migrant farm worker (NAFTA)—picking
up child at daycare

Figure 3.3   Migrant Farmworkers by Immigrant Era

THE JOURNEY—MIGRATING ON THE SEASON

Labour migration is a family affair that is highly routinised and conditioned by housing and employment. Families travel the migrant circuit
from as far away as Florida and Oaxaca for thousands of miles and
several days on end; others live within an hour's drive of the migrant
labour camp. They migrate in new and old cars, trucks, vans, SUVs;
some pull trailers, others carry their belongings in a single suitcase.
Many have calculated the cost of migration down to the cent and can
sustain themselves for the first month, while others arrive broke and are
forced to borrow additional money to pay for rent and food. Most are
anxious, not having safe, affordable, and temporary housing. This is a
primary reason that people begin preparing for the journey long before
the date of departure.

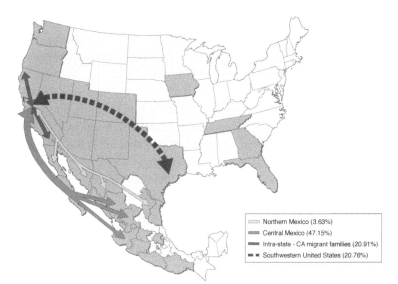

Figure 3.4   Contemporary migrant farmworker migration patterns.
Source: OMS, 'Migrant Families Housing Centers'.

A common theme that emerged from the interviews was uncertainty: migrant families never know what they will encounter along the road or at their destinations. Stories of accidents, broken-down vehicles, traffic tickets, encounters with unwelcoming people, and run-ins with police and immigration agents were repeated in all the labour camps. Each year, there are families who do not make it to their migration destination. Many turn back.

Parents frame the trip as an adventure to children. They get to see new sites, play games, and sing songs. Some get to eat in restaurants and even stay in hotels along the journey. The joy of travelling into another country is an adventure in itself. When they arrive at their destination, they will see and play with labour-camp friends from many different parts of the United States and Mexico. For the duration of the season, the Migrant Education Program will care for them; most children under eleven years of age will not labour in California's orchards or fields.

For children twelve and older, the fun stops when they arrive at the labour camp. They will have domestic duties within their temporary homes and will be part of the farmworker labour pool. In California, it is legal for twelve-year-olds to work alongside their parents in the fields and orchards, as long as they are not handling dangerous chemicals or machinery. Migrant children older than fifteen are allowed by law to work without parent supervision and can handle dangerous chemicals, operate machinery, and be employed by packing sheds and canneries.[33]

The OMS housing guarantee for returning families who arrive at the labour camp during specific dates at the beginning of the season plays a crucial role in migration and destination choices. If the migrant family does not arrive on the specified move-in date, that temporary abode is placed in a pool, raffled, and awarded to a new applicant.[34] Migrant families expressed a shared sense of urgency regarding making the move-in date. As a result, the most common reason for migrating into specific areas of California was not necessarily employment in a specific subsector of agriculture, but having access to affordable, safe temporary housing.

Jesus articulates how OMS move-in and move-out dates dictate their migrations:

> We need to leave everything prepared and come to an understanding with [family members] who will stay behind. This year my oldest daughter will stay in Mission [Texas] so she can finish her schooling. . . . My wife assures that we have everything we will need for the four months we will be on the migrant trail. . . . My oldest son helps with the packing of the small trailer and with driving . . . We depart Texas in the early morning and pass through New Mexico and Arizona before arriving in California. . . . We must be there when the camp opens.*

Upon arrival to the labour camps, a flurry of activity takes place. In Parlier, California, a procession of vehicles enters the gates into the main waiting area in April. Those with return passes are escorted through a series of booths where they are processed. First, they are required to fill out an extensive application that provides details on all family members and where they have been and will be employed and provide proper documentation (a W-4 tax form and immigration papers). Second, a series of nonprofit organisations host informational sessions as to their services. Finally, families go through a walkthrough of the dwelling and are allowed to move into their home for the next 180 days. These procedures take place at all OMS labour camps throughout California.

Families without guaranteed housing wait for the raffle. Those who are lucky are called and follow the same steps as returning families. According to the data, they will return the following year and for many years after. The fates of the migrant families turned away are less known. Many will stay in the area and reside in dwellings that are unsafe and unsanitary, such as apartments with other migrant families, or in homes as boarders, or live out of their own vehicles.[35] New OMS residents shared that they had travelled to other OMS labour camps that open later in the season hoping to win a space in one.

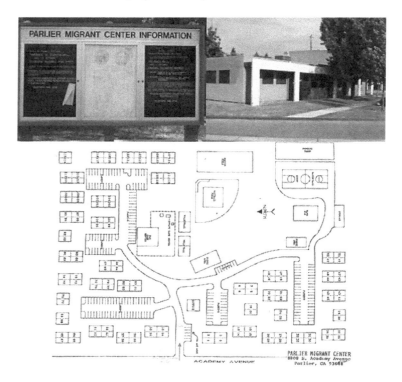

Figure 3.5　Migrant labour camp, Parlier, California.
Source: Multiple field observations, 2008–2009.

WITH THE OROZCOS

Major Spanish and English media outlets reported the death of seventeen-year-old Maria Isabel Vasquez Jimenez on 16 May 2008. The young farmworker, who was pregnant, had been pruning grapevines in hot weather (in the nineties Fahrenheit) and, in the sixth hour of the workday, collapsed and became disoriented from heat exhaustion and dehydration. The foreman and labour contractor refused to take her to seek medical attention and instead had her lay under the vines for several hours. When the labour contractor determined that she was gravely ill, he had a driver take her to a clinic, with explicit orders to lie about the circumstances of her illness. Doctors report that she would have had a good chance of survival if she had received treatment immediately. Instead, Maria was the next victim of agribusiness labour practices.

In the summer of 2008, we spent several days with the Orozco family, who have been migrating to the northern tip of the Central Valley for twelve years. Magdalena insisted, early in their marriage, that her husband apply for family-sponsored permanent resident visas on behalf of her and her two eldest children. After several years and thousands of dollars in application fees, they were awarded resident visas. Since then, they have been migrating for employment and searching for a place they can call home for more than a few months out of the year.

Magdalena Orozco, who is thirty-nine but looks several years older, wakes up at four in the morning and begins to prepare lunch for work. While she places leftover *chili con carne* in one Thermos and *frijoles* in another, she listens intently to Radio Mexico, 97.7 FM. During the weather report, she begins to worry. The temperature will most certainly reach the low hundreds, and the announcer reminds the listeners of Jimenez's death by dehydration earlier in the season. This concerns her because her two eldest will work alongside her and Simon in the peach orchard.

She wakes Victor, seventeen, and then Maria, fifteen. They need to have breakfast before they are picked up by the *contratista*. Raquel, seven, and Bernardo, a toddler, will be dropped off at the Migrant Education Center. *La escuelita* is outside the chain-link fence that separates their farmworker-housing community from another one next to the worker pick-up and drop-off points.

Simon, forty-five, has been married to Magdalena for eighteen years. He is outside, shaking the dust and peach-fuzz off the pick-bags while smoking a cigarette. This routine is not new to him; he recalls not having a choice the first time he migrated to the United States. Need forced his father (a former bracero) to decide that Simon's labour could contribute to the family's well-being. He migrated for the first to time to *El Norte* at fourteen. He felt ashamed for being afraid and for missing his mother, siblings, and grandparents. 'What else could we do?'*

Simon's first migration was to Fresno, California, where his father had relatives and was familiar with the employment circuit. They worked the very next day, picking grapes. This was brutal, backbreaking work for the most experienced and hardened farmworker, let alone a boy— ten hours a day, six days a week, for four weeks in a desert converted into a cornucopia. Since then, he has migrated to harvest strawberries in Florida, sugar beets in Michigan, cherries in Oregon, and apples in Washington. He has travelled for employment up and down California from the Coachella Valley to the northern tip of the Central Valley. Like most of his peers, Simon prides himself on being a hard worker 'who is not broken by the work'* and on being a *campesino*.

Magdalena speaks of the impact of migration on her children:

> Each year we migrate. . . peach and prunes here [Yuba-Sutter] then to Washington [state] to follow the apple season that lasts about three months . . . We return to this area and then off to Somerset [Arizona]. I believe that the most negative thing of all this movement is my children's schooling. They are never stable in any school because of our movement.*

The two older children are already working in the fields and will more than likely not finish high school. They will be tracked until they turn

Figure 3.6   Farmworkers in the fields and orchards.

Photos by the authors.

eighteen by migrant education programmes. Little is known about what happens to children of migrant farmworker families after they turn eighteen.[36]

The Orozco family's narrative is neither rare nor new. The commonalities between migrant families across the labour centres reveals patterns in migration and ways of living that have been path-dependent with employment practices and state policies for at least sixty-eight years.[37] These commonalities extend to other US migrant labour systems that are not solely supplied by Mexican labour. For example, the impacts of highly seasonal and labour-intensive migrant labour systems on working families are documented for African Americans in the South and Northeast,[38] Puerto Ricans and Caribbeans on the East Coast,[39] poor whites in the Midwest and California,[40] and Asian and Asian Americans in the Southwest.[41]

POLITICAL SOCIALISATION AND IDENTITY

On 25 March and 1 April 2006, immigrants, activists, their supporters, and protestors gathered in urban, metropolitan, and rural areas around the United States to voice their positions on HR Bill 4437, sponsored by Wisconsin Republican congressman James Sensenbrenner Jr. This law proposed further criminalising unauthorised migrants to secure the border from terrorists and the waves of 'illegal aliens.'[42] The protestors wanted, above all else, to express their disapproval of further criminalisation of unauthorised immigrants and the communities who would aid them. Most had been called to action by immigrant rights organisations because of proactive and transnational media networks (mainly Spanish radio and television). Part of the protest agenda was workplace and economic boycotts, with the intention of demonstrating immigrants' economic and social value. These protests were an opportunity to engage study participants in conversations about politics that affect the Mexican and Mexican American community. Unexpectedly, a large contingency of OMS residents participated in protests and boycotts to demonstrate their disapproval of HR 4437.

Alejandro González joined in the protests for two reasons. The first was that he wanted to show solidarity with his community to express his disappointment with this latest attack on immigrants. Second, he saw an opportunity for his family to become politicised by civically engaging in peaceful protest. They were connected to the marches through the Parlier

Catholic Church and informed by local Spanish radio and television. 'We awaken to the *Piolin por la Mañana* radio show',* he says, which throughout 2006 took the lead against anti-immigrant rhetoric. These were the largest political protests the United States had ever witnessed— families with children, high-school students, and men and women from all walks of life peacefully marched in protest.

   Alejandro recalls how well informed they were about the proposed law and the protests. 'They all knew'* the history of the law and of Congress-man Sensenbrenner, as well as where the protestors were to meet and what to wear and chant. The level of organisation and complex logistics that went into each protest speaks to the political awareness of those that organised these events, the complex communication networks that have evolved throughout the Latino community in the last sixty years, and the creation of a politicised, disenfranchised population that otherwise would not participate in formal politics.

   Alejandro speaks of his experience attending the protest:

> We marched through Fresno with thousands of other people. We arrived at City Hall where we demanded, in unison, that this law not be passed and for the passage of a just immigration law for all illegal immigrants. . . . We are not criminals.*

Alejandro and his wife Mariana are not US citizens. They cite what political scientists have found as the most common reasons for not naturalising—the application and process cost, the exam, and the language.[43] Another reason for low levels of naturalisation that emerged from the interviews was constant relocation. For international labour migrants who own homes in Mexico, US citizenship is not necessar-ily as important or integral to their immediate lives as for domestic labour migrants. On further examination, most expressed disdain toward mainstream US politics because of the negative presentation of immigrant labourers:

> *Alejandro*: My wife and I are permanent residents. . . I think we have not become US citizens because of the exam and because we do not speak English.
> *Mariana*: Well, I guess I could not tell you why I have not become a citizen, but I hear it is expensive.

Alejandro: It seems like it would be a good idea. But then, I have not needed it till now—so why become a US citizen if I have no use for it?*

In Watsonville, California, information is shared at the soccer field between the Migrant Education Center and the OMS housing units. On the outskirts of the field are benches with large shade trees used for recreation and relaxation. Soccer teams made of adults and adolescents have formed based on family relations and Mexican state of origin. On a brisk evening in July, a team with players from Jalisco took on a team of Michoacanos. After the match, we interviewed a couple in their late thirties whom we met during a mandatory community meeting to which the director of the Santa Cruz Housing Authority invited us; we would ultimately interview fifteen of the families volunteering there.[44]

Maria and Eufemio Marquez were quick to state that they were not political people: 'There is no time for formal politics' when you are struggling.* To them, the single most important issue was surviving the season and finding housing after the camp closed. This was their first year at the OMS centre and they felt fortunate to have won a unit during the raffle. They had been migrating to Watsonville for several years to work in the berry fields. They considered themselves fortunate because their migration only took them a little over two hours, and they secured housing quickly. They emigrated from Mexico in 2002. Their last home was in Oxnard, California, where they shared a two-bedroom apartment with another family. There they worked throughout Ventura County in lemon and avocado orchards.

They slowly began to share more about the reasons they did not engage with the marches more directly. Though they did not formally participate, they followed the coverage intently on the radio while at work and on television at home. They had high hopes that the marches would lead to comprehensive immigration reform, similar to the 1986 amnesty law. They finally shared in confidence[45] that Maria and their children Rosalio (seven) and Lizeth (four) were undocumented: they were scared of being exposed.[46]

Later in the season, Yesenia and Mario Salazar were interviewed at their unit at the Buena Vista migrant labour camp on the outskirts of Watsonville. Unusually for a migrant couple, they are highly politicised and vote in Mexican and US elections. Mario is the current president of the *comite directiva* at the labour camp and a member of the United Farm Workers union. They became naturalised US citizens in 1997 with the help of the union, which organised a citizenship drive and offered evening classes. For them, the decision to naturalise came soon after the passage of the 1996 Welfare Reform Act (officially the Personal Responsibility and Work Opportunity Reconciliation Act). They shared that the national debates about extending this law and limiting or even denying services to permanent residents scared them. Thus, their decision to naturalise was very much a pragmatic one.

Mario and Yesenia have been migrant farmworkers for decades. Since 1971, they have been returning to the Buena Vista camp as a family and have lived half of their adult lives there. Mario first came to Santa Cruz County with his father and brother (both former braceros and now deceased) at fourteen. His father placed him in a local high school so he could learn English. He went to school while on the season for two years, then decided to drop out. Yesenia has also been migrating to this area since the early 1970s. Her father (also a former Bracero) was friends with Mario's family, migrated to the same area, and worked in the same agriculture fields. They married and in that same year joined the families on the yearly migration from rural Jalisco to Buena Vista—both with *papeles*. They formed their family in the context of labour migration and now two of their three children have settled in California with their families.

The Salazars are part of a three-generation migrant-farmworker family stream that continues; their oldest son migrates with his family on the season with them. The two youngest live in the San Jose area, their daughter working as a teacher and their son in construction. They credit their children's ability to break from the migrant lifestyle to the opportunities afforded to them as US-born citizens. Early on, local and statewide education service programmes tracked them: the Head Start Program (healthy development of infant and toddlers), Migrant Education Program (middle and high school), and College Assistance Migrant Program (California State University—systemwide; their daughter attended San Jose State University). They are the lucky ones. Great disparity exists amongst migrant farmworker children within all immigrant status categories and at all levels of schooling. Yesenia speaks of her children's educational success:

> We allowed them to go to school and only took them to work when they were available. . . . The two youngest chose to continue. I am not sure how they did it, but they did [finish high school]. I believe that being citizens here helped them tremendously. I see many young and

smart children in the fields that cannot go to school because they don't have papers. . . . What for? they say. We will not be able to use it to get a job anyway.*

History has shown that when the Latino community perceives that it is being attacked, levels of participation and naturalisation increase. Ultimately, HR 4437 passed the House of Representatives but failed in the Senate. Immigrant-rights activists framed its defeat as a victory, but this left the immigrant community waiting for comprehensive immigration reform that did not come.

Figure 3.7   Politics, labour law, and integration.
Photos by the authors.

Migrant families travel to engage in a multitude of agriculture jobs. They stoop to harvest vegetables and fruits. They hoe weeds and thin row crops in the heat of summer from sunrise to sunset. They pick strawberries, run, stack, and load the product—as precise as any assembly plant. They run up and down fifteen-foot ladders with fifty-pound pick-bags attached to their bodies until they fill half-tonne bins. They follow shakers and catchers (mechanised harvesters) on their knees, picking from the dirt any prunes the machines drop. Men, women, and children cross international and state borders to tie, dig, plant, thin, pick, sort, weed, run, load, pack, can and process food in almost every region of California, urban and rural. Wherever land needs to be prepared for planting or crops tended and harvested, you will find migrant farmworker families.

Today, agribusiness is as dependent on labour as it was seventy-five years ago. The sciences behind the mechanisation efforts is nowhere near creating a machine with the same level of intellect, dexterity, or complex movement that humans have. Thus, farmworkers will remain an essential mainstay in agricultural production.

The economic, political, and social impacts of agriculture employment, housing systems, and state practices on migrant farmworker families are profound. The research presented here reveals that these macro-level structures influence migrant families' decisions about migration and how these families are integrated into local communities based on industrial agricultural production needs. The structures discussed in this research have institutionalised poverty: this is the core of the context of reception for migrant farmworkers. No matter how hard they work, most will never achieve the American dream. They will continue to work in the fields and orchards until their bodies no longer allow them to do so. They are bound to a system of agriculture production that thrives on labour exploitation. Workers know this. Bosses, politicians, pundits, academics, and many progressive thinkers know it, too.

4

Racism, Capitalist Inequality, and the Cooperative Mode of Production

INTRODUCTION

There was a steady line of people waiting to get their last-minute pastries before the bakery closed.[1] The workers joked and laughed as they worked. There was no one rushing them or telling them what to do. They all had tasks and knew what they had to do. The radio was playing a Spanish station with Mexican music. The bakery was on Valencia Street in San Francisco, which is the dividing line between the traditionally working-class Mission District and a more upscale community that has been moving in with the tech boom in the Bay Area. Mexican music playing in a business that caters to an upscale and largely white demographic seemed odd, if pleasant. It highlighted the diversity that this type of cooperative might seek to represent.

Before the Network of Bay Area Worker Cooperatives (No BAWC) meeting, it wasn't clear if the worker-owners understood the historical significance of what they were engaged in, but their mission statement— on the wall in very large and bold writing—read:

> We are a worker-owned cooperative that values and supports local community, social justice, and the environment. We aim to create the highest quality affordable baked goods; maintain an equal and positive work space; and provide workers with ongoing learning and skill development opportunities. We also support the creation of new cooperatives in the mission.

This bakery is one of seven independently run worker cooperatives that are part of a bakery association. Many things differentiate this business from others, including its culture, the collegiality among the workers, and the initiative and pride they take in their work, but the most important is that it is worker-owned and democratically controlled. While such enterprises have been around for several decades (the first bakery, named Cheeseboard, was started in 1971), they seem to be spreading and gaining steam as a viable and sustainable alternative to the types of businesses that led us into the 2008–09 economic crisis. They incorporate different values than those that give preference to profits above all else.

IDENTITY CHALLENGES WITHIN COOPERATIVES

While cooperatives provide more value for worker-owners and community members than normal businesses because they distribute earnings horizontally,[2] they are not without their fair share of problems. Because workers are socialised into the values and norms of a given society, they are subject to the problems that society perpetuates, including how perceptions of race and racism affect workers' interactions. Cooperatives within the United States, while attempting to change the economic structure of society, are still products of the US socio-cultural arena and its norms, including the often complex effects of racism.

Ron Schmidt argues that 'race plays a role in US politics because there is contestation over the political meaning and significance of so-called racial identities, and over inequalities and power relations between so-called racial groups.'[3] The literature on race, racism, and racial inequality is vast but necessary to explore in attempting to understand both how these types of organisations are affected by race on a micro-level within the organisation and also by how the cooperative national structure is affected by issues of racial inequality stemming from other societal influences. For instance, critical race theory (CRT) scholars argue that race occupies the central and most important position of oppression in the United States.[4] Specifically, they argue that 'racism is ordinary, not aberrational—"normal science," the usual way society does business, the common, everyday experience of most people of color in this country.'[5] The CRT arguments focus on placing race in a central position in any legal, educational, social policy, or institutional analysis.

Similarly, Omi and Winant's classic theory of racial formation places the same emphasis on race. For them, race is the primary factor in the development of US politics through what they term the 'racial state', which has operated according to the logic of the ideology of white supremacy. They argue that the state is inherently racial and that, 'far from intervening in racial conflicts, the state is itself the preeminent site of racial conflict.'[6] The racial state engages in racial politics through what was initially a racial dictatorship that completely excluded people of colour and exacted physical violence upon nonwhites to attain their subjugation.[7] This racial dictatorship eventually became a racial hegemony that operates on physical subjugation as well as consent through psychological fear of violence. This social hegemony, in turn, elaborates and maintains 'a popular system of ideas and practices—through education, the media, religion, folk wisdom, etc.—which [Gramsci] called "common sense".[8] The hegemonic system is achieved by what they term 'racial projects', which are defined as 'simultaneously an interpretation, representation, or exploitation of racial dynamics and an effort to reorganise and redistribute resources along particular racial lines'.[9] Their theoretical framework ultimately focuses on the hierarchical racial dissemination of resources that leaves people of colour, and specifically Blacks, on the outside looking in.

Intersectionality also provides a useful analytical tool for understanding the complexity of human interactions within organisations, especially within US contexts, as it specifically deals with how individuals experience different oppressions. In 1945, Claudia Jones introduced the concept of the 'triple oppression'—'the oppression of black women based on sex, race, and class'—that poor women of colour face in the United States.[10] Jones, a Trinidadian immigrant and member of the US Communist Party, challenged the party on its posing the essentialist question of whether to focus on class issues or race issues.[11] She argued that the layered identities of poor women of colour could not be detached from one another. They were all three different identities: gender, class, and race; having a conversation about which to focus on was simplistic and reductionist. In 1991, Kimberlé Crenshaw, building on the concept of multiple layers of oppression, introduced the now famous and heavily debated concept of intersectionality to highlight the essentialism existing within identity politics. According to Crenshaw, 'The problem with identity politics is not that it fails to transcend difference, as some critics charge, but rather the opposite, that it frequently conflates or ignores intragroup differences'.[12] Often, people's identities are essentialised into one-dimensional categories and put in contradistinction with one another.

Crenshaw begins to add more complexity to Jones's initial framework of multiple oppressions, focusing on how identities are multidimensional and situationally contextual and interact in different ways for different people. They are fluid and nonstatic markers of who we are, and they interact with each other in a myriad of very interesting complex and often contradictory ways. Thus, Jones's and Crenshaw's arguments bring to light the need to pay attention to the different layers of identity and how they interact. Patricia Hill Collins takes this argument and couples it with Black feminist thought, showing how images of Black women have a real-world effect on their lives.[13] How Black women are perceived interacts with their gender, class, race, and other identities to create conditions of different, intersecting layers of oppression of types and magnitudes that other racial groups do not face. In order to understand racial oppression, one must therefore understand the social complexity in which it is integrated and how it functions differently for different people. Peggy Macintosh adds to this debate by drawing out the different systems of privilege historically created by these dynamics, specifically highlighting how white privilege mirrors male privilege.[14]

These frameworks are instructive in attempting to understand the internal behavioural dynamics of work relations within cooperatives, even when there is an attempt to create an inclusive and equitable environment. Even though cooperatives, as collectives of workers-owners, are interested in creating a different economy and culture, one largely progressive and open, they still face social identity problems. Samantha, a queer Black Latina, for instance, argues that while her co-worker-owners are on the same page about the business and what kind of economy they are attempting to build, issues of race, class, gender, sexuality, etc., often surface within the organisation, even though she feels the group is intentional about addressing these and building solidarity around them. She argues that

as much as we may try, we will still see forms of oppression kind of springing forth here. It's disheartening but it's a good reminder that there is so much work to be done. . . . On one level, it's hard, because you see hierarchies sort of forming here in a way: like, some people's opinions could be taken more seriously than others, or some people talk more than others, or some people take on more responsibilities, or some people are more dominant in this workplace, and I think a lot of times it has a lot of overlap with race, gender, class, and you'll see that happening. So there's that, and it's not horrible, and we are constantly trying to work on it. Like you'll see people having a moment, 'I'm talking a lot here,' and step back at meetings. People are growing and learning and getting better at it with time, which is so

appreciated. . . . Then there is also a notion [that] our different sense of
priorities could be difficult. Because none of our priorities are all the
same. . . . But there was a large division in our [coop], it's still kind of
lingering, of like Latin American immigrants versus everyone else. . . .
There's these bohemian non-immigrant people and then there's Latin
American immigrants who are trying to hold it down, so there is a
definite cultural and definite social division happening here.[15]

In this exchange, Samantha is attempting to express the complexities of
identities and how they manifest in work processes. Even when people
are conscious about their identities and the different privileges they have,
and even though they may be intentional in addressing them in positive
ways, through open dialogues and conflict resolution, different issues
still surface. Osvaldo, another worker-owner at the coop, hints at the
same point:

You could see the divide in our [cooperative], you know, like pretty
clearly too, between the Latinos and the LGBT community, and
whenever we're making decisions and voting on them you can see a
clear line, you know, in terms of which way people are voting. It's very
visible and everybody sees it, and we're only now starting to talk about
it in terms of common vision, because I think that's what the biggest
problem is in terms of being able to work through these issues.[16]

Intersectionality helps in attempting to understand these issues within
the workplace. It is clear that the various workers at Samantha's cooperative all come from different backgrounds, all of which affect the
struggles they do or do not face individually. Samantha expressed differences between workers who are struggling to survive (holding it down)
and those she feels are privileged and are doing this work because it's
cool or trendy (bohemian). Osvaldo was a little more specific in pointing
at Latinos and LGBT people, but it is important to note that there are
no clear dividing lines. Osvaldo is specifically referring to white LGBT
worker-owners, but some worker-owners—like Samantha—fall into
both identity group categories. This points to how intersectionality helps
us understand the complex nature of work in an environment specifically designed to ameliorate societal inequalities. Samantha understands
that there is a life difference and a difference in the magnitude of struggle
between gender, national origin, class, and race and that this affects how

people interact at work and what they take for granted (their different systems of privilege). For her, the struggle of being a working-class immigrant in the United States has a different magnitude than some of the other issues.

To understand Osvaldo's position and why the line of demarcation for him within the cooperative is clearer, it is important to understand his story.

> So I grew up in Immokalee [Florida]. It's a small farmworker town, man, but it's big in terms of like, it's all farm work out there, man, tomatoes, bell peppers, you know. Watermelon season usually starts down there in southwest Florida and the town I grew up in, pretty much. I guess, like a lot of small towns, man, there are no opportunities there really. You don't really learn anything about the outside world, you know? When you're in a small town like that, you sort of live in a box. . . . You don't see the shit that is going on in the outside world, you just see your own little community and, like, I don't know, man. Like everyone that I grew up with pretty much has gone to prison or did some crazy shit or is like nowhere right now, man, because we are not sort of like the culture of like going to fucking college and shit. You know what I'm saying? It's mainly like drinking and hanging out in the street and shit. So that's pretty much where I grew up, and the thing that sort of changed for me, I think, was this organisation, man.
> When I turned about fourteen, you know, I was out in the streets . . . chilling and I see this group hanging out in front of a farm—maybe fifteen—and I see this group of people marching past the water, man, in Immokalee, and I'm like, what the hell is that? It turns out this farmworker was beaten in the fields for basically wanting to get a drink of water and I didn't know that at the time, I just see this group of people and I thought it was fucking cool. They were marching past and yelling and shit. Later on, when I found out about it, I don't know, I'd never seen anything like that in our community, man. It was like the beginning of something just different. . . . I had been a farmworker for a long time . . . and so since then, man, I've been sort of, I've been doing that [organising] off and on, 'cause I was still, even though the coalition[17] was a new window into a way of looking at shit, man, I was still kind of stuck in my own, like drinking all the time and screwing up in the streets and shit like that, you know what I mean? . . . Every now and then I'd go take off and do something

else for a little bit; then I'd come back and be in the coalition again. But I think who I am today, man, has a lot to do with the coalition, man, in terms of opening my mind to, like, see things in a different way. . . . I eventually ended up in prison any damn way and I did three years for some dumb shit. . . . I was, like, on the run in Mexico City for like a year during that time, too, and then I was away from my daughter. And so my daughter was born and I was fucking up so bad. I started drinking more and more and, obviously, you know, I ended up stealing a cop car and hauling ass and then went to Mexico for a year on the run. I ended up getting caught and coming back. I got caught on the border . . . that's when I decided, you know what? I need to go and do my time. I want to be with my daughter, you know? I don't want to be on the fucking run all the damn time. So I did my three years and said to myself, you know, while I'm in there, I'm going to do whatever the fuck I can to change the way I think about things and, like, I don't know, figure out how to do something with my life so that I can be a part of her life, you know what I'm saying? And so as soon as I got out of prison in Florida, my daughter had moved over here to Berkeley with her mother, and so I worked my way this way and just did whatever I could to get by.[18]

This history of struggle sets Osvaldo apart from the other people in his cooperative, especially those Samantha refers to as 'bohemian'. His struggle has always been about a lack of resources, which is a material struggle, not just an internal or personal identity struggle. His personal and identity struggles are all couched by the fact that he has lived in poverty his whole life; thus, the identity struggles he does encounter are all conditioned by this material reality. By the time he joined the cooperative he was carrying multiple levels of identity: farmworker, ex-convict, Latino, organiser, and father. All are conditioned by what material resources he has access to (monetary or otherwise). Such questions of economic survival undergird his understanding of the politics within the cooperative. He clearly delineates between those who are trying to survive—a struggle like his own, one of overcoming poverty—and those who are in the cooperative for a more welcoming space.

Highlighting these issues should not be taken as an attempt to rank any of the specific struggles, but rather to show the nuance and complexity of how they all come to interact within spaces that are supposed to be, and intend to be, 'an equal and positive work space'. For both Samantha and Osvaldo, the layers of struggle for the immigrants in the cooperative run deeper and are more complex because of racial dynamics and how immigrants are often treated and infantilised. What comes out clearly is a racial dividing line between what issues matter more and to whom. Based on interviews and observations, the brown and Black workers seem more concerned about material well-being because they come from vulnerable backgrounds of poverty. The white workers seem to be more concerned with issues of identity and process. Macintosh points to these dynamics, which she attributes to whiteness but which can also be interpreted as class-based.[19] What results from this is a contestation in the workplace over power. For Samantha and Osvaldo, the dividing line over that struggle for power is somewhat racialised, although intersectionality helps us see that this demarcation is not simple.

PATERNALISM IN A COOPERATIVE ENVIRONMENT

Gabriela, a Latina immigrant, reports that in her attempts to start a worker cooperative, she has been faced with a level of paternalism from the mostly white worker-cooperative developers[20] as well as superiors of the same ethnic background but different class position. She states,

> Since Freedom Café [a worker cooperative] existed already and we wanted to exist, we started talking with them to share information, what were their challenges . . . what were our challenges? One day the facilitator tells me, 'Hey, I'm leaving, but why don't you come and take my position in Freedom Café?' And I say, 'I have a commitment to these women at the Latina Center, I cannot leave them for that job.' But if you accept us all . . . we want to be part of a cooperative, and since you are a cooperative, maybe we can work with you.' So she spoke with Jane, and Jane said we would talk. All of the women from the Latina Center went to participate at Freedom Café. The problem was the people running the café had a different business idea than ours, which was selling healthy food. Not that we are against healthy food, because we also sell healthy food . . . but we wanted and were Latin fusion, and the food that we sell is very different and the concept is very different, even though the Latin food we sell is also healthy. Then, three months later, we decided that we no longer wanted to continue with their cooperative and instead we wanted to continue with the idea of our business.[21]*

This exchange calls into question several factors. The first is the democratic process of worker cooperatives. If Gabriela and her friends had joined this new organisation and now made up the majority, why couldn't they change the direction of the business, especially if they were going to be the owners of the cooperative? Why would the café not be willing to consider changes or a new direction in light of new membership? Based on observations made during the interview with Gabriela, it was clear that the people in positions to make such decisions weren't actually the workers but rather the people working for the nonprofits that funded these endeavours, who were largely white. This brings into focus a different aspect of race and racial paternalism. Gabriela did not say it outright, but it was clear from how she talked about it and her nonverbal communication that she experienced a racialised and class-based paternalism in her interactions with the white cooperative developers. Similar processes were observed in other cooperatives.

The study was supposed to initially focus on an organisation that focused on developing Latina cooperatives. That research could not be completed because of the organisation's inability to grant us access to the cooperatives. The people at the organisation, who were mostly white and formally educated, explicitly ruled out asking the cooperative workers themselves for access to interviews or observations. It was not clear at first why, if these worker cooperatives were in fact democratically owned and controlled and therefore autonomous, the nonprofit leaders would ask us not to talk to the worker-owners. Arguably, such paternalistic interactions were not just racialised but based on class status and assumptions about the type of decisions that workers could or could not make. In some of the interviews, especially those in which a worker cooperative was created by a developer organisation (usually a nonprofit), there was much less worker autonomy in decision-making, much like Gabriela experienced at Freedom Café. We argue that this lack of autonomy comes from base assumptions (often false ones) about the education and experience of these workers, assumptions that largely disempower and take agency away from the workers, especially low-income immigrant women. These organisations were empowering low-income Latina women with good and dignified jobs, but at the same time doing so through racialised paternalism. The fact remains that most of the people at the forefront of cooperative development, while well-intentioned, were educated white people; in their attempts to address economic issues of inequality, hard-working Latino/a worker-owners were being paraded around to workshops and presentations to tell and sell 'their' stories.

This is common in the nonprofit world, where good stories make for more funding. The concept is even called 'poverty pimping' by those critical of the nonprofit industrial complex, which often takes advantage of the dire conditions that people in poverty face. These stories are packaged into grant proposals and programmes intended to help alleviate the conditions, but never really deal with their root causes. A classic example that Mike Davis discusses is the drug and gang war in the United States, specifically Los Angeles, and how it fed the massive growth of police departments and nonprofit anti-gang programmes across the country. Gangs were extremely profitable for both of these industries. In 1992, during the Los Angeles Uprising, the Crips and the Bloods gangs declared a truce; the police department played both gangs against each other to get them to return to their antagonism. Selling the story of fear and gangs paid for SWAT tanks and equipment. It also funded anti-gang programmes that attempted to reform individuals rather than deal with the root causes of gang affiliation, namely lack of access to the kinds of well-paid jobs that had been available a generation before but had since been outsourced abroad due to neoliberalism.[22]

The difference in the case of the co-ops is that, although they focus on root causes, that doesn't preclude them from commodifying workers' stories in order to sell their brand. Gabriela experienced this multiple times with different organisations, including the one that trained her in organising and the one at which she was working when she began to research cooperatives but on her own time. With respect to the work she did building her cooperative, she says:

I did the work of organising [the cooperative] on my own time. There came a point where the organisation [Latina Center] wanted to take that. . . . I mean, they did not pay absolutely anything for my research, my work, my meetings. It was extra work I was doing. I met Saturday night with the leaders. None of that work I did was paid, but as it began to accumulate, the challenge became that they wanted it. They began asking, 'Okay, how is the cooperative going?' as if it was a project I was working on for them. I then notified them that I would be leaving work for the centre in July because I would be going with the cooperative full time. That process was not a positive one, because they tried to say that the cooperative began with them and was theirs, and it wasn't. I had to tell them it did not belong to them because they did not pay me for doing that job and it was a lot of work; it was my research that I did with my resources, that was it. Really, what the organisation was doing . . . all this, you know, they wanted to use to write grants to bring money to the organisation, but none of it would reach the cooperative, nothing. . . . They use that stuff to obtain more money, to apply for more support. And I said that I did not want that kind of paternalism because that's using people but without giving them the resources they need. So, in conclusion, I do not think that it would do us or anyone well to be under the umbrella of an organisation. At least we are truly empowered. For us, the decisions that we make are those of the members, not of an outside organisation.[23*]

The organisation she worked for attempted to commodify Gabriela's work and time because they saw potential in what she was doing on her own time. They saw it as a potential funding source for the work of their centre rather than as a good for the worker-owners who would benefit from the economic independence of co-owning their own business. That they felt they could assume ownership points to what they ultimately felt about Gabriela. The assumption that a project could be taken from someone who had put so much work into it is an attempt to exert power over that person; that is done only when someone feels that other person is weak. It points to an inherent paternalism and disjointed power relationships within the people involved. They thought they could get away with taking advantage of Gabriela because they ultimately did not see her as an equal.

What these comments from Samantha, Osvaldo, and Gabriela point to is that sometimes embedded in racial, gender, or sexuality categories are connotations of class and more; these are all conditioned by real circumstances. When Samantha and Osvaldo refer to *Latinos*, there is embedded in their use of the term the idea that people that come from difficult, and often poor backgrounds and are also often immigrants. Gabriela similarly confided that she felt that, although it came from people who meant well, the paternalism she experienced stemmed from their assumptions about her based on her working-class immigrant background, which is only her identity on this side of the border because of her immigration status. In Mexico, Gabriela was a college-educated teacher who worked in the countryside helping rural communities. Her actual experience working with cooperatives far exceeds that of the people who were paternalistic toward her. In Mexico, she dramatically changed a small, impoverished rural town over time by employing all the women through an embroidering cooperative:

I then noticed that the women of the village embroidered very nicely. But they only embroidered napkins, because they had lost the tradition of wearing embroidered blouses. . . . So I asked them . . . I went one day to Ocosingo [the nearest town] and I realised that they knew how to embroider and the women there did make blouses and sold at fifty pesos, which was quite a bit of money at that time. So I came back and I proposed to a girl, I said 'Hey, would you be interested embroidering blouses? You do a very nice job on your napkins'. She laughed and said, 'No, blouses, what for?' . . . and I told her, well, to sell. It was at that time that a young religious woman was visiting and I told her that they knew how to make those beautiful embroidered napkins and they could also make blouses. And she tells me, 'If we can make blouses, I will give them 500 pesos to buy fabric and thread'. . . . and we went [she and I] to buy fabric and thread and then we called that girl . . . and then we cut one blouse and I drew the flowers and told the girl, 'Can you help us embroider it and when we finish we will sell it and I will give half? And she says 'Okay'. And so she went, and in three days she came back with the finished blouse, and, boy, was it a beauty of a blouse. I tell her, 'You want to take another?' And, well, she took the other but returned three days later with another blouse and her cousin. Then the cousin took one, and then she brought another girl and then another girl . . . and when we had twenty blouses, three German tourist women arrived to visit the community. I told them, 'Hey, we are selling embroidered blouses,' and they said, 'Okay then, let's go to the school.' Well, we had put up a small school, and we put a display of blouses there and the German girls said, 'We want them all'. So we sold all the blouses, and half of what we made we gave to each of those who embroidered, and the other half was left to purchase more fabric. I finished my work there because my child was growing up and I wanted him to go to another place to study. And I think my cycle in the community was over, but the school was still there, the workshop was still there . . . and my contacts to distribute blouses stayed as well. They started to not only make blouses to sell abroad but they also began to sell clothes that they liked there in the community. And they distributed the earnings and had gatherings. . . . I tell you, the Indigenous community uses cooperatives as a way of life, it is not something new for them. So they had their strength of community, the strength of women and men. . . and they already use coopera- tives as their way of life . . . they know they should do meetings, they should report and they must reach agreements, there must be a vote, and no one needs to teach them this. They know—that is how their lives function.*

This experience was a formative one for Gabriela, as it showed her the power of working collaboratively. It allowed the women economic freedom, which wasn't just about money. This translated to something much more important than being able to purchase goods but rather the ability to not have to depend on men for their economic survival. This is a large accomplishment because, according to the National Coalition Against Domestic Violence, lack of income is a common reason victims cite for staying in abusive relationships.[24] Batterers often control victims' finances to prevent them from accessing resources, working, or main- taining control of their earnings, achieving self-sufficiency, and gaining financial independence.[25]

Gabriela helped develop a community worker cooperative that employed approximately one hundred women, yet in the United States she was being told by cooperative developers that she should follow their lead or hand the project over to them, even though in most cases they were leading failing enterprises like the Freedom Café and had little to no experience building cooperatives themselves. This paternal- ism was ultimately what led her to struggle from the very bottom with her colleagues to develop their own unaffiliated cooperative. What was important to the women was the autonomy to carry their vision forward, even at the expense of having to start from scratch, with few to no resources. This autonomy is a key factor in building cooperatives and in why they are important. The freedom of collective and autonomous decision-making is what many workers enjoy about cooperatives. They have the freedom to decide the fate of their business together. Worker-cooperative developer organisations ought to be mindful of this fact and allow the workers they are purporting to help the freedom to make decisions. This often is not the case, as workers of colour are often recruited to be part of a project by developer organisations rather than to build their own projects semi-autonomously. In such cases, power relations are clearly prejudiced by racial and other identity dynamics. These dynamics also play out within worker cooperatives themselves.

MOVING BEYOND A POLITICS OF DIFFERENCE

Samantha further deconstructed the complexity of identities and how they interact when she responded to a question about the identity make-up of her co-worker/owners:

> Almost everybody is a person of colour, almost everybody. . . . What makes it hard is that there [are] so many queer people here, but I actually don't count them as white in my head because they have another form of discrimination. So, yes, they benefit from whiteness, but there is also something that is so heavily going against them. . . . I think sometimes there's an 'oppression Olympics' thing that sort of happens here. It happens a lot in social justice circles, I think, where it's like, the person with the most boxes gets away with most shit. I feel like it happens here a lot. It's awful, right? If you're a woman, if you're trans, if you're an immigrant, if English isn't your first language. . . . Do you know what I'm trying to say? Well, then it's like, 'I can say whatever I want in this space now because I'm the most oppressed.' Like, shut up, it doesn't work that way.

Her comment here points to an interesting dynamic which she terms 'oppression Olympics': in essence, this is when workers compete for the status of being the most authentically oppressed, as if this earns one person more legitimacy or space to speak over others. While intersectionality can be useful in understanding and acknowledging the struggles of co-workers, which can be empowering and positive if used to build solidarity, when what Samantha describes begins to happen, it is much like tumbling down Alice's rabbit hole. The conversation or dynamics cease to be constructive and result in this 'oppression Olympics', or what Darder and Torres term a 'laundry list of oppressions'.[26] Where does a competition over who is more oppressed really lead?

Samantha confronted the positive way the cooperative dealt with intersectional issues like this from the very beginning of her experience at the cooperative. She recounted the very first time she was interviewed by only women:

They got back to me and I was in the interview, and I was already feeling the place because it was all women interviewing me. Number one, women were interviewing me, which I thought was interesting, because usually a couple of white guys are talking to me and I'm like rolling my eyes and you just mentally want to shut down. So it was all women interviewing me, first off. And then it was two women of colour. There was Cristy and Lulu, both, like, brown women, and then also Madeline, who's Eurasian, and then Jane, who's a queer white woman, and then I can clearly see this is kind of my spot. . . . Right off the bat it was super diverse, and so I said cool, and they were all really friendly and awesome and I felt really good about my interview, and it was nice.

Here, intersectionality is instructive in helping to understand the social processes of interaction and the power dynamics of getting a job. For the first time in Samantha's life she confronts a seemingly normal inter-action—a job interview—under completely abnormal (for our society) circumstances—being interviewed by only women. To Samantha, this changed the whole power dynamic of the interview process. For her it meant being asked questions by people she felt could relate to her and who might share similar struggles. Whether or not that was actually true is not necessarily the point; the point is that Samantha's perception of the situation—of understanding the different intersectional processes going on with the multiple people and identities in the room—changed her response to the situation. It allowed her to feel more justified in being herself, rather than attempting to fit into what her perception of a white, male job candidate might be. The fact that she could identify the dif-ferences and the layered politics (gender, race, class, sexuality) within the group of women interviewing her and how they mattered for her contextual situation was important in helping her navigate getting the job. Specifically, through understanding the intersectional politics at play in the situation, she could relate to the shared struggle and find a feeling of solidarity with the diversity of women in the room, especially finding common cause with the two women of colour in the room. This allowed her to interview for the job with a feeling of liberation and freedom she had never experienced before.

It is obvious that the cooperative was intentional in this process. Osvaldo confirms this: 'People were hired with diversity in mind, you know what I mean, because of the community that we're in, you know, in the Mission District and all of the history of gentrification there'.[27] Samantha was allowed to become an employee and has since been voted in and allowed to buy into the cooperative, becoming a worker-owner. In this way, intersectionality is useful in helping us and others understand how people navigate social situations. Similarly, it helped the people who were already worker-owners be intentional about interviewing new candidates and changing the power dynamics of a process that is often taken for granted.

It is also important to note that these social working relationships take place within a given arena, what Gramsci would call the structure. Samantha was in that situation because she needed a job. Osvaldo began his journey as a child-labourer and continues to define himself through hard work. Gabriela began her cooperative journey as a means for self-sufficiency. As such, intersectionality is useful in attempting to understand the complex nature of day-to-day social relations; as Samantha suggests, however, things don't happen in a vacuum. Similarly, for Osvaldo, the cooperative isn't *just* about creating a socially progressive alternative or building something for the future. While he cares about that also, the cooperative for him is about an immediate material impact on *his* and his daughter's life. While he cares about solidarity within his co-workers and respecting the different identities within his workplace, ultimately the cooperative form to him matters because it has provided him an opportunity that is rarely afforded to others with his background. For Osvaldo, these other issues matter, but they exist within a material struggle for survival. He argues, 'The thing is, there's a class difference, man. We really have to recognise how different people are in different classes. you know what I mean?' His understanding of these dynamics points to the knowledge that, while his co-workers are dealing with issues of identity, these issues are situated within a given economic social formation that conditions (but does not determine) how they all play out. Similarly, for Gabriela, cooperatives are a means of empowering women and helping them become self-sufficient to escape abuse and domestic violence. Thus, conversations about identity and intersectionality ought to be tempered and situated within the material context in which they occur.

Darder and Torres suggest that the legal system, education, identity politics, and all of the complexity therein are located in a given economic context and shaped by the imperatives of capital.[28] Therefore, when attempting to analyse issues of identity, it is important to always keep in mind that the complex social relations to which intersectionality and CRT attempt to draw attention all happen within that framework. Any analysis of racism in contemporary society thus ought to begin with the capitalist mode of production, classes, and class struggle. The processes intersectionality and CRT seek to understand and make central are themselves embedded within a context that is conditioned by people's economic (survival) necessities. In this respect, Darder and Torres argue that to focus explicitly on this 'politics of identity' rather than challenging the social construction of the category of race, which has been proven to be biologically false, only serves to entrench race as an identity. This is not to say that they argue for a colour-blind society; rather, they suggest that, instead of entrenching race as an identity category, we must analyse the processes of racism instead—in much the same way we argue that the category of 'Latino', rather than providing any analytical specificity, often obfuscates issues related to people's material conditions. Rather than debating what is and is not a Latino or Latinx or Chicano/a or the many iterations of identity labels, we ought more to focus on the ways in which racism functions within the system of capitalism to relegate brown people and other people of colour to the lowest economic positions in society. As such, Darder and Torres argue that an explicit focus on *only* race leaves CRT and racial formation theory lacking a systematic analysis of class or, more importantly, a substantive critique of capitalism.[29] In fact, Wood argues that these and other theories actually essentialise and conflate class and capitalism at best and, at worst, they reduce one (capitalism) into another (class).[30] She goes on to argue that it is important to understand that 'the class relation that constitutes capitalism is not, after all, just a personal identity, nor even just a principle of "stratification" or inequality. It is not only a specific system of power relations but also the constitutive relation of a distinctive social process, the dynamic of accumulation and the self-expansion of capital.'[31] It is important to note that Darder and Torres, in their denial of the centrality of race as a category, do 'not imply the denial of racism or the racist ideologies that have been central to capitalist exploitation and domination around the globe.'[32] For them, racism 'is *one of* the primary ideologies by which material conditions in society are organised and perpetuated in the service of capitalist accumulation.'[33]

An important contribution of cooperatives, then, that Samantha highlights is that those like the one she co-owns, which make a conscious effort to deal with difficult issues of identity and struggle, provide an avenue not just for identity but for structural economic equality. Darder and Torres make an important contribution in this regard as they highlight that intersectionality, and for that matter CRT and racial formation theory, all function and occur within the context of global capitalism. For them and for Wood, these plural identities exist 'within the determinative force of capitalism, its drive for accumulation, its commodification of all social life, its creation of the market as a necessity, and so on'.[34] As the dominant economic system, it permeates and conditions every aspect of the varying identities, rather than being reducible to class.[35]

What this means is that within the confines of the workplace, inter-sectionality, CRT, and racial formation theory help in understanding the different positions from which workers are operating. They help us acknowledge one another's struggles, as long as it leads to building soli-darity rather than becoming a type of 'oppression Olympics', as Samantha put it. She went on to state that, for her, the importance in understand-ing identities is in *acknowledging* the different oppressions, rather than using them as a trump card. She argued that it was important to use intersectional understandings of identity to 'build bridges' of solidarity in order to keep their eye on the big picture (economic equality), while also building identity equity. Osvaldo also weighed in, arguing:

I mean, you could be well-intentioned, but you're not recognising that there is a huge difference in culture, man, you know what I'm saying, and willing to work through the differences together as opposed to wanting your own sort of ideology to push through, then it's not going to fucking work, man. There needs to be openness in terms of like, on both sides, . . . working together to solve these problems to create something new. . . . And I do think something new needs to be created, you know what I mean, 'cause it's not just going to go one way or the other, in my opinion. It's going to be something different and something unique that has to come from dialogue from both sides and openness from both sides that I don't see happening right now and I see as a problem. And I think it's one of the things we've been trying to work through or work with at our bakery. I think that is why it's so important for us to start talking about what our common vision is with all of this stuff, man, so that we can be able to communicate more effectively in a more productive way . . . in a more understanding way of each other and who we are and where we come from. 'Cause without that shit, man, it's like we're going to be constantly fighting over stupid stuff, then not being able to talk about it, you know what I mean, because we don't understand each other. Anyways, it took us a while to get there, man, but we're now just starting to talk about that stuff and it's a good fucking thing, and it's only going to get better, hopefully.

Ultimately, they both feel that cooperatives that practice democratic decision-making and promote a culture of democracy, inclusiveness, and solidarity aren't just good for and effective at dealing with identity issues within the workplace; they also serve as a space for economic equality, especially for people of colour who lack access to opportunities because of structural discrimination.

RACISM AND THE MACROPOLITICS OF COOPERATIVES

Stepping back, we can begin to look at how these processes look on the macro-level, specifically in relation to cooperatives. One of the most accessible tools for introducing people to what cooperatives do and represent this is the film *Shift Change*,[36] which interviews workers-owners from several worker cooperatives, most in the United States. While this is an exceptional tool to show how these organisations function, some of the problems they face, and how they are resolved, one thing that becomes apparent throughout the film is the racial composition of the worker-owners in different industries. In the engineering cooperatives that are featured, most if not all of the workers seen are white and mostly male. When workers of colour are featured, they are doing traditionally low-wage labour work: cleaning cooperatives in the Bay Area or industrial manual-labour jobs in Cleveland.[37] This isn't to say that these companies have problems of racial discrimination (they may), but that these cooperatives are subject to and a microcosm of the racial conditions and contexts of the larger society. For instance, women make up the majority of worker-owners in cooperatives, yet find themselves on the outside looking in when it comes to accessing white-collar cooperative worker-ownership positions as well as leadership positions within their own cooperatives.[38] This is a result of the educational structure and the gendered and racialised labour force in the United States.

Latinas, for instance, 'are part of the largest and fastest growing minority group in the U.S. . . . [yet] earn a meager 60 cents for every dollar earned by a white man, representing the largest wage gap of any other group of working women'.[39] More than one-third of Latinas have less than a high school education. Latinas have the lowest employment-to-population ratio in the nation, at 52.7 percent. Latinas are also more likely to work in the low-wage service industry than any other population of colour; a lack of stable financial opportunities puts them in a very vulnerable economic position, and they experience one of the highest poverty rates of women in the labour force.[40]

Given this, it is not surprising to see that Latinas compose the largest segment of the growing worker-cooperative movement, but largely in service-sector industries. For instance, in the Bay Area, there is a complex of worker cooperatives devoted to helping Latina women whose focus is mostly in developing cleaning and food cooperatives. This isn't necessarily a negative development, because Latinas are largely doing that work already. Cooperative opportunities allow them to do it in a safer and better-paying environment. On an individual level, the cooperatives clearly provide better opportunities and working conditions for their female workers and workers of colour. For instance, the complex of cleaning cooperatives in the Bay Area pays, on average, 158 percent of what competitor companies pay; the cooperatives in the complex increase the median household income of their workers by an average 70 to 86 percent.[41] They also cover medical benefits as well as vacation time, sick days, and disability benefits. There is also less mental stress on women when they need to request days off, as there is no pressure that the supervisor will be upset. This is not a quantifiable benefit but it is extremely important. Peace of mind in the workplace is rare, but as stress is more and more linked to issues of health, it becomes an important benefit of working in cooperatives. That benefit provides the confidence and freedom to not have to stress over having to take time off to attend to a sick family member or one's own health. Cooperatives also empower the women with democratic decision-making that allows them to discuss, for example, whether to work with, toxic or organic cleaning products?

Similarly, Samantha notes that her cooperative 'pays fourteen [dollars per hour] on the weekdays and eighteen on the weekends. . . so it's really minimal, like super minimal, but you can live on it, you know?' She adds, 'If I had a family, no, that wouldn't work, but for me as a single woman it works'.[42] Her cooperative is one of the fairly new ones, but in her cooperative network, mature cooperatives pay thirty dollars an hour or more, a very liveable wage.[43] In relation to other workers' living and family conditions, she states that 'One candidate has two children, one of our founders has a kid, and two people recently had kids around the same time—each of them have one kid now, one little child. . . . I know I can live in Oakland easily, but over here [San Francisco], that's hard'. Clearly the cooperative is paying her what she considers a fair amount, especially given the benefits it provides.

However, another implication is that while her job provides a decent living for her, it does so only as long as she is a single woman without children. Also, she points to an interesting discussion over cost of living and specifically gentrification. The fact that Samantha makes enough to live what she feels is a life with dignity does not obscure the fact that she cannot afford to live in or near the area where she works. This highlights another important conversation on the role of cooperatives in building a different type of economy: What responsibility do cooperatives as a whole have in addressing structural issues like racism and even gentrification? While cooperatives benefit workers in a real material sense, as stated above, looking at them from a macrostructural perspective demonstrates that they face problems in achieving the goals that they seek for in the economy itself. If cooperatives are truly interested in developing social and economic justice, like the bakery suggests with its missions statement, then there needs to be a discussion about how to accomplish justice not just within cooperatives and for their individual worker-owner members, but also within the economy as a whole. For instance, what are the broader implications of perpetuating a largely two-tiered labour system that has historically relegated and still relegates workers of colour to manual labour jobs and has its roots in racial segregation, racial job competition, and structural inequality in educational attainment?

Statistically speaking, it is well known that African Americans and Latinos, because of lack of resources and access to quality education, have dismally low university enrolment and worse graduation rates. In the STEM (science, technology, engineering, and mathematics) fields, those numbers are even lower.[44] This isn't a problem of motivation but a failing of the larger society to promote and develop African American and Latino talent. Knowing this, though, cooperatives should make a concerted effort to recruit those few students of colour who make it out of their white-collar professional undergraduate training. Otherwise they run the risk of perpetuating the two-tiered labour system. The Economic Policy Institute estimates that, while the national unemployment rate fell to 5.6 percent for African Americans, it remains 10.4 percent in December of 2014 and is double that for people between sixteen and thirty.[45] Its report also argues that unemployment is more volatile for Black workers than for whites; wages of Black workers are on average 8 percent lower than those of white workers in the same industries. Latinos also hold a larger percentage of lower-income jobs.

As a result, dealing with incomes is only part of the macrostructural conversation. Housing is important, as Samantha noted. Thus, it is important to ask what sort of impact cooperatives have on processes of gentrification. Monica, the director of a national organisation for cooperatives, said:

> There's only so much profit margin you're going to get with retail, unless you're selling things at a huge mark-up to rich people, which is a strategy. We don't try putting bakeries in neighbourhoods in which people aren't going to pay four dollars for a scone. And it's like a wealth redistribution strategy. It's not necessarily meeting a community need, because that's not where the money is. So I think, with retail, it's an interesting strategic question. Are you trying to meet a community need, and create jobs, and make a stable institution, or are you trying to make a cash cow? And if that's that the case, then you probably don't want to meet a community need, because you don't want to try and extract that from people. I mean, I think you can do both. I mean somebody has to run a Laundromat, and that's a way to make money and still meet the community need. But I'm always interested in pushing it to the next level, beyond retail: what do we do that meets people's needs for real jobs and maybe also produces something people need?

Monica here points to a paradox facing cooperatives. In order to function, they need to be profitable. And in order for them to be profitable and pay what they want to pay worker-owners, they need to sell products at marked-up prices. This means strategically putting retail cooperatives in neighbourhoods where people can afford their products, or in communities that are 'up and coming' (in the process of being gentrified). They do this because rent is relatively cheap in these 'up and coming' neighbourhoods, but they still get the clientele that is moving in and will pay four dollars for a scone. However, this has a negative effect, driving housing prices up. So, while Melissa sees this process as redistributive—

taking money from wealthier people (customers) and giving it to working people (worker-owners)—it also works in reverse, as worker-owners and others are priced out of those same neighbourhoods. One bakery is in the middle of this paradox, as Osvaldo suggests:

> When I first came in I started seeing the difference between Mission Street and Valencia Street, which, I don't know if you—you saw the difference, right? It's pretty much all white, upper-middle-class people moving into the neighbourhood, pushing poorer brown folks out. I know there's a history between the African Americans who have been sort of pushed out of the community and so there's a lot of that, and I've been talking to a whole lot of different organisations around there about it . . . [and it's important to fight] for more inclusivity in the African American and Latino communities, man. Instead of us [the cooperative] just being part of the gentrification process, which is sort of what we are being right now because we are not really reaching out to the community in the ways that I think we can. Well, we kind of are, but I feel like we could be doing more and so, I don't know, man, I really feel like it's so, for me it's really important.[46]

Here Osvaldo points to the tension he feels about the role that his cooperative is playing in the gentrification process. To him it is important to use the cooperative to stave off gentrification rather than advancing it. He is very intentional in his thought process about how the cooperative should and can accomplish that:

> I think it's important to base the decisions on the community and put that shit first. One of the examples of that is when we are voting on whether or not to raise the prices on our products, you know what I mean, we could be raising the prices on our products because of the location that we are at, you know what I'm saying, and a lot of us don't go for that unless we see we really have to raise the prices, 'cause we want our products to be accessible to those who aren't loaded with money. . . . That is part of combating the whole gentrification shit.[47]

Another example of this that Osvaldo covers has to do with how his bakery can combat gentrification through hiring practices:

> I know there's this thing where you can't really base hiring on race or anything like that, but I feel like if we don't, the result will be gen-

trification—and there is a reason because a lot of it has to do with education. I mean, you have all of these upper-middle-class, really, white people who are moving into the area, so when they are applying for a job, you know what I mean, they are the ones who are going to get the opportunity. It's not going to be the people in the community, and so if we don't actively reach out and actively hire in terms of class and culture and race, then there is only one way that shit is going to go.

For this reason, cooperatives remain the most forward-thinking economic alternative to business as usual, especially when coupled with other policies that help tackle issues like gentrification from different angles. For instance, while cooperatives provide better wages, that only deals with one side of the issue. What good are higher wages if they are accompanied by higher rents and costs of living? Cooperatives accompanied by rent control and other policies, like implementing affordable nonprofit or even cooperative housing, all help collectively deal with issues of affordability in ways that allow communities to thrive without causing displacement. Communities are not made up of buildings; they are made up of people. What good is it to improve the infrastructure in a neighbourhood through redevelopment if it displaces the community that gave that neighbourhood its history and culture?

Cooperatives are therefore an important part of the economic democracy eco-system that is necessary to make communities more liveable and democratic in nature and practice. However, there needs to be a more concerted effort to deal effectively with some of the internal problems, like paternalism, identity and racial relations issues, and some of the more structural issues of systemic racism and gentrification, which are problems that confront all businesses. Those that deal effectively with these have, in our experience, been those that consciously engage in democracy and worker autonomy. These are necessary elements that these businesses need to promote in order for workers to actually begin to address these sorts of issues and talk about their impact on local communities. They also help workers to cope or deal with issues of racism and race in their cooperative and, more importantly, to tackle the material issues of inequality in their communities, especially working-class communities of colour. It will be important for cooperatives to ask these larger questions and deal with their macrostructural role in alleviating the history of racial inequality, especially if they are to be truly transformative models for people of colour.

COOPERATIVES AND A BETTER QUALITY OF LIFE

For the people like those interviewed here, cooperatives have had a fundamental impact on the material reality of their lives and opportunities. Their value comes across not in dollar amounts but in what this means to the workers: autonomy, democracy, and even the ability to confront systemic issues head on. This is especially beneficial for workers of colour, who are the most vulnerable demographic in the labour force when it comes to abuse and maltreatment from bosses. For instance, as Samantha noted, there was intention on the part of those interviewing her to provide a space that was amenable to and aware of the power dynamics of race and gender. This is important in helping people to thrive in spaces or situations of pressure. Ultimately, this is why Samantha enjoys working at her cooperative:

> I enjoy coming here, for sure. . . . Everyone can tell you that. . . . I walk in at that door with a giant smile on my face. . . . At the nonprofit I was working at before . . . it was always straight white girls and I had a really hard time being myself in that environment . . . they were all wonderful, though. It was about me, they weren't doing anything wrong. . . . They are all still my good, good friends and I love them all so much, but it was definitely a different place to be in . . . like, I had to play straight . . . raise my voice up a couple octaves and play into the surroundings I was in. . . . And here I can just be whoever, like, you look behind the counter, we are a really random group of people . . . and I feel like I can just paint a picture of who I am here and it will somehow fit in and be useful in some way. I also feel like I can just grow in whatever way I want to, compared to my nonprofit-world experience . . . just because, say I wanted a skill in a certain area, I can do that. I can bring it here, whereas at a nonprofit, if I had a set of tasks, I did those tasks, and if I sucked at it then I needed to get better, and if there was something else I wanted to bring to it, it wasn't as easy to just fit it in. But say, here, if I wanted to start taking up web design, I could easily start practising on the website here or, if I wanted to, I could easily start repairing stuff around here . . . or I could learn a bunch of stuff that could help this place out—and I probably should, now that I think about it—but . . . yeah, I can bring who I am here.

For her, working at the cooperative has been a liberating experience that has allowed her to develop her interests and helped her grow in any direction. Beyond her personally benefiting, she also believes that cooperatives are especially helpful in developing leadership abilities in people of colour, which for her has larger impacts. She suggests that she views cooperatives as especially beneficial for people of colour because:

> I see it as a way of how coloured people are working together . . . Of course, I'm not trying to say that it should be exclusive to people of colour only . . . but it could definitely work in favour of people of colour in terms of building a community, building skills, building a sense of leadership, because of course you have to be a leader and you can't just sit back, and I think it's great for people of colour.

Samantha sees cooperatives as not just a workplace to get better wages or a space of personal liberation, but as spaces where people of colour can develop leadership skills and training to improve their communities. For cooperatives that intentionally work toward providing skill building and training, it becomes an important space for workers of colour to learn skills and become educated in democracy and organisation, which they can then contribute to their communities. This is what Tim Huet refers to when he describes cooperatives as 'democracy demonstration projects'. What he means is that we need spaces where people can learn how to act and participate democratically in everyday life, so that we can live democratically on a daily basis.

For others, cooperatives are all of these things, but also opportunities to escape conditions that historically have kept people from thriving. For Osvaldo, an ex-convict with little education and minimal job prospects, it redefined his whole life:

> I got the job and it's been pretty awesome. But I don't know what I'd be doing now, man. I mean I went to ninth grade, basically, and I was only in ninth grade for like a few fucking months, man, you know what I'm saying, like I was kicked out of ninth grade when I was fifteen. I've just been working ever since. I just didn't have an experience with anything else, man. Like, right now, I don't even have a trade that, you know, I could fall onto. I don't have a lot of fucking options, especially since I'm an ex-convict now. If it wasn't for [the bakery], I don't know

what the fuck I'd be doing. I definitively wouldn't be the owner of a business, you know what I'm saying?

Working for the bakery has given him an opportunity afforded to very few people with his background. It has allowed him to thrive and develop intellectually. While he may not have formal education beyond ninth grade, in our interview we discussed gentrification and the system of capitalism, and he had a very developed frame of thought based on his life experience. Not only did the bakery give him a new opportunity at life, it did so by providing him a well-paying job that allows him to become a good father and live with dignity. The material impact on his life goes beyond dollars and cents:

> I never, ever in my life had health insurance or even thought about having health insurance, man, and now I have all of that stuff, and it's weird 'cause, like, at a time when . . . I don't know, it's just weird, it's like everything is falling into place. I never thought about having health insurance and now I do. I recently found out that I had a brain tumour that was like the size of a golf ball, that I wouldn't have known that I had, had I not been working here. They operated on it, took it out, I didn't have to pay shit for it, you know what I'm saying? It's like, I don't know, man, it's kind of crazy how shit works out, and so I'm really grateful.

In an era where workers' benefits and wages are being taken from them, this is a tremendous contribution for people like Osvaldo. Working at the cooperative literally saved his life, while also transforming his ability to change its trajectory.

Similarly, Gabriela sees cooperatives as not just income-generating spaces but a way to transform people's lives. Because of her personal experience she specifically saw cooperatives as a potential vehicle for women to gain economic independence and autonomy to escape domestic violence. After leaving Chiapas and the Indigenous women, she moved back to Guadalajara and worked at a nonprofit, where she met her now ex-husband. After that they moved to the United States, a tremendous change even for someone who was educated:

> I came in 2005 . . . and, as you know, I did not speak English or know how to drive and was undocumented. And then I started living with

domestic violence by the father of my children. But as I always used to look for resources, I started looking for resources for support and I found the Latina Center. When I visited the clinic for my children for their physical examination, I found a brochure about the Latina Center. I went to talk to the director and one day she answered the phone . . . and she had a thousand questions: Where did I come from? What were my skills? What were my dreams? What was my situation and how did I feel? She heard me for two hours. She said, 'Look, honey, you are going to take bus number 72 . . . and do not tell the father of your children that you are coming here'. So I started going to a support group, and I started to realise that it was the situation of all the women there. But the peculiarity of this organisation is that it has a leadership programme for Latinas. The programme lasts one year and gives a monthly training that is divided into three phases. The first phase was self-esteem. They work a lot to help women increases their self-esteem and know their worth, know their abilities, and recognise their skills and to help them see their full potential . . . and help with setting goals to start to look at goals, set them, fulfil them. The next phase is that women have to think of something that is affecting their life in relation to what is affecting their community. And so you have to choose a project to help solve that problem, and she has to write how that project will solve a problem. . . . how can it be a change. The third phase is to go into the community and put it into action, and after that you graduate as a community leader. So, according to what I had lived in Mexico and according to the challenges that I was being presented here and the challenges facing the people I met when I was in the support group . . . my project was . . . okay, I said, if in Chiapas by all us women getting together we developed a project with the cooperative, maybe here we can do the same. My approach was to develop a cooperative to help women in domestic violence that focused on helping to make them financially self-sufficient, so they could find independence from an abusive relationship . . . or if they were already out of an abusive relationship, that they could be economically self-sufficient.*

For Gabriela, it wasn't just about making a good living or being able to buy nice things, but what that good living meant for women in abusive relationships. It meant freedom from fear, the opportunity and ability to change direction when stuck in a difficult situation. Ultimately, it is the difference between living miserable, abused lives or living with a sense of freedom and possibility and the capacity to develop and grow as human beings. Gabriela sees cooperatives as an opportunity for vulnerable populations to overcome structural gender barriers, for her specifically Latina undocumented immigrant women. For women with very little opportunity and few prospects, this is a game changer. Words can't describe what this means for women in those types of situations, so much so that Gabriela in discussing this began to shed tears, both of sadness in remembering what she had been through and also happiness in the potential she saw in cooperatives for women like herself.

In the final analysis, this is why cooperatives matter for communities of colour: not just because of the dollar amounts involved but what those dollar amounts mean. They mean opportunity within a system that has relegated them to the bottom rungs of society. They mean opportunities not easily accessed unless you have the right education, the right connections or networks, or simply the right skin colour or gender. Cooperatives offer not just an opportunity within capitalism, but an opportunity to transform and shift the mode of production to something different, something that allows for people to develop their humanity. It allows the opportunity for people like Samantha, Osvaldo, and Gabriela to liberate themselves from racial, gender, sexual, and economic inequality.

COOPERATIVES, A CULTURAL WAR OF POSITION, AND THE FORMATION OF THE NEXT LEFT HISTORICAL BLOC

In her excellent book *Collective Courage: A History of African American Cooperative Economic Thought and Practice*, Jessica Gordon Nembhard recounts the history and practice of cooperatives among black communities in the United States. She situates black cooperative economics as an alternative form of economic development that grows out of racist exclusionary structures and a need in the black community to develop their own economy in order to access resources necessary for survival. She recounts how the US system of slavery and then, post-Reconstruction, Jim Crow left blacks in the US shut out of ownership as well as out of large segments of the labour force (especially those segments with advancement opportunities), which necessitated alternative strategies for communities to come together to provide the resources and services that were critical for their survival. She argues that she was interested in cooperative economic development as a community economic development strategy... and [her] focus was on how cooperatives help subaltern populations gain economic independence, especially in the face of racial segregation, racial discrimination and market failure...[she] began exploring ways in which cooperative ownership, particularly in worker cooperatives, is a strategy for community-based asset building, and [she] began to develop a concept of community wealth based on cooperative ownership and community assets.[48]

The book is fascinating and well researched and while she comes to the same conclusion as we have, in that for her cooperatives offer people of colour opportunities that they can't or don't have access to because of structural racism, there is one fundamental difference in our approaches to the topic. Gordon Nembhard situates cooperatives as a niche alternative within a framework of capitalism that has socially and economically excluded African Americans. For her, cooperatives are a solution to being shut out of a capitalist economy and labour market, and as such cooperatives become a way to enter the capitalist economy. She sees them as a means to develop black communities economically within the system of capitalism, as a corrective to 'market failure'. Cooperatives thus become a mechanism for accessing and becoming part of capitalism rather than a way to subvert it.

Our assessment of cooperatives suggests that cooperatives are themselves a counterhegemonic program that can transform capitalism into something else. The idea and praxis of cooperatives are part of the necessary conditions to create what Gramsci referred to as a new historical bloc. Gramsci argues that changing the socio-economic circumstances does not of itself produce political changes: it only sets the conditions in which such changes become possible.[49] Cooperatives and the cooperative mode of production provide the conditions for the possibility for political change in their practice of democracy. Because they are founded on democratic principles and focus on daily democratic participation, they become training grounds for democracy, or as Tim Huet suggests, 'democracy demonstration projects', where democracy and democratic culture can be practiced on a daily basis. In this sense they change the structure of our society in at least two fundamental ways. One, they change the ownership structure from one in which there is a separation between owners, those who extract profit and have control (power and decision-making), and those workers who only receive part of what they produce (and have no power to participate in decisions), to one in which the two are one and the same, thus eliminating exploitation from the worker-owner relation. Two, they impart a cultural transformation in the daily practice of democracy. They promote and disseminate democracy as a process in the very act of practicing it, expounding theory through praxis, leading through example. This second point is important and should not be overlooked.

People in the United States assume that they live in a democracy, but what is democratic about having democracy only in the 'civic' sphere, practicing it once or maybe twice a year and not in the economy, the arena which is the foundation of our society? How can we truly say that our country is democratic if people themselves aren't practicing democracy on a daily basis? If you define democracy as most political-science scholars do—having free and fair elections—then it appears we do live in a democracy. The problem with this definition, however, is that democracy is not about having choices: it is about having power. The two are not the same. Recall Helen Keller's comment about democratic choice: 'Our Democracy is but a name. We vote? What does that mean? It means that we choose between two bodies of real, though not avowed, autocrats. We choose between Tweedledum and Tweedledee'.[50]

Sheldon Wolin describes democracy as

> one among many versions of the political but it is peculiar in being the one idea that most other versions pay lip service to. I am reluctant . . . to describe democracy as a 'form' of government . . . in my understanding, democracy is a project concerned with the political potentialities of ordinary citizens, that is with their possibilities for becoming political beings through self-discovery of common concerns and of modes of action for realizing them.[51]

He understands democracy as being one form of the political that is rooted in action. He goes on to suggest that democracy is about how the political is experienced and asserts that it has a fugitive character. But this fugitive character only characterises democracy in our current society, where it is in fact rare. In an economy based on democratic cooperativism, it is practiced daily on a regular basis. In an economy with a democratic character and values as its founding principles, democracy becomes a verb, something to be engaged in regularly, where ordinary individuals realise they are capable of creating new cultural patterns of commonality and act accordingly.[52] Similarly, Lummis has defined democracy as its simple etymology: 'people power'.[53] How can you have democracy in a society whose whole economy is structured around keeping people from having power within the workforce?

The importance of cooperatives is not just in their power to transform working people's lives (which is extremely valuable), but in their ability to be part of creating a new historical bloc, what Laclau and Mouffe call a counterhegemonic program, that has the potential to challenge capitalism for hegemony.[54] Worker cooperatives provide the cultural training, the cultural activity, the ideological and value-laden discourse, and the potential for forming a cultural front to run alongside the changing economic and political structures. Worker cooperatives have the capacity to function as part of the ideological war of position between capital and labour, changing the conceptions of how people imagine labour relations can function. They change the terrain of what is possible, achievable, and necessary. In that sense, cooperatives don't just make sense as a niche market for people shut out of the economy or as a way into that very same economy as a corrective to 'market failure': they make sense as a more efficient and democratic 'new normal' form of organisation that has the potential to transform and change the capitalist paradigm to something different. Capitalism has already provided the space for their development.

NEOLIBERAL CRISES AND SPACE FOR COUNTERHEGEMONY

Marx asserted that internal contradictions within the system of capitalism lead it to provide spaces for change.[55] Marx and current Marxist scholars suggest that periodic crises within capitalism leave openings for new possibilities, or at the very least for other modes of production to challenge capitalism. This is because, as Maurice Dobb once wrote,

> Systems are never in reality to be found in their pure form, and in any period of history elements characteristic both of preceding and succeeding periods are to be found, sometimes mingled in extraordinary complexity. Important elements of each new society, although not necessarily the complete embryo of it, are contained within the womb of the old; and relics of an old society survive for long into the new.[56]

Capitalist crises provide spaces for these new or other systems to challenge it. The crises that the US has been experiencing since the 1970s have wreaked havoc on it and on the world. We are at the proverbial fork in the road, economically as well as biospherically, if you will; we can continue down the same destructive, predatory, profiteering, militaristic path or enact alternatives. One of the major problems with the current American economy is that it no longer manufactures anything. The American economy used to be such a world power because it was built around industrial production: 'Until the latter part of the twentieth century, US industries were world-class producers of basic industrial equipment'.[57] This is no longer the case; we have moved to a post-Fordist economy that outsources production to other countries. As a result, we have become a 'post-industrial economy' with very few tech jobs and a whole lot of low-wage service-industry jobs. This has had a disastrous effect on the average worker's purchasing power. More and more people have to work longer hours at jobs they never thought they would have, and sometimes multiple jobs, just to get by. According to Melman, the design and the production capabilities for ships, propulsion, navigation, and infrastructure, as well as the classes of equipment and the skills required for manufacturing heavy railroad equipment, have disappeared from the United States.[58]

Without this capability, the United States must rely on other countries to provide its technological infrastructure. It has a massive need to manufacture the innovative ideas and products that individuals and companies are developing to meet the growing need for greener and advanced technologies. From hyperloops to solar roadways and playgrounds to moisture-capturing billboards, the opportunities are endless.[59] For each of these ideas there are many others which our manufacturing capacity is ill-equipped to produce on the scale necessary to fix our crumbling infrastructure or create a prosperous new economy. What led to the dwindling of the manufacturing economy, though, ironically, is also part of the 'embryo' that can help develop a new, cooperative economy. A rebuilt manufacturing base need not be a massive Fordist operation with smokestacks everywhere. While neoliberalism has been devastating in many respects, it has also shown that decentralisation is not only possible but can also be efficient. David Harvey defines neoliberalism as:

a theory of political economic practices that proposes that human well-being can best be advanced by liberating individual entrepreneurial freedoms and skills within an institutional framework characterized by strong private property rights, free markets, and free trade . . . the role of the state is to guarantee, for example the quality and integrity of money. It must also setup those military, defense, police and legal structures and functions required to secure private property rights and to guarantee, by force if need be the proper functioning of markets. . . . Furthermore, if markets do not exist (in areas such as land, water, education, health care, social security, or environmental pollution) then they must be created, by state action if necessary.[60]

The turn towards neoliberalism since the 1970s has led to three key new features of this form of capitalism: deregulation, privatisation, and decentralisation.[61] In the first instance, governments have retreated from regulating businesses, letting markets 'self-regulate'—which has been disastrous for the conditions of workers and communities the world over, especially because average workers and citizens have no input into the decisions companies make. There is no discussion within corporations about moral or ethical practices nor of their impacts, much less space for such dialogue, as people's livelihoods are at stake. In the second instance, it has led to a move away from the conception that the state has a role in providing citizens with any sort of 'public good'. This has caused a series of state sell-offs of formerly government-provided services that were and are essential to establish a fair market. Government public services, in many ways, keep private industry honest by providing affordable not-for-profit competition that keeps private-sector prices down. Imagine what the cost of mailing a letter would be if the US Postal Service was privatised. Where companies are meant to compete, they often collude to raise prices; this is especially apparent with the oil industry.[62] In the third instance, neoliberalism has decentralised the economy by outsourcing manufacturing to countries where labour is cheaper. In the US this has meant a shift away from industrialisation to a post-industrial paradox of high-tech knowledge-labour jobs and a no-tech service sector, with a very minimal intervening economy to bridge the two. Currently, the majority of US workers, 79.9 percent, are employed in the service industry, most at very low wages.[63]

This transformation has resulted in union autoworkers and other manufacturing workers who made middle-class wages and had middle-class lifestyles being sacked and put out on the street, struggling in minimum-wage jobs and fighting to escape poverty. While this is tragic, the mental-health impact on a generation of older men who used to be able to support their families is heart-breaking. Hit in higher proportion to their numbers were workers of colour, historically the last hired and the first fired in the process of transformation.[64] This de-industrialisation has been one of the major reasons for the continued decades-long urban inequality that is today being brought to light by protests and uprisings in places like Ferguson and Baltimore.[65] According to Robert Pollin, neoliberal policies have led to 'deeper vulnerabilities' being exposed, 'problems of *American capitalism itself*—the system as a whole'.[66] How is a system that continues to impoverish working people efficient? It isn't, and Engler argues that 'the capitalist market is the problem, not the solution'.[67]

While neoliberalism has created conditions that have eroded workers' wages and conditions and structured a declining standard of living for many Americans, it also provides some opportunities for moving forward and has opened up spaces for change. It has shown that local, decentralised production is not only possible but can be efficient. What we mean by efficient is not only in getting products from production to market but also in stabilising local economies where production takes place, in a decentralised and democratically organised form. Worker cooperatives are primed to develop within this framework of decentralisation, and if they do, they could also empower local communities. Neoliberalism has laid the foundation for a decentralised, cooperative mode of production that is controlled democratically by workers at the point of production. In decentralising the economy, neoliberalism has provided space for workers to control the operations at the point of production; this has the potential to change the structure of the economy from the ground up. The challenge now comes in changing the mode of production to one where workers own the means of production while at the same time deploying the culture and values of democracy in an effort to challenge the dominance of the profit motive and capitalism itself.

An example of this arose in a discussion with a professor about the outsourcing of the University of California–Irvine janitorial staff. There had been a few-years-long campaign to get the custodial staff insourced so that workers could receive benefits and fair wages. Workers and students were finally successful in convincing the administration to insource the workers, but this created a problem for workers who had immigration status issues. We suggested that it would be interesting if, rather than insourcing the workers, someone could organise them into a worker cooperative that they controlled and ran democratically. This would allow them to cut out the nonproductive owners of the business who created no value, and solve the issue of the university not wanting to insource the workers as well as its requirement to document immigration statuses. The workers would be outsourced, but would own and control their own business and focus on their specialisation and have the opportunity to grow their market share; the university would support that form of community support (with some pressure from students and faculty as a way of supporting living wages).

The move towards outsourcing, while a neoliberal practice, doesn't need to be a negative. It is only negative in that in its current orientation it leads to diminished wages, but its need comes from a business's interest to shed nonessential functions. In the case of the University of California, that means shedding non-knowledge-producing or transmitting functions, like custodial work. As currently practiced, this is detrimental to workers, as they are outsourced to private, low-wage-paying companies. But this need not be the case, as worker cooperatives can compete effectively in that market because they don't need to subsidise the wealthy lifestyle of the owner or their family. However convincing people that this is possible and also appealing as a form of empowering working communities is a large task, in that even though we have been through this crisis, politicians continue to promote the same old remedies to our economic problems. Brendan Martin argues that

> slump, financial instability, collapsing infrastructure and public services, deeper and wider social divisions, record homelessness, declining sense of community and national morale—these have been among Thatcherism's legacies, compounded by its eponym's successors. Reaganism has bequeathed similar millstones in the United States, and what is there to show for it? In both countries, the rationale was cut public spending. In both countries, it ended up deeper in the red than ever before. If that is success then failure is hard to imagine, and yet the free market triumphalists appear to have learned nothing.[68]

This includes President Obama, a Democrat, who continued this line of detrimental economic development and sought support for the Trans-Pacific Partnership, a free-trade deal involving twelve countries that would further the damage that other trade agreements, like NAFTA, have done to US workers. President Trump has done the same thing by signing a tax cut to the wealthy.[69]

MOVING FROM AN ANTI-AGENDA TOWARDS
A COOPERATIVE MODE OF PRODUCTION

Osvaldo believes the shift towards cooperatives is immensely important:

I feel like cooperatives, like that's the future, like the future of human society.... I feel like that's what we should be working towards, because the current situation, I mean, capitalism just doesn't fucking work, man! I mean, it works for a few people, it doesn't work for everybody, and people get left behind and, yeah. I mean, I think I feel like cooperativism is like the answer to that shit and maybe it's not cooperativism in like what it looks like today, but I feel like we're sort of evolving towards like whatever it is that it's going to be in the future.

This comment is poignant for a few reasons. In the first instance many would be surprised that someone with his background could make a statement about the totality and the failure of American capitalism. But why would anyone be surprised that someone who has been part of the backbone of the capitalist economy, a worker who has worked various jobs, understands the nature of the system? Osvaldo, like many workers across the country, understands the system and who it is meant to work for. When you begin to pick fruit in the fields at the age of eight, you know instantly that this system was not meant for you, nor will it ever work for people like you. Second, his critique of capitalism evolves beyond an anti-systemic sentiment.

This seems trivial but is of immense importance. Often, as scholars or critics, we focus on what is wrong with the current system or structures and attempt to pinpoint problems—what has been termed a 'tinkering politics'. There is a slew of movements or loose associations tied to ideas of anti-systems or anti-structures: for instance, people who care about and do work on anti-racism or anti-capitalism or anti-patriarchy. But rarely do these associated ideas and people confer around ideas of what their visions of the future are; rather, they focus on what they are against. It is easy to see the problems of our current society because we are living them, but if we are anti-racist, anti-capitalist, or anti-patriarchy, what would we replace these things with once we have done the work of toppling them? What are we for? This also begs the question of process. Is the goal to topple these discourses and practices first and then to replace them with something else, or does the replacing happen as a process leading up to the destruction of the old? One only need look at history to answer this question. In this book we argue that Latino/a workers are at the forefront of asking these questions and of envisioning these alternative futures.

Capitalism developed during and within the system of feudalism, only to become the dominant form once it had gained enough traction, supporters, and wealth to challenge the aristocracy. With this in mind then, one of the important findings of my research is that it isn't enough to be anti-systemic; rather, much like Tim Huet suggests, we must begin to build that which we seek to replace our anti-systemic proclivities. For Osvaldo and others, that means growing and building the cooperative movement with social justice ideals and democratic culture. This means moving beyond a critique of capital and even beyond looking to the state to ameliorate the effects of capitalism. It means there must be a move towards building that thing we wish to see replace what we currently have.

Worse still than being anti-, Wendy Brown argues that today, too often, 'leftists have largely forsaken analyses of the liberal state and capitalism as sites of domination and have focused instead on their implication in political and economic inequalities. . . . [Instead they] turn to the state for protection against the worst abuses of the market'.[70] In doing so, Brown argues, 'they decline to consider the state as a vehicle of domination'. While in many ways it is important to force the state to open up and become democratic, as the women's movement and civil rights movement and the anti-Vietnam War movement have done, it is also important to begin to live democratically. While many leftists emphasise agency through social movements and seeking redress in the social or political sphere, i.e., the state, it is ultimately the mode of production that is the source of exploitation and injustice. As long as the mode of production remains the same, any political victories will be minimal, as political candidates and office holders may differ on social policy but never really on economic policy. E.P. Thompson notes that a central concept of Marx is 'that a given productive system not only produces commodities, it also reproduces itself, its productive relations and its ideological forms and legitimations'.[71] Therefore the capitalist mode of production reproduces capitalism, and always will as long as that mode or form exists. The only way to change the reproduction of the system, then, is to change the way the productive system itself is structured. If we look at democracy as a process and practice, then we can't look to the state to give it to us: we must begin to practice it, and the only agents capable of doing so are those who produce—the working class. Thompson suggests that the connection between historical process and the mode of production is human experience; praxis (human experience through agency) is what allows change in the mode of production in a historical process.[72] Therefore any change in the structure will have to take place in the restructuring of the mode of production itself and not necessarily in the political sphere. Simply, what this means is that we have to change our mode of thinking and being: we need to begin to live and practice democratically.

There is a fine philosophical line here that merits discussion as far as what role worker cooperatives have in reproducing versus restructuring the mode of production. Are the hegemonic projects of anti-racism, anti-capitalism, and anti-patriarchy about seeking inclusion and fixing the current system? Are they working within the system rather than trying to challenge it and, even more, replace it with something? As posed by well-meaning scholars like Gordon Nembhard, cooperatives are a means towards achieving inclusion for those who have been excluded or correcting the problems of capitalism. This can be seen in how some people write about cooperatives under the topic of 'shared capitalism'. They talk about expanding ownership and granting access to private ownership to more people.[73] For these scholars, cooperatives offer better access to the American dream without necessarily changing it.

While Brown is accurate in her analysis of leftist proclivities towards inclusion at the expense of critically challenging the established order, in the case of cooperatives it doesn't have to be a choice between the two. Worker cooperatives can engage in a double project, in that they seek a better standard of living for their workers in the short term but also call on others to seek these same rights and mobilise to create a true democracy, a radical economic democracy that challenges the 'new world order' in the long term. In a war of position against the current hegemonic ideology there are short-term battles and long-term battles. It is just as important to win short-term battles as it is to win the war itself. Cooperatives call on others to democratise the economy as a means towards emancipation. Cooperatives seek rights for themselves; for example, in California, AB 816, the California Worker Cooperative Act, provides a business entity specifically for worker cooperatives within the existing Consumer Cooperative Corporation Law.[74] Worker cooperatives and those invested in them do this not as an end in itself but a means towards a specific end. Worker cooperatives, especially those based on fundamental discourses of social justice and democratic ownership, work for such rights in the hopes that they will open up a rupture, a political space that will allow others to engage in a real, democratic economic project. It may seem paradoxical to look to a liberal state for rights while at the same time using these rights to challenge the very state that grants them. But if worker cooperatives are intentional about the end goal—to transform our current system into something else—then it will achieve that goal by preparing the capitalist system to give birth to something new. This intentionality, though, is a necessary cultural precondition for a paradigm shift. It can't just be a diffuse scattering of different worker cooperatives doing their own thing, without some cultural or ideological goal. If that is the case, we run the risk of just creating a community of capitalist cooperatives.

This is where the cultural discourse of democracy becomes key. The goal isn't just to develop shared-ownership enterprises that provide a better standard of living for their workers: it is to institute what Huet calls 'democracy demonstration projects'. It is to normalise democratic practice in the economy, to make democracy not just a system or form of power-sharing and decision-making but something that occurs regularly. That is what real democracy is: a process, a verb, something to be engaged in regularly. Democracy is a perpetually ongoing political moment of the potentiality of citizens to have and execute power on a daily basis.

The disruption caused by the daily practice of democracy is a rejection and therefore alternative against what Rancière calls the 'police', which he describes as 'an order of bodies that defines the allocation of ways of doing, ways of being, and ways of saying and sees that those bodies are assigned by name to a particular place and task; it is an order of the visible and the say-able'.[75] It is thus also a challenge to the concept of 'normal' ways of being and doing. Foucault argues, 'The normal is established as a principle of coercion in teaching . . . normalization becomes one of the great instruments of power'.[76] Thus worker cooperatives, through their existence and daily practices, de-normalise and challenge on a daily basis, in ways that regular people can see and experience, the dominant discourse of how to organise businesses. They show democracy in action.

This cooperative duality is what is so transformational about worker cooperatives. They empower workers to practice democracy and they show the public (their clients) that it is possible. Much like the radical democratic project of the Zapatista movement, worker cooperatives that aim to change the economic structure have a dual role: they seek for their workers a part of today's American dream, but they also work towards changing the dream into a 'world where many worlds fit'.[77]

In doing this, worker cooperatives proclaim themselves as 'a part' of today but also of tomorrow. Just like 'the Zapatistas speak for a time further on . . . [their] words do not fit the present, but they are made to fit into a puzzle that does not yet exist',[78] Osvaldo similarly makes this reference with worker cooperatives when he states, 'I mean I think I feel like cooperativism is like the answer to that shit [capitalism] and maybe it's not cooperativism in like what it looks like today, but I feel like we're sort of evolving towards like whatever it is that it's going to be in the future'. The 'puzzle does not yet exist' and it is 'evolving towards, like whatever it is that it's going to be in the future' because we do not know what it will be. We do not know because democracy is a process—a contingent one, at that, one that involves discussion and deliberation and context. All of that depends on people and will hopefully result in not just one form of being and doing but a variety of forms, what Esteva and Prakash call grassroots post-modernism, how the world's social majorities are escaping from the monoculture of a single global society and regenerating their own cultural, natural, and economic spaces, resulting in 'a world where many worlds fit'.[79]

Ultimately one cannot speak of any project of change without at once speaking of humanity, agency, and praxis in creating that change, for it is humanity that necessitates the kind of change Marx envisioned. Capitalism is inhumane and therefore there must be a move towards more humane and democratic forms of relations of production, culture, and engagement. Humanity itself, real men and women, will move us towards more humane forms of the relations of production. E.P. Thompson reminds us 'that people can [and do] assert their humanity'.[80] Such assertions are what have historically led to change. And the kind of change that Marxists speak of and envision must occur not just in the political sphere but especially in the economic sphere, in the mode of production itself. Only by transforming the relations of production through economic and workplace democracy where workers actually own and control the means of production will workers be dis-alienated and the structure thus transformed.[81] Transforming the workplace will also transform how the economy engages the social and political. After all, capitalism began with the reorganisation of production; shouldn't that be where we begin the process *out* of capitalism? The potentialities engendered by actual men and women and their capacities to reconstruct society are tantamount to any theory or philosophy of change. Abstractions can be helpful, analyses of structures useful, but only when connected to material reality and the experiences of human agents, who at the end of the day always have and employ the capacity to change their conditions. Only then does change occur. Of central importance to accomplishing this change is the concept of agency; workers should be done waiting for politicians to fix their problems. They should, and in many cases have, decided to fix the problems themselves, to have responsibility, dignity, and self-respect, which is why they have been and will be successful. They are invested in their enterprises, as are the communities they stem from; they have a personal stake in success; their lives depend on it. There is no greater power than a community collectively working together to accomplish the goal of a better life for each other and for the future. These different movements, then, provide living examples that another world is possible.

Economic democracy as an idea and a project provides immense potential for empowering whole societies and, more importantly, allowing them better standards of living through fairer distribution of wealth and, ultimately, more control over their daily lives. The practice and process of democracy is the only real alternative based on freedom and liberation and, as such, should be taken seriously as a—if not the—method of improving and ultimately eliminating the degradation in our world. The worker cooperative that Osvaldo co-owns has given him the experience that Fromm discusses: 'freedom to create and to construct, to wonder and to venture. Such freedom requires that the individual be active and responsible, not a slave or a well-fed cog in the machine . . . it is not enough that men are not slaves; if social conditions further the existence of automatons, the result will not be love of life but love of death.'[82] Osvaldo makes this clear when he describes the magnitude of economic democracy and specifically worker cooperatives in changing his world:

This shit is really important to me. When I think of my history as a worker, you know, a farmworker and, you know, I did other stuff too, like construction and shit, I've milked cows before at a dairy farm, I've been in so much different shit, you know, man. I'm a worker, you know what I'm saying? And in every single one of those fucking jobs, that's all I was, I was a worker and it meant something different to me and I definitively took pride in the work I did, 'cause I've always been a hard worker, but I was always just, I don't know, right now *worker* has a different meaning. Before I was a worker, which meant, you know, that I was working for this person and I worked hard and that was how I had job security, but here [at the cooperative] it's like I'm a worker and an owner, too, man . . . It makes me feel like that's how all workers should feel because . . . when you don't own it, it takes something away—the pride aspect of it, man, the joy of being a worker, it just takes, I don't know, I can't explain it. It just feels different. As a worker I feel fulfilled, like I have a purpose. In every other job I didn't have a purpose. . . . [With the cooperative] I have some say in where our business goes, you know what? I mean I have really like a lot of control and power, like I feel really empowered right now, man. In terms of [the] direction that our coop is taking and, you know, the decisions that are being made, you know what I mean. I'm like, I'm a part of that process, where as in other ones I was just like following orders, man, and whether I liked it or not, it is what it is . . . you feel that sort of disempowerment. . . . I mean this cooperative is my life . . . it's not just my work, and that's like just another huge difference. Like, when I'm working at some other place, man, for somebody, it's not mine, you know what I'm saying? . . . Here, like I have a sense of ownership here . . . even when I'm not working, man, I'm working, you know what I mean? I'm thinking about it and I'm doing it and I like it, the fact that I'm thinking about it and doing it when I'm not even there, you know what I mean, 'cause it's just become such a big part of who I am.

In many ways Osvaldo, through his experience in his cooperative, is describing a pedagogy of the oppressed:

a pedagogy that is forged *with* not *for*, the oppressed, in the incessant struggle to regain humanity . . . [one where] the oppressed unveil the world of oppression and through the praxis commit themselves to its transformation . . . [and where] the reality of oppression has already been transformed, this pedagogy ceases to belong to the oppressed and becomes a pedagogy of all people in the process of permanent liberation.[83]

The worker cooperative has become the vehicle through which Osvaldo and his co-workers practice a pedagogy of liberation within themselves, as well as disseminating it to those they interact with in their communities and exposing them to the liberating practice of democracy. It is their form of struggle in the war of position to create an alternative hegemony, a world where many worlds fit. But it all begins with spreading the idea of economic democracy through praxis because, as Carnoy and Shearer argue, 'Ideas have power that can free untapped hope and energy in a people. The democratic idea of America has been and can again be a powerful weapon. It is a living heritage, which we can apply to the economic system in which we live, and with it we can build a new reality'.[84]

5
Working but Poor in the City of Milwaukee: Life Stories

Finding a job in Milwaukee is hard. Finding a good paying job and with benefits is close to impossible.

—David, twenty-two, low-wage worker

BACKGROUND

The action research detailed in this chapter was funded by a coalition of Milwaukee based social justice movement organisations who seek to address and dismantle the root causes of inequality. *Action research* can be defined as 'a participatory, democratic process concerned with developing practical knowing. . . . It seeks to bring together action and reflection, theory and practice, in participation with others, in the pursuit of practical solutions to issues of pressing concerns'.[1] This research was conducted in the tradition of Ernesto Galarza, who modelled action research methods and documented its importance for social movement agenda setting. Galarza provided future action researchers an action research manifesto grounded in research, action, and advocacy: 'research with a purpose'.[2]

This action research assessed the lives of working-but-poor Milwaukee residents and noted commonalities and challenges this population faces in their everyday working-class lives. The research findings provided the funding social-movement organisations a deeper understanding of the impacts that low-wage jobs have on working but poor communities in Milwaukee and how to best to support their organising efforts.

We found that low-wage Milwaukeean workers come from many different backgrounds and live in communities throughout the city. This labour force is racially and ethnically diverse, made up of women and men, young and old, single and married, some parent, many not. They are part of extended-family units, homeless and homeowners, students, high-school dropouts, and college graduates. Some were born in the United States;

many are foreign born and hold different immigrant statuses. Many live in co-ethnic and co-racial communities. Despite this diversity in the characteristics of the low-wage labour pool, they are connected as workers to a system of labour exploitation that has essentially institutionalised poverty. They make up the working but poor workforce in Milwaukee and across the country.

INTRODUCTION

The Wisconsin Latino population has substantially increased in the last three decades. From 1990 to 2015, Wisconsin experienced a threefold increase in its Latino population, from 93,000 to 370,000. Latinos now make up 6 percent of the Wisconsin population, making them the largest minority in the state; they surpassed African Americans in 2014. Of this group, 75 percent self-identify as being of Mexican origin, 55 percent are foreign-born, 67 percent primarily speak Spanish, and 34 percent live below the poverty line. Wisconsin Latinos have a median age of twenty-four, and 48 percent are younger than seventeen.

The Latino workforce is a vital and essential component of the Wisconsin economy. In this aspect, they play a similar role to Latino working populations throughout the country. They are not marginal but central to the Wisconsin political economy. The industries that employ the largest share of Latinos are: manufacturing, 27.4 percent; educational services, health care, and social assistance, 14.9 percent; agriculture, forestry, fishing and hunting, and mining, 14.3 percent; retail trade, 9 percent; construction, 8.9 percent; and transportation, warehousing, and utilities, 7.9 percent.[3] In agriculture, 90 percent of migrant and seasonal workers are of Mexican origin and 55 percent of the dairy-industry workforce is composed of Latino immigrants.[4]

Low-wage workers are one of the most disadvantaged working groups in the United States. They experience poverty wages, seasonal employment, weak attachment to the labour force, and limited employment opportunities and are neglected by policy makers and labour-enforcement agencies. This paradox of 'poverty amid the plenty' has created continual growing inequality that has restricted opportunities and stagnated the civic integration and upward mobility of low-wage workers, their families, and future generations.[5]

Globalisation has led to outsourcing manufacturing jobs and declines in construction and building industry employment. In the last thirty years, globalisation has left a void of well-paid union and nonunion jobs with benefits. Today, Milwaukee is continuing an economic restructuring that is shifting traditionally stable manufacturing jobs with high wages and benefits to light manufacturing, food production, home health and nursing care, and service industry jobs that primarily offer lower wages, less job security, and no employment benefits.

Low-wage jobs are jobs within any industry that pay less than $11.19 an hour, which is the threshold at full-time year-round employment to keep a family of four out of poverty.[6] Simply stated, these jobs cannot provide enough income to meet the basic needs for a family. They offer little job security or retirement security; limited (if any) health insurance, sick leave, and vacation time; and much lower pay. The vast majority of low-wage jobs are nonunion. All too often, temporary employment ('temp') agencies act as the quasi employer. The impacts that low-wage jobs have on workers and communities are long lasting and devastating.

Low-wage jobs have become endemic to the economic order of the city and a mainstay in working-but-poor communities.[7] Nearly 100,000 workers—35 percent of the city of Milwaukee's labour force—are low-wage workers who live in poverty.[8] This report reveals key narratives from communities of Milwaukee's working poor, whose daily employment struggles affect every facet of their lives—where they work, where they live, with whom they interact, and their very survival.

This chapter is based on twenty one-on-one in-depth thematic interviews conducted with people of colour, immigrants and low-wage workers in Milwaukee, WI. Interview subjects were identified by the Open Places Milwaukee (OPM) coalition partners and set up by the lead investigator. Interviews were conducted from June 26, 2013, to July 20, 2013, and administered at a place of each interviewee's choice, including their homes, coffee shops, libraries and other public places.

The principal investigator and coalition partners developed the questionnaire used for the interviews. The questionnaire is thematic and includes several probes per theme. The themes focused on personal background and characteristics; neighbourhood and movement; employment, unemployment, and underemployment; future outlook; discrimination and segregation; civic participation; and immigrant communities and immigration reform. It ended with an open-ended self-reflection question. Interviews were conducted in English and Spanish.

The data from the interviews is used to contextualise working people's narratives within larger structural employment and demographic trends.

Their centred narratives give us a deeper understanding of the impact of low-wage jobs on working-but-poor communities in Milwaukee.

POPULATION DESCRIPTIVE

Table 2 displays the diversity among the low-wage workers interviewed for this research and describes demographic and social variables that offer insight into a substantial portion of Milwaukee's working population. The interviews revealed that, on average, low-wage workers who participated in this study are thirty-two years old; most have at least a high school diploma or its equivalent; and 40 percent are in committed relationships and have one child under the age of eighteen within their household. Most interviewees are currently employed, make an average of $9.84 an hour, work thirty hours per week, and have no employer-provided benefits (i.e., medical, dental, vision insurance, vacation, sick leave). Over half currently receive government assistance, such as medical (Badger Care), rent and housing assistance, FoodShare, job assistance (Wisconsin Works W-2), or childcare services; three-quarters use food and clothing pantries provided by public and nonprofit organisations such as churches. Most of the interviewees feel that they live in unsafe and failing communities, citing violence and deteriorating housing. In

Table 2   Milwaukee Low-Wage Workers: Descriptive Statistics

	Mean	*N*
Age	31.65	20
Gender (Female)	70 percent	20
School	3.70	20
Relationship Status (Married)	40 percent	20
Children under 18	1.10	20
Currently Employed	2.10	20
Weekly Hours	30.59	17
Hourly Rate	$9.84	17
Employer Benefits	15 percent	20
Recently Unemployed	75 percent	20
Immigrant	25 percent	20
If Immigrant, Status (Authorised)	40 percent	5
Neighbourhood Safe	35 percent	20
On Gov't Assistance	55 percent	20
Use Food and/or Clothing Pantry	75 percent	20
Hopeful about Personal Future	85 percent	20

sum, the interviews reveal a paradox of work and poverty that is directly linked to community planning and economic development.

EMPLOYMENT

The low-wage workers interviewed are employed by a number of 'big box' retail centres, food production and packaging companies, security companies, in-home healthcare providers, nursing convalescence homes, fast-food chains, and/or temp agencies that provide labour to multiple industries. None expressed that they were paid a living and fair wage, had good working conditions or benefits, or were guaranteed long-term employment, and most felt their work environments were unsafe and openly hostile.

They perform many job functions: physical labour on construction sites, handling fragile patients, preparing and delivering food and beverages to customers, loading freight trucks with food and other manufactured products using heavy machinery. Workers employed directly by a company expressed a sense of stability with regard to work hours, days, and job site; this was not the case for workers hired by temp agencies.

Donald

'I am a cashier and collect the carts at Target. I hate my job. They treat me with such little respect. Sometimes I feel that it is because I am a Black man.'

Donald, a twenty-two-year-old, has been working for the Target in West Allis for fifteen months. He earns $7.89 an hour and works fifteen hours per week, which puts him 200% below the poverty rate for one person, which is an annual income of $11,490.

Prior to Target, Donald was unemployed for three years and attended a for-profit university. He was dropped from the school for nonpayment and lived on what his father—himself a low-wage worker—earned. He describes this time as one of the worst experiences of his life. He currently lives with his father and three unemployed adult brothers (ages nineteen to twenty-five) in a neighbourhood with no jobs and where his best friend was recently murdered.

The constant search for employment is central to the lives of the interviewees. It is a complex process layered with barriers based on favouritism, racism, sexism, and multiple forms of discrimination. The employment process involves identifying jobs, assessing whether one qualifies and/or has a 'proper' background, filling out and submitting an application, and interviewing. They described the process as difficult, cumbersome, and unrewarding and shared that it produces personal anxiety from knowing that they are relegated to low-wage jobs that only help maintain the status quo of poverty.

Temp agencies have become a mainstay within the low-wage employment system. Employment by temp agencies has grown to pre-recession levels, to an estimated 26,200 workers in the greater Milwaukee area. These companies thrive in the low-wage labour market by acting as intermediaries between a worker and employer; they profit indirectly from the work performed by the worker. Temp agencies do not offer permanent employment or opportunities for advancement and are used to contract pooled labour that is cheap, exploitable, and replaceable. Interviewees described temp agencies as their last recourse to enter the labour market. They expressed a deep sense of dissatisfaction with their lives stemming from maltreatment on the job by the company, which bypassed direct employment responsibilities, and by the temp agency.

Tracy

'Temp work sucks . . . I want out!'

Tracy, thirty-seven, is a middle-aged single mother who has worked for temp agencies for the past eleven years. She is a general labourer at a factory, where she packages cookies. She works between twenty-five to thirty hours a week and is paid eight dollars an hour. She describes her workplace as a diverse one where Latinos, whites, and African Americans work side by side. She also notes that the temp agency uses race and immigration status to create divisions between the workers. 'There is tension at the workplace. The managers at the plant and agency say all the time [that] Latinos are better workers and the Blacks are lazy. So they pit us against each other.' Tracy also notes a negative culture with regard to work safety: 'I cannot report any workplace hazards or injuries because you will be fired.'

Temp-agency employees reported that they are required to purchase their own uniforms and must use the agency's transportation to and from the job site. The cost of uniforms varied depending on the type of industry and job to be performed. These costs include work gloves, shoes/boots, shirts, pants, and other protective clothing. The fees for transportation averaged seven dollars per day. Emiliano, a thirty-year-old Latino immigrant and BG Staffing worker, states, 'If I am lucky I can work five days in a week and make $250. Minus the cost of transportation, lunch, and other expenses, I am lucky to bring home $190 a week.'

Job seeking does not end once the person becomes employed. It is a daily activity that continues for those who are successful in completing the employment process, for those who complete the process and are not hired, and for job seekers who begin the process but are unable to complete it. In sum, the low-wage employment system is central to their lives and dictates major life activities, including decisions that involve their immediate families, whether to attend school, where and how they live, and with whom they interact.

NEIGHBOURHOODS

Good neighbourhoods are well planned and maintained by city and community members. They connect people to places and jobs and offer mixed-use development and safe, open areas where community members interact (i.e., green space). They do not just happen organically. They take vision and planning, with input from public and private stakeholders—including community members from all walks of life. Good neighbourhoods act as long-term social and economic engines for their residents.

Table 3 offers a centred narrative with regard to how the interviewees described their immediate and surrounding neighbourhoods. Milwaukee is a segregated city with regions of co-ethnic and co-racial communities where African Americans live in the Northside; Latinos live in the Southside and Whites live in the suburbs and along the lakefront. The disparate trends in economic and social outlook, neighbourhood safety, and employment opportunities within the boundaries that separate these communities are troubling. Few described their neighbourhoods as 'good and/or safe' or as offering employment. Instead, they describe their neighbourhoods as areas with high police presence and criminal activity that range from loitering, to drug dealing, to murder. The North and South side residents pointed to economic insecurity as the root of this type of activity in their neighbourhoods. Tracy states: 'There are many young brothers and sisters hanging out on the block because of the lack of jobs and other opportunities. People need to make a living somehow and this [crime] is what is available in the inner city.'

Table 3 City of Milwaukee Neighbourhood Descriptors

- Northside/Inner-city: Harambee and Arlington Heights neighborhoods. Predominantly African American, high crime and poverty rates, low home-ownership rates, deteriorating structures, few to no jobs in the immediate area.
- Southside: Clarke Square and Layton Park neighborhoods. Predominantly Latino (mostly Mexican and Mexican American), high crime and poverty rates, low homeownership rates, many low-wage jobs in immediate area.
- Eastside: Shorewood and Brady Street neighborhoods. Predominantly white, safe and well-maintained neighborhoods, more affluent part of Milwaukee (Shore Hill, Marquette University, and UW Milwaukee in particular), above-average homeownership rates, businesses with white-collar jobs.
- Westside: Washington Park and Merrill Park neighborhoods. Most diverse neighborhood with many homeowners, shopping centers; considered an emerging region of the city.

The interviewees identified many neighbourhoods; we chose to reference areas by region.

Employment and housing are intrinsically linked. The ability to pay for household living expenses determines length of stay at a home and in a neighbourhood. The interviewees averaged living four years at their current home and had lived in five different homes since turning eighteen, which puts them on pace to exceed the national mobility average.[9] Their life narratives reveal the relationship between low-wage employment, underemployment and unemployment, and home displacement, family insecurity, and life opportunities.

Melissa is a twenty-year-old African American low-wage worker and has moved eleven times since being on her own. She and her child have not been able to establish roots in any one neighbourhood. She has been forced to move by landlords for nonpayment or late payment of rent, not by 'choice.' For her, the ideal living situation would be to stay in one place where her children can grow up in a stable household, attend one school per school year, and have the same opportunities as children do in the surrounding affluent communities. Unfortunately, she earns minimum wage as a home healthcare provider and is employed part time, which places her at extreme risk of being constantly displaced.[10]

Interviewees shared their neighbourhood experiences and reasons for staying. Many live where they live because it is home. This was especially the case for Northsiders: many are second and third-generation Milwaukeeans with deep roots in their communities. Immigrant and other study participants stated that a major reason for living where they do is because of the existence of co-ethnic and co-racial communities that reflect their own lives. Within these community spaces they receive services and entertainment and interact in neighbourhood affairs in ways that are culturally and linguistically appropriate.

Affordability and access to a home are universal reasons for staying, as indicated by repeated responses in all narratives in this study. However, housing options for Milwaukee's working poor are dramatically limited and concentrated in areas of the city where opportunities for living-wage employment are close to nonexistent. As Linda, a twenty-nine-year-old white woman, puts it, 'Milwaukee is good at mapping demographic differences but bad at breaking down economic and social barriers.'

LOW-WAGE IMMIGRANT WORKERS

As noted previously, Latinos are the single largest immigrant group in the city.[11] A part of the research was to assess attitudes of nonimmigrant and immigrant low-wage workers toward immigrant labour and immigration reform.[12]

Graph 1 summarises this population's gender, age, nativity, and citizenship status.[13] Overall, Latinos are evenly distributed by gender (52 percent male, 48 percent female). Those under eighteen are predominantly native-born (91 percent), while adults are predominately foreign-born (90 percent). Naturalisation rates among the foreign-born are low, with 18 percent of adults and 10 percent of immigrant youth having become naturalised US citizens.

Immigrants face an array of difficulties that are not common among other workers. These difficulties intensify based on official immigrant status. On the individual level, status affects everything from social to economic integration. On the societal level, rigid status categories weaken the long-term economic and civic health of communities. Although we conducted interviews with immigrants of different immigrant statuses, we focus on the unauthorised Latino immigrant experience.[14]

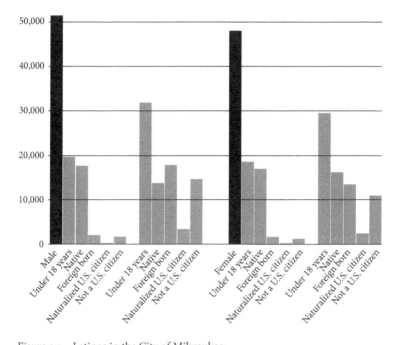

Figure 5.1   Latinos in the City of Milwaukee

Unauthorised low-wage immigrant workers revealed that they are subject to higher levels of job exploitation, including severe mal-treatment, wage theft, labour violations, health and safety violations, discrimination, and deportation. They are subject to E-Verify by many employers, and do not qualify for Wisconsin driver's licences or public social services.[15] They are completely shut out of legal employment structures and relegated to a different standard of survival.

Outside of work, being unauthorised influences almost every aspect of their day-to-day activities. Interviewees shared that they are fearful when they go to work, drop children off at school, go shopping, attend church, or have any other outing. Any interaction with authorities can result in *la migra* (Immigration and Customs Enforcement) becoming involved, which can lead to deportation proceedings that would make them ineligible for future status adjustment.

Emiliano is representative of many unauthorised immigrants in Milwaukee. He is part of a mixed-status extended family who live in a two-bedroom, one-bathroom home on the Southside. He, his wife, and her parents are all low-wage unauthorised immigrant workers that are employed by a temp agency. Their two children are US citizens and attend Milwaukee public schools. 'Any time I drive to work or wherever, I can be deported. If I complain at work, I can be deported. What will happen to my family—my wife and children? They depend on me. It causes me great pain to think about this but I have to shut it out and continue', he says.

Though interviewees noted various immigration routes and modes of crossing into the United States, they all stated that they immigrated because of need and not by choice. For example, Noelia, forty-three, says, 'I am here because of need. I am both a father and mother to my two children and care for my mother as well. I almost died crossing the border and witnessed horrible things. It took me twenty days to cross and get away from the smugglers. All because I need to work to survive. I have paid the price. . . . I have not seen my family in more than thirteen years. I am here alone'.

None had prior knowledge of Milwaukee, its weather, or local employment structures; they came because they had family who had settled there. Upon arrival, their priority was to find work and begin to pay the loans they had taken to immigrate and send money back to family.

Since 2006, a pro-immigrant-rights social movement has taken root in the United States. It seeks to change immigration policy so that an estimated 11 million unauthorised immigrants can adjust their immigration status. Milwaukee has become a hub of this movement and has gained national recognition for community organising efforts whose agenda is to influence the national debate on comprehensive immigration reform (CIR).[16]

Not surprisingly, immigrant interviewees are attuned to this national debate. Immigrant status is the single most important issue that affects immigrants in the United States. Nonimmigrant interviewees had little to no knowledge of the national debate and movement for CIR. Although many spoke negatively of having to compete with undocumented and documented immigrants for jobs and expressed concern about undocumented immigrants breaking the law, there was consensus that the current immigration system was broken and needed to be fixed. African Americans empathised with undocumented immigrants based on their experiences as minorities who struggle with employment discrimination, societal racism, and the criminal-justice system.

SURVIVAL STRATEGIES

Low-wage workers do not earn enough to meet the essentials for survival: food, shelter, clothing, and medical attention. Because of this economic insecurity, most have developed survival strategies such as budgetary approaches and decisions made on the immediate needs of the individual and or the family.

Interviewees prioritised food and rent above all. Many live in extended-family households to reduce their cost of living. Most noted not paying for heat, water, or electricity, not buying clothing for themselves or children, and not being able to afford internet access or phone services. For many, it is a paycheck-by-paycheck existence that is subsidised by public safety-net programmes.

Public safety-net programmes are important survival components for working-but-poor Milwaukeeans. They supplement wages by helping workers meet their food, clothing, medical, and other essential needs that would otherwise go unmet. These programmes are for US citizens and eligible immigrants and are widely advertised by the city and county.[17]

Using the averages from Table 1, a single person with one child under the age of eighteen, working thirty-two hours a week, earning $9.84 an hour, and paying $750 a month for rent would qualify for the following benefits in Wisconsin: FoodShare, WisconsinWorks, school meals, The Emergency Food Assistance Program (TEFAP—food pantries), the BadgerCare Plus Standard health plan, and Home Energy Assistance for winter heating.[18]

Interviewees expressed a shared sense of shame and embarrassment of having to supplement their work income with the use of public services. Justice, a thirty-year-old African American woman, said, 'Two weeks ago I did not get paid all my check and couldn't pay rent because I had to feed my children. Feed my children or pay rent? I choose to feed my children. It makes me sad and embarrassed to get food and clothing [from the pantries]. There are a lot of people in my situation'. They work—sometimes multiple jobs—continually search for better employment and life opportunities, and still cannot afford the basics, let alone have residual income for planning for the future or leisure. They have become part of the pooled labour supply for low-wage employment that perpetuates interdependence between low-wage earners, employers, and public-assistance programmes. In short, they are representative of the workforce that makeup the US underclass.[19]

Interviewees noted that formal education was both a survival strategy and a way out of poverty wage employment. As a survival strategy, they applied for school and were eligible for student loans. This aid, along with part-time work, helped them get by, whether they were attending community college or public and private universities. They set educational goals toward professional careers in education, social services, healthcare, law, criminal justice, and private industry.

For select unauthorised immigrants, formal education is a way to temporarily adjust their immigration status under the Deferred Action for Childhood Arrivals (DACA), also known as the Dream Act, implemented by executive order by the Obama administration in June 2012. Under this policy, unauthorised immigrants who entered the United States prior to 15 June 2007 can qualify for status adjustment if they have had no criminal activity and have attended or are enrolled in school (K-12 or an accredited higher education institution).[20] From 2012 to 2017, approximately 800,000 people qualified for temporary relief from deportation under this executive order. The Trump Administration has rescinded Obama's executive order and 'Dreamers' are beginning to roll off this program, ending their stay in 'legal status' and returning to their 'illegal' lives.[21]

Norma, twenty-three, is a Dreamer who recently adjusted her status. She is a senior majoring in sociology at the University of Wisconsin at Milwaukee. She has been living in Milwaukee's Southside since she was five years old. Her parents brought her and a brother to the United States from Mexico in search of economic and educational opportunities. She says, 'I didn't know I was unauthorised until I was fifteen. It was time to talk about college and financial aid and I found out that I didn't qualify.' Since adjusting her status, she has left her previous jobs (server and house cleaner) and has found a steady full-time job that helps pay for her college expenses. She now is excited and hopeful about her future.

Despite being integral to the city's social and economic well-being, these workers live in poverty and have had to develop survival strategies to mitigate their positions. This context of work and poverty is the common ground that all working-but-poor share despite demographic or status differences. The important issues that arise from the interviews with regards to this working-but-poor context are community and labour organising issues. We will see in the following section and book chapters, examples of the actions workers and organisations have taken to change this context.

HOPE-ACTION-CHANGE

Despite the many life challenges and employment barriers faced by the Milwaukeeans interviewed for this research, they continue to be hopeful about the possibilities for positive change in their personal lives. Most are involved in their communities with organisations with long-term social and economic justice agendas, such as Voces de la Frontera, Wisconsin Jobs Now, 9to5, Wisconsin Voices, and others. Some face retribution for this work: Emiliano states, 'My daughter was at a pizza party at her school. She refused to eat the pizza because it was from Palermo's. She told the teacher, "Palermo's is a very bad company. My daddy made pizza and they fired him. They fired him because he was fighting for justice"'.

Low-wage workers are invested in their communities. Many are active in grassroots campaigns that seek to raise the minimum wage, protect women's and workers' rights, increase civic participation, and pass pro-immigrant-rights legislation. They are also involved in campaigns to end violence in their communities; create bridges between Black, Brown, and white communities; collect food for pantries; and operate literacy programmes for adults and children. Many joined the 2011 Wisconsin Uprising protests at the state capitol in solidarity with public workers who lost most of their labour rights. They lobby at the state capitol and in Washington, D.C., and canvass their communities during elections. Georgia, fifty-one, a recently unemployed low-wage Latina worker, finds inspiration in this work: 'I am involved with the Raise the Minimum Wage campaign; we are learning how to connect [and] organise to fight back', she says.

6
Latina/o Labour in Multicultural Los Angeles

It is by eating the Other . . . that one asserts power and privilege.
—bell hooks, *Black Looks*

The symbolic production and consumption of the Other[1]—of minority and historically disenfranchised cultures—is perhaps mostly rampantly perpetuated in Los Angeles by style-setting nouvelle-cuisine restaurants that cater to elite surveyors of multicultural cuisines. Such restaurants embody those spaces where the critical infrastructure[2] and the largely immigrant Latino service workforce converge in a stark pairing to market and produce the multicultural cuisine that unassumingly defines Los Angeles as a global city.

GLOBALISATION AND THE CULTURAL CAPITAL OF MULTICULTURAL CUISINE

That nouvelle restaurants help manufacture the edible multicultural symbols upon which a global city's pluralistic self-image is constructed is not surprising. The metropolis of the industrial age has long been identified as the style centre that generates cultural models which are then emulated in the suburban and rural periphery. In the postindustrial global city of today, moreover, that function has intensified as cultural production has become a chief economic activity. The formation of the ubiquitous field of cultural studies and the study of what Pierre Bourdieu once called 'cultural capital'[3] indicates the emerging implications, scholarly and otherwise, of this phenomenon. Studies abound that assess cultural iconography, culture industries, popular culture, and the commodification of culture (to name only a few subjects). Yet, as Mike Davis claims in *Magical Urbanism*, a certain invisibility of Latinas/os persists in high-end urban studies charged with examining such cultural phenomena from the vantage of the world economy's impact on the metropolis. Davis contends that 'For more than a decade urban theory has been intensely focused on trying to understand how the new world economy is reshaping the metropolis. . . . . Yet most of the literature on 'globalization' has paradoxically ignored its most spectacular US expression'.[4] The present chapter proposes not only to bring visibility to Latinas/os within urban studies, but also to speculate on the implications of having the labour of a largely immigrant Latina/o workforce support nouvelle multicultural restaurants in a postindustrial, postcolonial urban landscape like Los Angeles, where the marketing and availability of multicultural cuisine has become symptomatic of a certain postcolonial desire of the elite to possess the Other by symbolic measures in lieu of territorial and geopolitical expansion.

Building upon her earlier studies of gentrification, Sharon Zukin advances the concept of the 'symbolic economy' in *The Culture of Cities* to more thoroughly explain this transformation of the metropolis. She argues that urban elites appropriate the images, narratives, and symbols of multiculturalism and inscribe them into the built environment to communicate their tastes, values, and desires to their cultural peers and the citizenry at large. These signs are meant to uphold the misguided assumption that one can have unmediated access to the world of the cultural Other—to establish the illusion of cultural transparency. Homi Bhabha characterises such instances of transparency as taking place when 'the semantic seems to prevail over the syntactic, the signified over the signifier'.[5]

This prevalence can come about since texts do not merely reflect reality; rather, and perhaps more significantly, they create reality. A text, Fredric Jameson argues, 'articulates its own situation and textualises it, thereby encouraging and perpetuating the illusion that the situation itself did not exist before it, that there is nothing but a text, that there never was any extra- or contextual reality before the text itself generated it in the form of a mirage'.[6] The texts woven by the symbolic economy of multiculturalism in effect perpetuate the illusion that certain timely signs (though, to the conscious minds of surveyors of multicultural cuisine, they appear as anything but signs) paradoxically provide for unmediated passage into the world of the cultural Other. In the context of multicultural nouvelle restaurants, the texts of cuisine, with all their ethnic flair and flavour, signal access to this different world.

LABOUR IN THE NOUVELLE RESTAURANT

Restaurants function as important gateways and clearinghouses for global labour recruitment. The size of a city's restaurant workforce, 'the countries of origin of participants, and the volume of monetary transactions that pass through them', Zukin writes, 'make restaurant work an important transnational activity—and one that is mainly undocumented.'[7] In Los Angeles, multicultural nouvelle restaurants straddle a paradox: Latina/o immigrants provide unskilled physical labour, while college- and academy-trained chefs exhibit the role of culinary artists. In such an intellectual division of labour, a cadre of mostly non-Latino elite chefs appropriate and reinterpret the Latina/o ingredients and recipes their Latina/o staff members assemble into nouvelle creations; this ghettoises unskilled Latina/o workers, many of whom remain employed in the same positions indefinitely. Tens of thousands of Latina/o immigrant workers ensure that these places operate profitably and smoothly. That these ubiquitous contradictions of multicultural commodification do not seem more jarring is due in part to the very idealism of the multicultural discourses that obscure them. As Rey Chow contends, 'In the problematic of cultural otherness, the two senses of idealism come together: idealism in the sense of idealisation, of valorisation of non-Western "others", we witness a kind of tendency to see all such "others" as equivalent, as a mere positive idea devoid of material embeddedness and contradiction.'[8]

There is indeed a contemporary repression of contradiction from public knowledge about this intellectual division of labour, which can be partly attributed to a vigorous anti-immigrant discourse that seeks to silence any consideration of the complexities and compromises that permeate the daily lives of individual Latina/o immigrants. The proposed resolutions to the ongoing US immigration issue imply a vacuous programme of assimilation that, in the long term, would only maintain the current division of labour and preserve control of the symbolic economy for those in power. Even in the most humane legislative proposals, this immigrant Latina/o workforce would be permitted into the United States on the condition of, as the saying now goes, 'filling the jobs Americans don't want.' They would, in effect, occupy a silent, expendable, and exploited niche within the symbolic economy, confirming Herbert Marcuse's prescient claim that in the technological work world of the twentieth (and now the twenty-first) century, the working class would no longer appear 'to be the living contradiction to the established society'.[9] This potentially critical social agent has, in the postindustrial era, continued to be silenced—in part by the discursive efforts of urban elites trying to remarket urban landscapes like Los Angeles as unequivocally 'multicultural.' Such efforts have simultaneously attempted to accomplish the incorporation of Latina/o cuisine *and* the marginalisation of low-wage Latina/o culinary workers. The fact that new digital technologies now encourage the proliferation of industries based solely upon the commodification of cultural artefacts spurs local critical media, which particularly depend on and identify with their audiences, to normalise elite culinary representations by translating them into popular vernacular and to negotiate a city's 'look and feel,' designating which cultures 'should be visible' and which should remain invisible.[10] As Latinas/os emerge as the Los Angeles area's majority population and workforce, particularly in the growing service sector, the discursive juncture conjoining the representation and production of multicultural cuisine offers a critical site for gauging Latina/o cultural power—or, more precisely, relative lack of such power.

To be sure, immigrants have their reasons for seeking out the industry's low-paying, often dead-end jobs. Lack of English-language skills and US educational credentials, willingness to work unusual and long hours at subminimum wages, 'and the restaurant industry's traditional barriers to unionization' make immigrants a 'pliable' labour force preferred by employers.[11] In her ethnographic survey of New York restaurants, Zukin also found that those immigrant workers who were permitted direct contact with the public were more European in appearance and had mastered English and middle-class manners. By contrast, Mexicans dominated 'the lowest-skill kitchen positions', a fact that she attributes to the rural origins of immigrant workers who had not yet acquired 'urban job skills'.[12]

Several structural factors explain why style-setting restaurants prefer to employ Latina/o immigrants in unskilled and less visible positions. First, the celebrity chef and assisting sous-chefs and line chefs represent the greatest part of these restaurants' kitchen labour costs. Industry insiders note that restaurant owners do not spend money to train immigrant Latina/o workers. And the language barrier between the skilled, generally non-Latina/o chefs and unskilled Latina/o dishwashers and bussers reinforces the social distance that separates these groups. Traditionally, even skilled restaurant employees received their training and experience on the job; today, however, the preferred career path to becoming a style-setting chef begins with a university degree, followed by vocational training in a European-styled culinary academy and an apprenticeship in a chic kitchen.[13] Few Latinas/os receive elite professional training, although they represent the majority of Southern California's restaurant workforce. Most enter the restaurant industry by the back door, through referrals or recommendations; they get their on-the-job training at middle- to low-end restaurants, whether full-service or fast food—a career path that does not prepare them for work in a chic restaurant. Also, the high failure rate of restaurants and the undocumented status of many immigrant workers both increase their vulnerability. From the immigrant worker's perspective, the obstacles to advancement are indeed discouraging.

Figure 6.1   Restaurant Worker

Latina/o restaurant workers' functional relationship to the symbolic economy is one of near exclusion from the critical infrastructure and structural subordination in the workplace. The social relations of restaurant production and the representation of Mexican cuisine mutually constitute Latina/o immigrants as a subordinated workforce while normalising the commercial and aesthetic appropriation of

Mexican culture. Inadequate educational preparation discourages these workers from effectively contesting the representation of their labour and their cuisine inside the restaurant, while racialised media representations of Mexican culture devalue immigrants in society at large. This structural-cultural symbiosis explains why the Latina/o flavour of Los Angeles—a city with a Mexican population second only to that of Mexico City, with more than 30,000 restaurants where Latina/o cooks prepare myriad cuisines and with a Latina/o workforce large enough to shut down the city's restaurants if it stayed home—remains marginalised in the city's culture wars.[14]

Despite their seeming pluralism and populist disdain for class snobbery, the multicultural nouvelle restaurants of Los Angeles are its most representative elite institutions. Once inside the restaurant, the tourist or overseas businessperson experiences a safe and highly aestheticised encounter with the multicultural city before heading off to an evening at the Dorothy Chandler Pavilion, a private screening on the Universal Studios lot, or an afternoon at the Museum of Contemporary Art. In other cases, dinner at Patina Restaurant is the evening's theatrical event. The multicultural style-setting nouvelle restaurant thus functions as an entertainment niche in its own right or as a prelude to another cultural experience. Its workforce, however, operating silently behind the scenes, serves as the condition for that experience. In Los Angeles County's food-services industry, Latina/o immigrants outnumber Anglos by a ratio of more than two to one and make up as much as 70 percent of this workforce.[15] Their sheer numbers suggest the kinds of serious economic disruptions that would take place without them.

CONSTRUCTING THE 'HISPANIC' FANTASY

It must be noted that this neglect to acknowledge the critical role of the largely Latina/o immigrant workforce sustaining multicultural dining has been an ongoing historical blind spot, extending from past efforts by elites to invent a cosmopolitan identity for Los Angeles through a very selective Hispanic fantasy discourse. A process of selective inclusion and exclusion has allowed for the incorporation of a mestizo Mexican culture into a generic and romanticised conception of Spanish culture; ultimately, this created a sophisticated origin myth to be exploited by the patrician class of Los Angeles as a means of symbolic conquest.

While walking west from Ohio in 1884, writing about his journey in instalments for the *Los Angeles Daily Times* (as the paper was then called), Charles Fletcher Lummis, California's most influential booster-journalist, delivered accounts of Mexicans and Indians that reiterated a well-established anti-Mexican and anti-Indian discourse. Throughout the Southwest, publishers of dime novels, travelogues, and newspapers used culinary imagery to illustrate Mexicans' 'savagery' and 'depravity' to mark this community (along with Native Indians) as racial Others. Similarly, implicitly referring to the effects of Mexican cooking, Lummis once remarked that 'not even a coyote will touch a dead Greaser, the flesh is so seasoned with the red pepper they ram into their food in howling profusion'.[16]

However, less than a decade later, Lummis excused himself for his 'silly' Anglo-Saxon prejudices in his 1892 travelogue *Tramp Across the Continent*.[17] His ideological transformation began a personal and professional campaign to produce narratives and symbols with which Mexican Los Angeles could be revalorised as a fantasy landscape of Spanish romance. In contrast, Lummis's subtler Hispanic fantasy appropriated those Mexican cultural images that could be interpreted as 'Spanish' (read: white and European) or as dependent on Anglo leadership and protection, while excluding others. Los Angeles restaurateurs and cookbook writers, swept up in Lummis's Mission revival movement, made their enchiladas and tamales more palatable for non-Mexican diners by affixing the 'Spanish' label.

Lummis, however, cannot take all the credit for the symbolic reinvention of California. In 1884, Helen Hunt Jackson published *Ramona*, a novel she wrote to denounce exploitation of Native Americans; *Ramona* became, in the hands of D.W. Griffith, the perfect libretto for selling his vision of Spanish California. Griffith's 1910 film version of the novel deployed the standard Hispanic fantasy discourse to elevate *Ramona* to the level of respectable art for middle-class audiences. Jackson had originally made her protagonist, whom she identified as Mexican, the offspring of a Scottish father and an Indian mother, which Europeanised the character for readers who perceived mestizos as degraded 'half-breeds'. Griffith encouraged male members of the audience to fantasise about a 'Spanish' beauty, yet still portrayed Mexicans and Native Americans as innately inferior beings too powerless to impede progress, represented as white conquest and capital expansion.[18] By 1916, the novel had generated as much as $50 million in publishing, stage, and screen revenues (equivalent to the amount generated by a Spielberg blockbuster today), as well as providing the mythic rationale for a landscape transformation already in progress.

That picture would change after the 1940s, when Mexican American activists began to win important social victories in the local labour movement as well as a few local elections during the 1950s. After the 1960s, these modest gains would be bolstered by the emergence of Chicana/o political activism, a burst of mainstream and grassroots book and magazine publishing by and about Chicanas/os, and the rapid expansion of Spanish-language television, along with the grudging admittance of a handful of Mexican journalists into the mainstream English-language media. In East Los Angeles, a resurgence of Mexican cultural pride hastened the disappearance of 'Spanish' restaurants. The numerous *puestos* (food stalls) of the First Street Mercado, the introduction of pescaderías or seafood restaurants serving steaming bowls of *siete mares*, Mexico City style taquerías serving *tacos al pastor*, and *birrierías* serving slow-roasted goat would offer new spaces for the social construction and expression of Chicano and Mexican identity. Neighbourhood eateries such as Manuel's Tepeyac in East Los Angeles, La Golondrina in Olvera Street, Lucy's El Adobe across the street from Paramount Studios, and Barragan's and La Villa Taxco on Sunset Boulevard continued to serve as 'third places' for political discussion and deal-making between an emerging Mexican American middle-class political leadership and the Democratic machine. Meanwhile, the spread of Mexican restaurants followed the movement of Mexican Americans into the suburbs. Central and South American restaurants would continue a slow but steady acquisition of cultural space in the Pico–Union/Westlake area, Hollywood, and Echo Park. Incremental increases in Latino political, economic, and media empowerment accompanied these conquests.

But after the 1970s, the government and media diluted these gains by reviving the term *Hispanic* and other aspects of the fantasy legacy. Suzanne Oboler points out the reductive levelling of the complex and diverse histories under colonialism and postcolonialism by this term:

The ethnic label *Hispanic* began to be widely disseminated by state agencies after 1970. . . . The adoption of the ethnic designator *Hispanic* is commonly understood in terms of Spain's presence in the hemisphere for over three hundred years. . . . Thus, it is important to ask to what extent the appeal to the legacy of the Spanish colonial rule can justify the homogenization under the label *Hispanic* of the subsequent experiences of at least 23 million citizens, residents, and immigrants of Latin American descent. Can this appeal account, for example, for the legacies of Mexican Americans/Chicanos and Puerto Ricans, whose respective post-Spanish colonial histories and cultures have since been differentially shaped by their experiences in the United States? . . . And is it rooted in an accurate perception of the diversity of Latin American populations in their *own* countries of origin? . . . It is important to note that contact and relations among Latin Americans and between them and the United States have historically been limited primarily to the interactions between and among their state representatives.[19]

CALIFORNIA CUISINE

Beginning in the San Francisco Bay Area in the 1970s and continuing later in Los Angeles, the West Coast staged a culinary revolution called 'California cuisine'. The new label acknowledged recipes and ingredients from European and Pacific Rim culinary sources. Soon afterward, Los Angeles began to emphasise its Mexican and Native American influences. Despite its international scope, however, this explosion in culinary innovation was dominated by a single culinary aesthetic: nouvelle cuisine. The new cuisine perfectly suited such emergent global cities as Los Angeles in their transition to economies of cultural production.

Like the European modernists of previous decades, the elite French chefs who initiated the nouvelle revolution in the early 1970s utilised the images, flavours, and associations of the exotic Other to critique a preceding generation of French haute chefs. Like the nouvelle chefs who had rediscovered and reinvented France's regional cuisine, the American nouvelle disciples applied their techniques and aesthetic to local ingredients and recipes, a gentrifying impulse that explains an initial interest in regional culinary history. The practitioners and promoters of California cuisine, nouvelle cuisine *mexique*, and Cal-Mex, Southwest, and Tex-Mex cuisines, as well as of other variants of the new American cuisine, mined the past to feed a commodifying aesthetic, but few of these chefs felt compelled to engage in a critical dialogue with Mexican and other so-called Third World cuisines. The appropriation and rejection of local ingredients and recipes gathered from around the world represented, at a symbolic level, the rhetorical assertions and counter-assertions of an argument occurring within a culinary tradition. The haute and nouvelle partisans did not seriously attempt to engage the practitioners and advocates of non-European, non-nouvelle culinary discourses in their dialogue.

This was true, of course, for Los Angeles, which emerged as a hotbed of nouvelle experimentation in the 1980s. With rare exceptions, the city's nouvelle disciples were not interested in incorporating Mexican cuisine as a fully realised cultural or aesthetic subject. Instead, the poststructur-alism of the nouvelle style appeared to vanquish historical memory and freed chefs to fill their tamales with smoked salmon or caviar without having to worry too much about the cultural ramifications of how they appropriated recipes or combined ingredients. The nouvelle chefs also discovered that they could make Mexican cuisine more palatable to their upscale clientele if they called it *Southwestern*, a term that simultane-ously evoked New Age appropriations of Native American mysticism and the Hispanic fantasy legacy while and de-emphasising overtly Mexican influences.

The food writers who fussed about 'exotic' new ingredients and the ingenious ways nouvelle chefs painted on plates legitimated the chefs' cultural appropriations. Few of the critical infrastructure's members noted the imperial way a new generation of European-trained chefs had detached Mexican and 'Third World' cuisines from their social and cultural histories. More important, the one-way conversation of a postmodern French aesthetic imposing itself upon New World foods and ingredients was held up as a sophisticated urban metaphor of 'salad bowl' multiculturalism or, more technically, 'liberal multiculturalism'.[20] David Rieff, a New York writer and the son of Susan Sontag, takes the culinary metaphor quite literally when he writes:

Indeed, it was on the . . . far more basic level of what people ate that this multiculturalization of the Southland had progressed the farthest. Ethnic restaurants and fast-food restaurants, only recently . . . confined to particular neighbourhoods or immigrant-owned minimals, seemed to be sprouting up everywhere. . . . A generation of Anglo kids whose parents had been raised on steak and baked potatoes could comfort-ably tell the difference at a glance between Thai and Cantonese food. A previously exotic prospect like, say, a Szechuan dinner now seemed almost tame, a Mexican burrito as American as a hamburger. In other words, their bellies were growing up multicultural.[21]

The city's hosting of the 1984 Olympic Games, preceded and followed by two Los Angeles Arts Festivals that included artists from the Pacific Rim and redevelopment projects rationalised as cultural improvement, drew upon multicultural motifs to engender wider public support. A 'liberal multiculturalism', as defined by McLaren, emerged from the cultural events taking place in Los Angeles during the mid-1980s and early 1990s. Lisa Lowe writes,

> Los Angeles was represented as a postmodern multicultural cornu-
> copia, an international patchwork quilt, a global department store;
> although the 'signifiers' were the very uneven, irreducible differ-
> ences between these diverse acts [cultural festivals], the important
> 'signified' was a notion of Los Angeles as multicultural spectacle. In
> the process, each performance tradition was equated with every other,
> and its meaning was reduced and generalised to a common denom-
> inator whose significance was exotic, colourful advertisement of Los
> Angeles.[22]

The city's style-setting restaurants and the food writers who reviewed them played a prominent role in the 'revalorisation' of LA culture. The critical infrastructure fostered the convergence of Hollywood-style glamour with poststructuralist 'multicultural delectation'. Restaurateurs, chefs, architects, and interior designers marshalled music, lighting, celebrities, and 'attractive' waiters and waitresses, as well as tastes and aromas, to stimulate and normalise the experience of consuming the multicultural Other. These new culinary spaces, in other words, sym-bolically fetishised a kind of cultural cannibalism. This mode of cultural production ran on more than symbolic appropriation, however; as has already been stated, the commodification of multicultural cuisine reinforced and relied upon a division of labour that trapped Latina/o immigrant workers in the role of brute physical labourers.

Some scholars see the growing Latina/o middle class as the solution to the cultural silence of Latinas/os in the city they will soon dominate numerically. These scholars expect upward social mobility, which they confuse with the ability to earn middle incomes, to resolve this paradox: either assimilation will reinforce the current hegemonic order or majority political and consumer buying power will allow Latinas/os to construct a mainstream version of their culture.

But if a numerical majority is to lead to the formation of a cultural class, the core of that class will emerge from working-class immigrants and the popular culture they create and consume. There are a few reasons for this projection. First, Spanish remains the language of the service sector; behind kitchen doors, the immigrant workers who rely upon the well-established social networks that maintain their access to restaurant jobs ensure the dominance of Spanish in the workplace. Second, the purchasing power of a growing immigrant population has expanded Spanish-language media and provided the Latina/o community with the resources to satisfy its cultural appetites; an expanding economy of nostalgia supplies these immigrants with the raw ingredients to maintain and elaborate upon a vibrant culinary culture within the home and the neighbourhood. The memory-driven side of the market is sustained by the region's indigenous Latina/o cultures, new immigrant arrivals, and second- or third-generation 'retro-Latinas/os' trying to recover what they have forgotten.

UNIONS AS CULTURAL INSTITUTIONS

Developing unions as cultural institutions would begin to invest the immigrant majority of restaurant workers with the intellectual authority to represent their own cuisines. Although such a future may seem far off, a variant of this model already exists. In France, the best chefs come from the working class and acquire mastery through on-the-job apprenticeship. Such a system cannot work here as long as the service sector divides workers into first- and second-class wage earners. But the unions could pursue their own institution-building strategy to make service-sector work more economically and culturally rewarding. While increasing their Latina/o and Asian memberships, they could assume more responsibility for cultural training and draw upon the expertise of neighbourhood arts organisations. At the same time, these Latina/o-led unions could mobilise voters to strengthen and reorient their local educational institutions. The schools would have the task of building a worker-oriented cultural class that would challenge and open the local critical infrastructure while democratising restaurants' social organisation and allocation of representational power.

CONCLUSION

Los Angeles, a veritable tangle of culture industries, exemplifies the global city as arbiter of cultural meaning and investment, but also as a postcolonial territory subject to reinterpretation by its Latina/o majority. The nearness of its postcolonial past thus presents certain risks to elite efforts to incorporate, reconfigure, and commodify the city's multi-cultural landscapes. 'The colonial aftermath', says Leela Gandhi, 'is marked by the range of ambivalent cultural moods and formations which accompany periods of transition and translation.'[23] These periods are ongoing and never finally resolved. So it can be expected that Los Angeles's elite and elite-striving culture industries will continue to create narratives and images that seem to render harmless whatever oppositional tendencies its inhabitants preserve in their memories: the elites know they cannot fully control and exploit the landscapes of the present without also patrolling the landscapes of the past. The creative destruction of landscape formation is more than a material process; it is the language of power, the means by which elites include and exclude symbols to construct and communicate the urban images, narratives, and visions they hope to make appear real. To Zukin, for instance, the symbolic economy speaks especially clearly in restaurants.

One cannot expect the ambitious attempt of urban elites to make transparent and accessible the cultural and historical world of the Other to go uncontested. 'Despite appearances', argues Bhabha, 'the text of transparency inscribes a double vision: the field of the "true" emerges as a visible sign of authority only after the regulatory and displacing division of the true and the false.'[24] Although urban elites use the critical infrastructure to attempt to dominate the means of symbolic production and distribution, they do not control this absolutely. To begin with, the huge costs of constructing their grand narratives depend upon the consent of the culture-consuming, tax-paying, and voting public. Moreover, their texts are continually contested and thus subject to the give and take, the inherent ambivalence, of a cultural dialectic. We learn from Jameson that self-consciousness is the driving force behind dialec-tical thought: that it is 'thought about thought. Thought to the second power which at the same time remains aware of its own intellectual operations in the very act of thinking.'[25] Effective dialectical thought includes consciousness of one's complicity. After a while, exposure to the symbolic economy of multiculturalism, whether one is of the elite class or not, is likely to yield private and public considerations not only of what the associated signs of culture mean but of the very conditions of their meaning.

7

Latino Futures? Cultural Political Economy and Alternative Futures

This chapter makes a general case for grounding a twenty-first-century critical Latino studies and politics in something we shall provisionally call 'cultural political economy'.[1] It makes that case by attempting to resolve lingering theoretical tensions between socioeconomic (structural) and culture-based (semiotic) approaches to our neoliberal present.[2] This postdisciplinary interpretation reaffirms the centrality of capitalist formations in the study of the Latino question by embedding social and cultural categories in the lived spaces of our macroeconomic order. The kind of cultural political economy we posit strives for a theoretically and empirically useful analytic with which to approach the urban question for our changing times.

From the above approach, we sketch a few strategic lines to confront changing class formations and deindustrialisation in neoliberal capitalism's period of indefinitely prolonged crisis. Our cursory review then explores the ways our current economic crisis implicates the scholarly projects of Latino and Chicano urban studies—and how our interpretations of cultural political economy might reconfigure these projects to answer the continued attacks from the populist right.

We picked up some of our critical thread from theoretical themes previously addressed by Valle and Torres in *Latino Metropolis*.[3] From our perspective, this work was foundational in exploring the strategic political and discursive opportunities that Los Angeles offered as it emerged as a majority Mexican and Latino city. The context in which the city reached this demographic tipping point was as important as its passage through the socioeconomic minefield of industrial transformation. The maturation of what was then a hardly noticed transition to a post-Fordist mode of production in the nation's largest manufacturing centre spelled the most important element of that irreducible difference. The emergence of a majority-Latino immigrant working class in both the new manufacturing enterprises and the growing service sector was a symptom of the wrenching deindustrialisation and reindustrialisation of the region, a thoroughgoing reorganisation of production in which neoliberal globalisation imported the *maquiladora* model to industrial sectors that were too expensive to relocate to Latin America or Asia. More important to the lived experiences of that emergent Latino working-class majority were the socioeconomic and cultural consequences of that new industrial order: its ever-harsher regime of class inequality, misery, and marginalisation.

Like Valle and Torres, we recognise the obvious: that attaining a supernumerary status would not guarantee diminished social inequalities so long as the region's symbolic economy continued to racialise, and therefore devalue, Latino immigrant labour. The means of cultural production, in other words, played a powerful role in reinforcing and reproducing the new social relations of post-Fordist production and its disciplinary requirements. There were, for example, subtle interactions between the recurring moral panics directed against 'illegal alien' workers, the postmodern commodification of Mexican cuisine and ethnic tourist enclaves, and a huge restaurant industry that depended on the exploitation of a Latino/a immigrant workforce.

We recognize that there was a confluence of economic, political, and cultural changes meshed with the consolidation of a progressive Latino labour leadership and the day-to-day practices of Latino hybridity as aspects of a contestatory and pragmatic survival strategy in all arenas of representation, including practices of place-making. Making sense of these enmeshments, or what Marx called the metabolism of social and material conditions, required a degree of theoretical and methodological experimentation on our parts. Marx, after all, never developed a full-blown theorisation of culture deduced from the logics of communicative processes. Instead, he saw the 'natural' environment as a seemingly endless yet two-sided metabolic dialectic with humans, who, in modifying it, evolved new social relations to survive the environment they had changed.

That metabolism cannot function without the coordinating and interpretive cultural membrane through which human societies appraise, modify, and adapt to their environments: an approach to the symbolic order that Marx lacked, but intuited, when he proposed the logic of his biological metaphor. He brushed up against the symbolic order again when he acknowledged the seeming mysteries of the commodity fetish, an object of socially produced value that is nevertheless a bearer of multiple connotative secrets: 'A commodity appears at first sight an extremely obvious, trivial thing. But its analysis brings out that it is a very strange thing, abounding in metaphysical subtleties and theological niceties'.[4] Slavoj Žižek argues that the social relations that produce the commodity 'fetish as a solid object' nevertheless carry within them the ideology that hides the social costs of the commodity's creation, a spectral parallel of pure 'ideology' that hides the commodity's contradictions in plain sight. He convincingly uses the ways digital technology has taken the 'dematerialisation' of the money fetish, its transformations from gold bullion to paper currency to the transfer of the digital bank draft, to illustrate the extreme literalness with which these spectral transformations now occur, transformations that Marx would scarcely recognise. Our interpretation of the dematerialised fetish simply translates Žižek's notion of the 'spectral aspect of capitalism' as one aspect of the cultural life of capitalism, theorised from the more nuanced perspective of discourse and discursive practices.[5]

Our reading of the contributions of cultural studies has led to our exploration of Marx's biological metaphor and to look for the genealogies of social metabolism. Culture, in our version of this trope, functions as a medium and a by-product, a lived neural network, and a physical archive of knowledge from which societies formulate and test new social forms and conceptual and material technology. Our formulation of culture does not distinguish between its resemblance to a living organism and its transformations into market commodities or technology. It tries instead to sense the organic life of culture in those moments when lived neural networks and the residues of the symbolic order obey the genetic and viral logics of language mutation. It proposes a conceptual language that tries to detect a dynamic process, namely those instances when the network's residues materialise in the archive of the known and knowable and blur the boundaries with which we try to distinguish the contaminating human trace from our idealised images of nature. The combined, synergistic effect of medium and residue can powerfully influence our social and so-called natural environments by exerting an inertial force that retards social adaptation to new environmental conditions or by generating new knowledge with which to transform those conditions. That the cultural function's dual aspects fill the seemingly minimal interstitial gap that articulates the linkage of the social to the material environment does not diminish its power. Great effects often occur at a seemingly microscopic scale, a subtlety that allows us to envision cultural processes occurring within an ecological model of the biosphere.

We could go further, arguing that living organisms cannot sustain themselves without mediating communicative systems—membranes, if you will—through which they interact and do something that resembles learning from the environment. Human society, in such a reformulation, would then emerge in that place where the spheres of culture, political economy, and biology overlap, a triangular arrangement that situates the lived 'materiality' of Henri Lefebvre's theorisation of 'the everyday' within an ecology of human and nonhuman communicative communities.[6] Such a reframing would allow us to resituate Marx's notion of metabolism within the most recent theorisations of ecology and evolutionary biology, but that task taxes our theoretical abilities and takes us far afield from our critique of the decreasing relevance of cultural studies.

What we are concerned with on this point is continuing to recalibrate the field's formidable critical tools for a new task: building the conceptual equation that would balance the discursive and the structural material realities of globalised capital accumulation. What could Stuart Hall and Michel Foucault tell us about the cultural-economic metabolism of post-Fordist political economy, and can we extrapolate a category that would fuse political economy and a critical theory of culture, a field since named *cultural political economy?* We, like our predecessors, are attempting to take the critical turn in the global metropolis seriously and to bring cultural critique to power and class relations as they occur in the globalised city—a messy, fluid, and densely meaningful place, and therefore the ideal arena in which to study the processes of globalisation. We are also interested in the global city's radical cosmopolitanism, a space of lived hybridity in which the immigrant subject's virtuoso experimentation with that environment's multiple political and cultural codes fosters new ways of thinking and acting around, under, and beyond the nation-state's rigid categories.

That cosmopolitanism underlies the implicit logic of *Latino Metropolis.* Valle and Torres expressed this by simultaneously running a positivist analytic alongside a critical interpretation to give each a reciprocal role within an overarching interpretive construct, which was Los Angeles's entire symbolic and built landscape. Like them, we cannot talk about Latinos, the city's ethnic majority, without a totalising theory of the city that could correlate a specific cultural process to every social relation within the context of market capitalism. Doing this, however, requires us to redirect cultural studies away from its customary preoccupation with the subaltern subject and its myriad processes of identity formation. We believe that all subjectivities, including the varieties of 'whiteness' embodied by the city's corporate elite, merited the critical gaze of cultural studies. If these critical approaches hold any validity, they should allow us to interpret identity formation for all social classes and racialised ethnicities, and to locate the cultural effects we theorised within the totality of existing social relations of late global capital.

We therefore seek the reciprocal translatability between analytic and critical approaches, between the dialectical and the genealogical, to identify those points of structural articulation where cultural effects were unambiguous. Valle and Torres also strove for an approach that would allow us to plot the intersection of spatial and temporal planes from which indigenous local memories and their subjective spaces erupt from global capital's urban matrix. In sum, they have provided us with a powerful way to theorise the knowledge strands that construct a cultural political economy.

THE CITY AS NARRATIVE OBSERVATORY

Michel Foucault's theory of 'governmentality,' however, provides one method of doing the improbable—identifying the knowledge strands that encode the global city's assembly instructions. Each of its knowledge strands began to be instrumentalised and codified as a strain of governmental technology in the fifteenth and sixteenth centuries, when emerging European states used the administrative apparatus of the medieval justice system to organise new governmental offices. These relatively small institutional innovations began to 'governmentalise' the state by increments.[7] Liberalism's eighteenth-century inauguration stimulated new government innovations to ensure the modern state's survival. Governments rapidly borrowed the new techniques of disciplining the populace they sent to prisons, hospitals, factories, and the military. The new census-taking methodologies established a concrete basis for imagining and implementing a national political economy. Obtaining accurate counts of the population provided a practical way to monitor a nation's demographic wealth and health and the material conditions and social relations that contributed to or detracted from its productivity.

As inventory-taking methods improved, it also became possible to monitor the lives of individual citizens. Birth and death certificates; school, tax, criminal, and military records; and a growing list of other documentary procedures allowed government to envision a state of perpetual surveillance initially devised for controlling prisoners and hospital patients but applied later to the full citizenry. Methods used to contain contagion in cities or reinforce the military chain of command also found their way into rationales for reorganising government bureaucracies. Innovations in the surveillance and regulation of mental illness, sexuality, and female fertility allowed bureaucracies to narrow the application of that technology from the general populace to discrete social groups until focussing its gaze upon the body of the individual.

The modern state's tendency to apply these disciplinary techniques to different classes of objects led to another innovation: one could more thoroughly manipulate and disseminate the abstract discourse of the state by ascribing to it human corporeal qualities. The state's metonymic association with the body grew from an earlier metaphor—the medieval city as corporate or fictional person.[8] Each innovation in governmental technology incrementally modified the state's forms and political rationality, a process that expanded the state's power while increasing its dependence on the invention and reorganisation of existing governmental institutions to consolidate its gains and neutralise challenges to its authority.

In time, the proliferation of governmental functions and organs not only produced internal contradictions that undermined older governmental functions but revealed that the state did not possess a coherent, essential core of truth upon which it was based, only a collection of different and sometimes incompatible administrative techniques that the populace experienced as the unitary state. Foucault called the state's ever-changing governmental adaptations: governmentality, or that 'ensemble' of 'institutions, procedures, analyses and . . . calculations and tactics that allow the exercise of this very specific albeit complex form of power, which has [the population] as its target, [political economy] as its principal form of knowledge, and [the apparatuses of security] as its essential technical means'.[9]

From the eighteenth century onward, the formerly distinct spheres of 'government, population, and political economy' gradually fused into 'a solid series' of social practices we today call the economy. Foucault's spectrum of effects theorised the production of wealth, the security of the state, and the control of the population as an integrated whole. However, rather than stress the Orwellian notion of a centralised state under the control of a single, all-knowing entity, Foucault envisioned the state as a field of effects generated by an ensemble of governmental technologies that naturalised that state's political hegemony. His theorisation would allow others to more than simply speculate on the vague possibilities of a genealogy of the present. It would give those with sufficiently rich archives the means to identify and disentangle the governmental technologies that shape the state and its inhabiting subjectivities.

A key observation, one half-explained in *Latino Metropolis*, was the role capital plays, via its power to create and implement laws and generate and circulate its necessary truths, in re-creating the governmental technologies that generate the state 'effect'. (Valle would take the next step and make that formulation of the cultural technologies of capital accumulation explicit in his next book, *City of Industry: Genealogies of Power in Southern California*.[10])

That was then, the more than a decade old 'then' of *Latino Metropolis*, in which Valle and Torres generally predicted the inevitability of our present economic collapse and resurgent anti-immigrant Latino hysteria. They recognised the potential for that crisis in the contradictions of a US capitalist system that cannibalised itself in successive crises of financialisation rather than reinvesting in the production of new wealth. It is therefore now understood, given that these conditions are recurring and intensifying, that Latino scholars and activist organisers accept social dislocation as a certainty they should plan for in their scholarship and praxis. We believe that the economic meltdown of 2008 and its effects validate the continued pursuit of the scholarly project we envision for Latino studies and politics: its interdisciplinarity as a field of study and its focus on interpreting the Latino working class within the totality of an urban landscape and experience.

The city, as the localised arena of global processes and changing class relations, is still the conceptual space in which to continue those experiments. The present-day context of economic collapse and resurgent anti-immigrant hysteria, however, also suggests that we remain vigilant to new possibilities of scholarly activism, that we look to the critical turn for more than monkey wrenches and cultural technologies of discontent. We should also consider using those tools to identify new opportunities of strategic urban intervention and to create moments of emancipatory rupture with which we might free ourselves to imagine another urban future in the space opened up by the social and cultural equivalent of a cosmological singularity.

Genealogy offers another way to revisit our revolutions for the lessons their successes and failures teach, and for traces of the singularities that rupture and reset the clock of capitalist hegemony. We are not talking about reviving boring Stalinist hagiographies of worker heroes but of producing cultural genealogies of settings in which emancipatory subjectivity erupted in specific individuals, social movements, or class formations.

The various genres of narrative art, whether written, performed, or lived, represent one way of observing and exploring the fusion of these spaces and subjectivities. Entering that narrative observatory requires recovering the seemingly disconnected stories Latinos and Latinas told themselves when they encountered each other and reinvented themselves in the sweatshops, boulevards, slaughterhouses, and movie houses of the last century, when they dreamed of other radical futures, few outside the immigrant and exile communities seemed to hear or see. Making an inventory of revolutionary remembering could be that first step in preparing ourselves to identify, and if possible, cultivate new revolutionary subjectivities in the cities that Latina/o immigrants know best. We could start, in other words, by identifying the low-hanging fruit of an abandoned neighbourhood 'tree' and then making plans for that tree's pruning, watering, and feeding.

ANSWERING THE CALL TO ACTION

We borrow from a speech Mao gave on 29 May 1939 as a kind of ideal to which we should aspire in the aftermath of the rise of the Tea Party–led state censorship of the Latino/ethnic studies high-school curriculum in Arizona, an episode which, in the final analysis, contributed to today's anti-immigrant Trump era:

> It is good if the enemy attacks us, since it proves that we have drawn a clear line of demarcation between the enemy and ourselves. It is still better if the enemy attacks us wildly and paints us as utterly black and without a single virtue; it demonstrates that we have not only drawn a clear line of demarcation between the enemy and ourselves but also achieved a great deal in our work.[11]

Could it be that these high-school educators deserved the epithets of the populist right, especially being accused of fomenting a postcolonial critique of the United States' conquest of the Arizona territory? As we all know, many of the attacks were fevered projections of an ethnic *reconquista* that our colleagues do not teach. We also know that they meant for these attacks to distract Arizonans from the ruling majority's failure to prevent the state's fiscal collapse. They chose to blame the racialised other they strove to recreate—Mexican and Latino immigrants and their children, who will indeed alter the state's balance of political power, if only modestly.

The 'Tea Party' populists needed to turn the Latino/a immigrant into a terrifying threat. It did not matter to them that the community's integration into the state's electorate, and their attendant acquisition and exercise of civil rights, has been painfully slow. The symbiotic media-state representations of immigrants' border violations had already produced the appropriate intensity of moral sensitisation. They targeted teachers who taught the modest virtues of ethnic and racial diversity and the Latino community's well-documented contributions to Arizona's wealth as agents of subversion. The teachers who had had the audacity to urge the next generation of Latino/a voters to act as first-class rather than alienated citizens were a terror too good to pass up. Why calmly accept that inevitability, one that would not fundamentally alter the state's neoliberal underpinnings, if you could orchestrate a major distraction? Cultivating a panic was much better than acknowledging that Latino immigration was a symptom, not a cause, of the economic globalisation that had destroyed the high-wage manufacturing Arizona had secured during the Cold War, or that the low-wage, no-benefit post-Fordist regime that had replaced it depended on a surplus of 'unskilled' immigrant labour. Such is the racist logic of populist xenophobia: it obsesses over the impure outsider that would threaten the purity of the polis, its innocent 'we' of (white) natives, the indispensable ingredient of 'whiteness' that the Tea Partiers, the 'birthers', and the anti-immigrant Trump supporters presume in their tribal construct of citizenship.

Perhaps it is time to earn their scorn. Perhaps it is time to search our political and cultural memories of failed revolutions, as Žižek recommends, for the antipode of the populist pole, a position around which a viable left could coalesce and offer a coherent alternative to the populist right. The next generation of Latino/a studies scholars has a particular role to play in the search for that new positionality. We hope they will show that a viable left in the United States cannot emerge if it does not embrace the quintessential 'part of no part,' the undocumented immigrant, and others effectively stripped of citizenship as its core constituency, the future majority that will embody and express our deepest democratic values and impulses.

Place matters in this continuing enterprise. We assert an emphasis in *The Latino Question* on the places of production to imagine a new politics, one that would cut across districts and working-class neighbourhoods: community politics are not principally the politics of neighbourhoods but the politics of work, class, and culture. We should advance this line further now and reconsider what the category of class can mean in US cities when the immigrant-dependent restaurant industry scatters the place of production throughout the urban landscape. That same question applies more directly to the Walmart clerks and subcontracted warehouse workers symbiotically connected to Asian manufacturing via that vast trans-Pacific system of commodity distribution known as logistics. Not only does understanding immigrant workers' role in global manufacturing clarify their labour power's strategic significance, it forces us to question the notion that consumption is the new point of production, an implicitly nationalist orientation that tends to privilege the welfare of the 'American' worker-consumer over all the others, while ignoring the urgency of building transnational worker solidarity.

The organisers of Warehouse Workers United are, as of this writing, attempting such a re-centring of working-class citizenship amidst the world's largest concentration of warehouses. Global trade in the Pacific Rim and Southern California's north-south mountain corridors has created a new battlefield clustered around the rail, truck, and air infrastructure of San Bernardino and Riverside Counties. Geography has funnelled the huge increases in cargo pulsing from the ports of Los Angeles and Long Beach through the historically depressed region misleadingly named the Inland Empire. The transformation of the logistics industry, which was touted as the cure to the region's chronic job losses and housing foreclosures, actually raised particulate air pollution to the world's fourth-highest while turning temporary employment agencies into the new growth sector.[12] These permanently temporary agencies eagerly refined 'sweatshop' subcontracting technologies to the retail industry's specifications. They drastically lowered wages, job security, and safety standards for more than 53,000 workers (most of them undocumented) by creating a barrier of deniability for warehouse retailers to evade responsibility for creating those conditions.[13]

The Change to Win[14]-supported campaign's answer to the atomising technologies of outsourcing has been to build an impressive coalition of environmental, labour unions, church groups, and West and East Coast Occupiers in support of immigrant Latino workers battling for union representation, living wages, and safer working conditions.[15] It attempts not only to create that tipping point at which Latino immigrant workers can make the transition from racialised minority to empowered working-class majority, but also to neutralise the demoralising effects of labour subcontracting by representing the entire transportation corridor as a continuation of the warehouse. Its strategy is to expose the industry's vulnerabilities to a variety of community actions, from regulatory and legal interventions against safety violations to blockades of key trucking arteries, by revealing its complicity in degrading the region's social and natural ecology.[16]

Obviously, a handful of Latino scholars will not lead this constructive political project by themselves. Already, many academics of seemingly marginalised tendencies (such as critical ethnic studies, postcolonial studies, cultural studies, women's studies, and gender studies) as well as independent scholars, artists, and activists are asking questions of this sort and engaging in emancipatory scholarship that seeks to expose the imbalance of power embedded within the social relations of production.

What lies ahead for this next generation of would-be scholars, and how do they pursue it? We believe that Latino/a urban theorists can perform a great service through research and practice that explains to their would-be colleagues, and progressives generally, why they must see their futures in creating class relations based upon complete identification with the emergent urban and rural immigrant majorities. They can also help by excavating the discursive legacy, those genealogies of knowledge and practice that have directly contributed to mass mobilisations of Latino immigrant workers. They can set an example by acknowledging the radical and revolutionary Latino/a intellectuals, workers, and scholars who shaped the agenda and narratives that reacquainted organised labour and today's movements with the feasibility of a national general strike by achieving a scale that spoke more loudly than its rhetoric.

Cultural processes were crucial in producing that result. The use of Spanish-language media, above all radio and print media, to mobilise millions in 2006 validated the importance we gave to that strategic resource in previous works and which we give it now in *The Latino Question*. The content and forms of their appeal to Latino workers also betrayed a genealogical moment overlooked in the scholarly studies that interpreted the 2006 mobilisations. Immigrant-rights organisers formed in the Los Angeles Marxist-Leninist circles of the 1970s led that first push to prevent the passage of HR 4437, legislation that would have set the stage for deporting millions of undocumented immigrants and prosecuting anyone convicted of sheltering them. That generation's historical formation was especially evident in 2006's May Day demonstrations as well as in the ongoing Dreamer movement. They had orchestrated a mobilisation in which supposedly 'conservative' immigrants in immaculate white T-shirts denounced racism, sexism, class inequality, borders, imperialism, and neoliberal globalisation—a concise inventory, in other words, of a discursive formation we can call the Latino left.

Two immigrant-rights activists, Jesse Diaz and Javier Rodriguez, deserve recognition for their intrepid leadership in initiating, organising, and framing that day's unprecedented demonstrations. In addition to the million or so marchers who mobilised in Chicago, New York, Milwaukee, and dozens of smaller cities across the United States, a million more went to the streets of Los Angeles in two separate marches. That first wave of marches demanded immediate and unconditional amnesty for all undocumented immigrants, an immediate halt to border-fence construction, decriminalisation of the undocumented, and an immediate cessation of factory raids and deportations. More importantly, the mobilisations emptied the work place. As many as 75 percent of the Los Angeles industries employing Latino labour shut their doors, while as many as 90 percent of the day truckers hauling goods from the ports of Los Angeles and Long Beach stayed home. 'On farms in California and Arizona,' Rodriguez said, 'fruit and vegetables went unpicked, and across the country, meat-packing and poultry farms, fast-food franchises and other businesses were forced to close. In a lot of cases, employers supported their workers: all over Los Angeles businesses started putting up signs saying they would be closed on May 1'.[17]

Those events deserve further study, starting with the so-called mainstream Latino organisations and unions that fragmented and weakened the mobilisation's initial message by prematurely supporting the Democratic Party's pragmatic path to immigration reform. A new generation of scholars and organic intellectuals must also give itself permission to question the institutions from which they should expect bolder leadership. Would it be reasonable for them to ask, for example, why the discipline of Chicano/a and Latino/a studies, especially its bureaucratic apparatus, seemed to take such a reticent stance toward the self-organising immigrant energy recently displayed on the streets? That institutional ambivalence (not the independent scholars who met in the streets) also suggests itself when a few scholars and administrators still try to reconcile the uniqueness of Chicano/a identity, as asserted in the 1960s, with the growing immigrant presence that has transformed Latino/a communities everywhere. We will not go into all the twists and turns of that reticence here. Suffice it to say that, except for the sober concluding pages of Michael Soldatenko's *Chicano Studies: The Genesis of a Discipline*,[18] only a fraction of works within the discipline seem to have mustered the courage to discuss the widening fissures of this ideological debate directly. Strangely, that silence continues, as Soldatenko observes, even though a growing number, perhaps a majority, of scholars sheltered under the rubric of Chicano/a studies practice strains of scholarship that have already outstripped the discursive boundaries of its most generous disciplinary definitions. That silence means that the pressure to re-radicalise Chicano/a studies has also come from the students and their sisters and brother academics outside the discipline.

We can hear that prodding to revisit pre-Chicano-movement origins in works such as Gilbert G. González's *Guest Workers or Colonized Labor? Mexican Labor Migration to the United States* (2007), Mike Davis's *Magical Urbanism: Latinos Reinvent the US Big City* (2000), David R. Diaz's *Barrio Urbanism: Chicanos, Planning, and American Cities* (2005), and William David Estrada's *The Los Angeles Plaza: Sacred and Contested Space* (2008), especially for his masterful recontextualisation of the plaza's Magonista, Wobbly, and anarchist synergies. Raúl Homero Villa's *Barrio-Logos: Space and Place in Urban Chicano Literature and Culture* (2000) and Ignacio López-Calvo's *Latino Los Angeles in Film and Fiction: The Cultural Production of Social Anxiety* (2011) push upon that reticence from another direction. López-Calvo challenges the long-held myths that authentic Hispanic 'cultural identity was to be found outside the urban context' and that the early 1970s had somehow birthed a fully formed Chicano literature from the preceding decade's radical protest. López-Calvo's work does an especially effective job of debunking Chicano/a literature's pastoral image and uncomplicated identitarian origins. Not only does that literature draw from deep

Indigenous, Spanish, and African roots, but its late-twentieth-century energy is urban and therefore modern in its questioning of imposed or 'traditional' tropes of racial, gender, and sexual identity. Its polyvocal, restless, questioning energy will continue in this century, López-Calvo writes, given that 'the massive migration of Latinos to Los Angeles has turned this late-capitalist metropolis into a privileged site for Chicano and Latino cultural production. It is no longer the Babylon where Mexican immigrants inevitably lose their "authentic" national traits and roots,' but the imaginary in which they radically remap the city's democratic possibilities.[19]

Ernesto Galarza's cryptic Magonista and Wobbly references in his classic autobiography, *Barrio Boy*, represent another contribution that urges a critical look back to the early Chicano movement's preoccupation with identity formation. Galarza would say as much in a series of interviews he gave in 1977 to 1978 and 1981, when he questioned the way Chicano scholars and activists in the 1960s and 1970s tried to represent themselves through the single prism of ethnic identity:

> I try to stay away from terms that rely on ethnicity. I use terms that represent what people do for a living. *Occupation* is a much more meaningful term. Academics at UCLA have worked on this theme. In Arizona and in New Mexico there is a great deal of scholarly interest in this problem of choice of terminology. I don't think it leads very far, because if you look at these terms—you'll find people who are called Chicanos in San Jose; they're called Chicanos in Imperial Valley; they're called Chicanos in San Francisco. But if you know those people, the occupational differences are more important, to me, anyway. It may be because I have a certain bias against ethnic identity. I don't think people should be handled that way . . . should be catalogued . . . because it's not a permanent characteristic other than to those who believe in very strong racial, ethnic characteristics—and I don't.[20]

The Chicano/a-studies project would eventually catch up to Galarza's formulation and embrace his understanding of social constructivism. However, the discipline retains a certain ambivalence regarding the utility of Galarza's cautiously expressed class analysis (one informed more by Weber than by Marx).

Does the bureaucratic imperative to defend Chicano/a studies in some of the same institutions Galarza mentioned more than four decades ago still trick us into a scholarship that imbues Chicano/a identity with a transcendent quality, one that defies the historical flux that transforms all others? Do we harbour a deeply buried assimilationist wish when we expect new Latino immigrants to act as Chicano/a in the making, a vast transitional population reliving the traumas and joys of inventing a bicultural-bilingual citizenship? Discovering the common experiences with which different immigrant communities have reclaimed their humanity in a system that denies it is indeed valuable. But do lingering notions of identity politics freeze us in a neoliberal status quo that acknowledges diversity while preventing us from facing the brutal economic reality of our time? Will celebrating diversity challenge the state in its current embattled corporate configuration to countenance the continued naturalisation of millions of immigrants? Does not the current depth of the crisis require that we rethink what a 'Chicano/a' politics can mean in an economy that will stagnate for decades to come, in which even the most modest, most humane immigration reforms or defence against rollbacks on minor legislative victories require massive, broad-based national mobilisations to implement? It would seem that the manner in which Galarza's work slowly disappeared from the curriculum has answered these questions. His were not deemed interesting questions.

But an ideological debate that erupted in the 1970s, outside the academy: on Los Angeles's picket lines, its sweatshops and Immigration and Naturalization Services— *La Migra,* detention facilities—would revive Galarza's line of questioning. Laura Pulido's *Black, Brown, Yellow, and Left: Radical Activism in Los Angeles* (2006) touched that nerve when she credited the Marxist-Leninist cadres of that decade for pushing the movement in a more radical and ultimately more fruitful direction. Pulido, who does not ignore the failures of Bert Corona[21] and Centro de Acción Social Autónomo (CASA), nevertheless recognises their undeniable impact on the city's present political landscape: 'Former members of CASA had not only created a network of like-minded people but seeds of resistance within the 'old' labour movement that would blossom with advent of greater institutional support.'[22] That cadre's most important discovery was to recognise the likely impact of the emergence of a majority immigrant Latino workforce on all other class and power relations in the city, a realisation they obfuscated when they tried to replace Chicano/a cultural nationalism with Mexican nationalism as a means of achieving a new working-class solidarity. But even the seeming half-measure of representing CASA as the Marxist-Leninist vanguard of workers unified by a crudely constructed theory of nationalist loyalty had the benefit of loosening up the ways Chicano/a academics and activists had represented class relations and self-awareness until that time, and of recognising the possibilities of Latin American worker solidarity. The seeds they had sown would bear fruit in the 1990s, when former CASA members assumed pivotal positions of leadership within the local and national labour movement, the legal arm of the immigrant-rights movement, and the political class that began to reshape the city's entire political culture. Their emancipatory intentions, moreover, did not simply respond to that decade's material conditions; their practice would create the conditions of another struggle, one that re-appeared to fill the streets of Los Angeles and other major cities in 2006.

But the relative silence with which the Chicano/a-studies standard-bearers have received the work of Pulido and her urban-studies colleagues underscores the subtle rift in the discipline's ethnically focused bureaucratic project. The edge of that rift reappears each time Latino/a students treat the glories of the 1960s with more reverence than the mass immigrant mobilisations that have occurred since the 1990s, a nostalgic gaze that prevents them from recognising the radical possibilities of the present. That is what made Bert Corona so remarkable. If he were with us today, would he gently coax those students and nostalgic faculty to overcome their fears and tell them that the present is the best time and place to struggle and that the scale of the immigrant-led labour movement he helped create dwarfs anything the Chicano movement achieved?

We must also acknowledge the limits Pulido imposed on herself. Her understandable focus on the field from which the three ideological configurations of Los Angeles's ethnic left emerged necessarily gave less attention to Bert Corona's biography. Nor did she have the space to adequately address the subtle ways these revived 'Lefts' owed their successes to the city's early- and mid-twentieth-century leftist radicals. Perhaps we should put the responsibility for that silence at the feet of a prior generation of scholars and journalists who succeeded in distancing Corona from the early-twentieth-century left that formed him and made him a recurring target of Red-baiting. Perhaps we should also question those efforts to remake Bert as a wholesome ethnic leader of generic progressive tendencies and only the slightest 'socialist' sympathies.[23] These revisions illustrate the ways the ghosts of the left still haunt the Chicano/a movement's ideological project, a squeamishness Bert understood and patiently tolerated but ignored when it came time to take the courageous political gamble of challenging the early Chicano/a movement to embrace the cause of undocumented Mexican, Central American, and South American immigrant workers.

The effect of Bert's strategic choices and his consistent critique of corporate capitalism, still cause some Chicano academics to agonise over whether they should embrace the immigrant workers who demonstrate a willingness to put their class loyalties before ethnic, racial, or national allegiances. That ambivalence persists when Chicano/a and Latino/a scholars look past the 1970s, that crucial decade in which the organisational and discursive foundations of the Latino immigrant mass mobilisations of the 2000s began to appear as a complicated, largely urban response to brutal worker exploitation, the government's policies of immigration terror, and the limitations of the previous decade's Chicano/a radical discourse. It was in that decade that the first women and gay artists began to express their dissatisfaction with constraints of Chicano/a cultural nationalism, and Chicano/a activists confronted the immigrant and political refugees who would alter the demographic composition and social relations that characterised what they had once understood as a predominantly Mexican American 'community'. Not only would Mexican and other Latin American immigrants soon emerge as the barrio's new majority, they would eventually emerge as urban America's working class, a realisation that obliged the more farsighted to see the sweatshop or factory floor as the crucial arena of struggle.

The ideological effects of Chicano activists, intellectuals, and artists travelling to Cuba, Mexico, Central America, and other destinations in Latin America, as well as China, in the late 1960s and continuing through the 1970s and 1980s provoked another series of discussions that would further erode the movement's insularity. They exposed themselves to a variety of Marxist and socialist critiques and debates centred on US capitalism and imperialism would acquire more nuanced understandings of how they fit into a larger anti-imperialist front, as well as of the left's failures and defeats. The pace of these conversations increased in the 1970s, when brutal military repression from Mexico, Chile, and Argentina sent Latin American refugees and intellectuals to the United States. These conversations continued in the late 1970s and 1980s with the arrival of Central American political and economic refugees escaping US-funded terror and counter-revolution.

These intellectuals often arrived with their books, given the popularity of Latin American literature experienced during the 'boom' years, a reception enhanced by university courses that assigned them and Spanish-language print media that covered and interpreted them. Whether they passed through as touring performers or as lesser-known artists, writers, or professors who came to stay, young Chicano/a and Latino/a intellectuals found it easier to stay abreast of Latin America's political and cultural debates when they socialised with their Latin American cousins, dialogues that pushed that generation into a deeper exploration of their movement's pre-Chicano/a radical revolutionary roots.

These subversive influences and contradictory tendencies shared a geographic constant: they had converged in the major cities of the United States. The acknowledged centrality of the urban experience, as David Harvey's recent work suggests, therefore underlies the future study of the formation of Latino subjectivity. The recent studies that contextualise José Martí's New York, the city that witnessed Puerto Rican Bernardo Vega's political formation two decades later, represent a sample from that small number of postcolonial works that explore the US city's role in co-authoring a transnational, hemispheric Latino intellectual legacy. We would expect Chicago to have exerted a comparable effect upon Lucy Gonzales Parsons, a possibility only marginally appreciated by the identity-based projects of recent African American and Chicano/a scholarship. Where else but in that brutal cauldron of industrial exploitation and anarchist protest would the emancipated and fluently bilingual *mestiza* former slave be able to reinvent herself into a radical labour activist who would convince Martí in 1887 of the possibilities of a Latina feminism? Laura Lomas, in her indispensable *Translating Empire: José Martí, Migrant Latino Subjects, and American Modernities* (2008), helps us see that other Lucy, the one the poet witnessed through his emerging postcolonial gaze in New York when she spoke in defence of the Haymarket Martyrs. Her oratorical art, because it equalled his, forced him to question his macho prejudices about women made 'mannish' because they dared speak in the public sphere, and to recognise her as the unexpected female incarnation of the *mestizo* revolutionary he had begun to envision in *Nuestra America*. The following passage further illustrates the transformative spell she cast on Martí:

There were moments when not a sound could be heard in the assembly except her inspired voice, which flowed slowly from her mouth, like spheres of fire, and the gasping of those who had stopped breathing momentarily in order to hear the sob in her throat. When this Indian and Mexican *mestiza* stopped speaking, all the heads were inclined, as if in prayer upon the benches in church, and the room seemed to fill, like a field of wheat bending in the wind. . . . Everything in her appears an invitation to believe and to rise up. Her speech, in its total sincerity, is literary. Her doctrines wave like a flag; she does not ask for mercy for those condemned to death, for her own husband, but denounces the causes and the accomplices to the misery that leads men to desperation.[24]

Lucy's performance, however, embodied not only a glorious beauty but also the necessity and possibility of a revolutionary, anti-capitalist politics rooted in the hemisphere's indigenous soil, and thus the seed of an organic, autochthonous society for which Martí still searched. There was one important realisation Lucy's anarchism seemed to lack, one that Martí possessed but did not live long enough to share: that the existence of modern capitalism depended upon the discourse of 'race' refined in the conquest of the Americas, a cultural technology re-adapted to that brutal task of dehumanising, dividing, and subordinating late-nineteenth-century workers.

Asking and answering these questions, when contextualised in the cultural political economy of the urban scene, not only will provide a way of revitalising the institutional purpose of Chicano/a studies but will suggest the role an urban Latino/a-studies agenda can play in transforming progressive national politics: Davis's 'magical urbanism'. These interventions can articulate new forms of critique and struggle through which labouring Latino/a classes, including the fragile first-generation middle class, might go beyond the limits imposed upon them by the logic of market capitalism to propose a Latino/a power of constructive and lasting effects, one through which a class teaches itself to think about capital while acting against it.

Conclusion

To make a real difference we need to shift common sense, change the terms of debate and shape a new political terrain.

—Doreen Massey[1]

Ideas have power that can free untapped hope and energy in a people. The democratic idea of America has been and can again be a powerful weapon. It is a living heritage, which we can apply to the economic system in which we live, and with it we can build a new reality.

—Martin Carnoy and Derek Shearer[2]

WORKING-CLASS LATINOS

The Latino Question documents truths about working-class Latino lives, their trials and tribulations, and how they connect to the larger structures embedded within cultural political economy. Similar truths have been documented by scholars like Gilbert G. González, Ernesto Galarza, Vicki Ruiz, Mario Barrera, Rudy Acuña, and other academics whose scholarship has influenced our theoretical approaches considerably. Their scholarship highlights macro-level structural processes that result in the displacement of entire communities, forcing them onto the labour migration trails and then into different systems of production relations. They also document the very personal negative life experiences of working-class Mexicans and Mexican Americans, caused by a system of labour exploitation built on a cultural ideology informed by capital and class relations, racial supremacy, xenophobia, and sexism. We found that contemporary Latina/o workers, including youth, experience similar struggles because they face structures and cultural ideologies very much like their predecessors. Our scholarship also exposes what at first seems to be a paradox of abuse, exploitation, and the positive contributions of the diverse Latino working class. We conclude, however, that it is not a paradoxical contradiction but rather the outcome of a precise system of social relations in which capital defines the sum of material products, the sum of commodities, their exchange values, and their social magnitudes.³ In short, capital conditions the lives of Latinos in very specific ways that demand from them a position relative to their labour and material production, more so than any specific social identity.

Throughout *The Latino Question* we have discussed various Mexican and Mexican American working-class historical periods that have been shaped by US foreign policy toward Mexico and linked generationally. We trace this economic-engineering agenda to the turn of the 1900s and argue that it continues and is reflected in today's political realities. During Mexico's modernization era (at the turn of the 1900s), Mexican and Mexican American labour was instrumental in building the economic and industrial infrastructure that capitalists and elites continue to utilise. Mexican and Mexican American workers, through their labour, literally transformed blood, sweat, and tears into the economic and industrial infrastructure that is still present today in the United States. The model of conquest employed during this era used financial manipulation backed by military threat. Modernisation through direct foreign investment was sold as the only economic model that would save Mexico's frail democracy. The irony is that Mexico's democracy came at a cost, which was a complete loss of economic sovereignty.

We introduce the Bracero generation. This generation of Mexican workers is often overshadowed by the narrative of the Mexican American and white workers labelled the 'Greatest Generation' and characterised as the generation that recovered from the Great Depression and protected democracy by defeating fascism in World War II. We remind the reader that the unsung heroes of the Greatest Generation are its millions of Braceros and undocumented workers.

Post-Bracero labour migrants are also a part of our analysis. This generation of workers followed the historic labour trails to El Norte that most of their family and hometown friends had previously undertaken and continue to follow. They are not seen as part of the Baby Boomer generation but as an appendix to the American working class that continued to provide the sustenance for national consumption and survival. Although these labour migrants continued to work in the agri-cultural industry, they increasingly became a part of the workforce in other low-wage secondary labour markets such as the construction, service, and hospitality industries, while dispersing to nontraditional states like Michigan, Illinois, New York, Georgia, and Wisconsin. We offer narratives of workers from this generation, who share that, although they are of retirement age, cannot afford to do so because they belong to a racialised working but poor class subjected to endless work by capitalism. Many will continue to work until their bodies no longer allow them to do so.

The contemporary labour migrant community is constituted by displaced people who are the victims of continued imperial practices that have been in place for at least a century. These practices have met the economic interests of the empire by making both natural and human resources available for exploitation. A notable difference within this working-class generation is their increased activity in social-movement organisations seeking to democratise workplaces and pass comprehensive immigration reform.

We chose to rearticulate the mechanisms that link labour migration to generations of Latinos in the US working class to (1) explain how Latina/o populations in the United States share a common experience based on historical and material relations imbedded in their position within relations of production (that is, political and economic subjugation); (2) dispel the myths that often frame Latino working communities as new and or foreign; and (3) discuss how working-class Latinas and Latinos participate in building workplace democracy and economic and social justice movements.

We explicitly posit that the working class has been at the centre of both Mexican American and US history, culture and gender relations. This common class interest, albeit defined and shaped by different historical periods, is and remains the primary antagonism in contemporary capitalist society. We are very cognisant that our approach contrasts sharply with that of many of our friends and colleagues in the academy, especially in political science, where heterodox political economy is treated with scepticism and behavioural models and neoclassical economic analysis represent the underlying ideological orthodoxy.

THE ELECTION OF TRUMP

The Republican and Democratic parties, or, to be more exact, the Republican-Democratic party, represent the capitalist class in the class struggle. They are the political wings of the capitalist system and such differences as arise between them relate to spoils and not to principles.

—Eugene V. Debs[4]

As we write this conclusion, the Latino working classes are feeling the sting of inequality, austerity, and grave uncertainty in these perilous times under the administration of Donald Trump. What follows are our collective thoughts on the 2016 presidential election. Though there is so much to ponder, we focus on a few broad ideas and possible implications for working communities that have already been unleashed by the current administration.

Our Introduction offers a brief analysis of the elections that led to Trump's election as the forty-fifth president of the United States. We argued that the established neoliberal political parties failed in understanding the 'silent majority's' message to working communities that are constituted by immigrant and native, women and men, young and old, people of colour and whites, secular, religious, and atheist.

A month after the election, NBC News offered a working definition of the 'silent majority' that stated:

> Trump's power famously came from his 'silent majority'—working-class white voters who felt mocked and ignored. . . .
>
> Trump's appeals to the economic, cultural and racial fears of his supporters were widely perceived as offensive to women and minorities. Many GOP leaders warned it would be impossible to win a national election by polarizing the electorate and focusing so intensely on a shrinking segment of the population, even as the country is becoming more diverse, educated and culturally tolerant.
>
> Trump proved them wrong.[5]

Though this definition seems to capture elements of this population, it falls short of explicitly stating the ideological underpinnings that made them feel 'economic, cultural and racial fears'. We address this shortfall throughout *The Latino Question*, which supports the argument that the frame employed by the Trump campaign was nothing more than a clever political ploy organised by elite interests that used a racialised discourse rooted in the ideology of white supremacy and its fear of otherness. This discourse continues to guarantee production and maximise profits. In other words, the 'silent majority' is a recasting of a tried-and-true social hierarchy that pits workers of the same class against each other by perpetuating fear through perceived identity differences. This 'new normal' is not new; in fact, it is a standard divide-and-conquer practice used by capitalists and the elite within the structures of social injustice.

Our concerns are focused on the rhetoric of hate that was publicly placed into action on January 20, 2017. They include concerns for our community, future generations, labour, and the environment. These concerns are exacerbated by what we learned from our case studies about the destruction and social disintegration that previous attacks on undocumented people and their families have caused.

THE NEXT LEFT: MOVEMENT-BUILDING FOR THE FUTURE

The Latino Question offers case studies and theoretical framing that challenge the established orthodoxy of Latino identity politics, which argues that the 'self', in the absence of material conditions, is the most important unit of analysis for understanding and explaining complex social relations. Though we agree that identity politics is a good primer for discussion, it ultimately lacks specificity and thus cannot explain the material conditions of the contemporary Latino working class, as we state in our Introduction. It is much less subject to a capital critique, since it barely accommodates the very idea of Marx's critique of capital. We agree with Ellen Meiksins Wood's position of 'identifying the specificity of capitalism as a system of social relations and power',[6] which we argue manifests itself in class inequality.

As Raymond Williams has theorised, the condition of subaltern groups is fragmentation. If this is the case, then how can we discuss 'Latino social movements'? Do they exist? The answer is both yes and no. Latinos and Latinas have organised against various forms of injustice and domination, but not always in terms of being 'Latino and Latina'. Some of the political and economic circumstances they face are ascribed to class relations. We are reminded here of the seminal work of E.P. Thompson in his analysis of the English working class: 'We cannot understand class unless we see it as a social and cultural formation, arising from processes which can only be studied as they work themselves out over a considerable historical period'.[7] As we have noted in this volume, 'Latino and Latina' social movements are social and cultural formations that arise from conflicts within capitalist social relations embedded in production.

Many of the social movements (or social formations) that involve Latino and Latina agency are based on issues that directly affect poor or working-class people. Many of the best-known Latino and Latina social movements have been intricately linked to material conditions and class struggle. Given the diversity of Chicano and Chicana and Latino and Latina historiography, it is important not to render noneconomic relations invisible or fall into the analytical trap of so-called economic determinism. However, the utility of the categories of political economy Karl Marx devised remain central to this treatment and understanding of social movements and the wider political economy of the United States. In the previous chapter, we advance an approach informed by the Lancaster school of cultural political economy to overcome economic reductionism by finding a 'middle ground' that recognizes the dialogue between culture and capitalist social relations. Our explicit class and economic structure intervention is a response to many in Chicana/o and Latina/o studies (with or without the gender-neutral signifier 'x') of abandoning questions of inequality, class relations, and most importantly, the normative methods of a critique of political economy.[8] These were essential points of interrogation in the development of Mexican American studies in the late 1960s and early 1970s.

It is important to make clear that there were strands of ultra-leftism, dogmatism, and sectarianism on the Chicano and Chicana feminist left which often undermined a more democratic socialist left critique to ethnic and cultural interpretations of the 'Latino Question'. However, many of these differences were never part of the dominant discourse on the Chicano left. Although these ideological trends were marginal in the overall landscape of the Chicano and Chicana left discourse, these theoretical debates were very important steps in shaping and articulating a diverse movement with healthy tension. One healthy movement strand was the Chicana socialist challenge to both male-centred politics and everyday experience and its theoretical contribution to the overall body of Chicano and Chicana politics in and outside the academy. Here we are speaking of the seminal and important, but neglected, work of Rosalinda González and Linda Apodoca, who engaged in collaborative work as well as independent Marxist-inspired scholarship.[9] Many subsequent works by Chicana feminists that represented a different pathway; one particularly influential work that was indifferent to the historical materialist analysis represented in the work of the above two scholars is *The Decolonial Imaginary* (1999), by the Foucauldian-informed historian Emma Pérez, which represented the wider cultural turn in history and cultural studies. This work established a distance from so-called orthodox Marxist political economy, with its class analysis and strident critique of capital. The essential and thoughtful commentary on this linguistic turn that Pérez represents is Ellen Meiksins Wood's *The Retreat from Class*

(1986). Wood posited that true democracy, economic democracy, can't be merely the goal of building a civil society and strengthening its infrastructure but must involve a major transformation and restructuring of the entire capitalist political economy.

The subsequent 'cultural or linguistic turn' in the social sciences, a shift that was embraced by a significant number of scholars in Mexican American studies, found a receptive intellectual space in Chicana feminist theory, and more broadly in Chicano and Chicana cultural studies, with its focus on race, gender, class—intersectionality. This theoretical shift in direction reflected a new orthodoxy that not only rendered capital and labour invisible but also declined to subject the capitalist system to nuanced and profound critique. While this new focus on intersectionality and how individuals experience oppression and exploitation is important, there is an irony in focusing on individual selves at the expense of neglecting capitalism as a system of social relations and power in a time of unprecedented growth of wealth inequality and stagnant wages. This retreat to how individuals experience oppression is indicative of large social phenomena in the social sciences and humanities that move away from system analyses of power and economic structures and relations. If Latinos are to combat the growing inequality and economic subjugation in the unrepentant economy, then their response must be based not on individualist or self-focused analyses but rather on a collective and solidarity-based understanding of their position within the economic power structure as a class, a working class.

Latino and Latina social and economic movements encompass both 'traditional' and 'new' social movements. Formal labour organisations and workers' rights groups continue to be an integral component of activism in many Latino and Latina communities. In the early 2000s, when the labour movement was waning in other segments of society, US-born and immigrant Latinos and Latinas represented a significant portion of organized labour's membership, especially in large urban centres such as Los Angeles and New York. These social movements were organised around improving lives and working conditions for all workers and their families. These groups are highly structured and have quite formal rules for membership (dues, routine meetings, and so forth).

The Latino and Latina social movements that differ from this model are those whose membership is not as 'naturally' occurring, as it is in the case of factory workers who work in the same place. These new social movements are at times based on gender, neighbourhood issues, or social themes (ending violence, better schools, and so forth). These groups employ traditional tactics of social movements such as mass mobilisation, but they utilise them as means to change values or attitudes. Furthermore, some rely little on 'organisation'. Membership and group rules are flexible and fluid. Others still focus on developing new and innovative relations of production implementing democratic cultures of participation and ownership within the economy itself. Furthermore, Latino and Latina social movements as 'social formations' are not formulaic or identical. They are time- and context-based. If we are to take the concept of democratic participation seriously as these movements all do, they will be disparate, because when workers have voices and freedom to be creative in their participation and decision-making, they will have varied outcomes and models. Ultimately this is what we suggest will drive a new generation not just of resistance[10] but rather—and more importantly—a new generation of movement forward, of progress. This empowerment, led by grassroots projects that focus on not just promoting participation but expecting it and requiring it and knowing that workers are capable of it, is what will move working-class movements forward.

Some of the social movements organised by Latinos and Latinas are massive and awe-inspiring; others are mundane and quotidian. What they have in common is the desire to transform an unjust situation into a more just one. The collective spirit of benefitting the many instead of the few serves as a reliable vehicle for action. Paulo Freire reminds us in his analysis of anti-dialogic action that oppressed groups must liberate themselves from many oppressive ontological and epistemological structures. Freire identified two key tactics of oppression: 'divide and rule' and 'manipulation'. A divided or fragmented group will not work toward unity or build community; instead its members will believe they lack shared goals, values, or agendas. The condition of manipulation is perpetuated by dominant national 'myths' that protect the elite's interests in society. Hegemony, after all, is maintained through both consent and coercion, and the tactics Freire points out have functioned historically through race, ethnicity, and gender to cleave and divide working classes. Divide and rule as well as manipulation, as tools of oppression, destabilise progressive organising and unity, because many individuals believe the problems they face are individual problems, not social or structural ones. Furthermore, they are led to believe that they have no shared interests (political or economic). Overcoming this situation within a changing and shifting terrain of struggle—namely, an ever more neoliberal economy—has pushed Latinos and Latinas toward what Gramsci would call a strategic war of position. Latinos and Latinas have had to use creative strategies and methods for organising and building mass movements and new economies rooted in workplace democracy, solidarity, and class-consciousness. The goal is to be strategic in the struggle to attack as Adolph Reed posits, the specific material manifestations of capitalism, not just grand concepts like racism or oppression, but instead their manifestations at their roots, which of course are conditioned by, embedded in, and the result of the economic relations of production.

Cesar E. Chávez was once asked, 'How did you all build the UFW?' His response was, 'One person at a time'. So, we ask, what can working-class Latinos achieve in the near future? Our response is simple: organise and find common ground with other social movements that have been for far too long divided by ideological boundaries. Organize to end the onslaught of capital and to end economic exploitation, for better wages and working conditions, for affordable and community-owned housing, and for fairer, more democratic, and more just workplaces.

Only by engaging in a strategic war of position, organising, and advancing a collective agenda that encompasses diverse social movements can communities build the society and economy of the future, one where everyone can live and work with dignity. In this manner, working people can build a base that can be mobilised for power.

There are a great many in today's American working class who do not see the relevance of the labour movement, let alone other social movements. There are many reasons for this situation, but as long as social movement organisations focus almost exclusively on their own agendas, we cannot expect it to change. Mainstream social and economic justice movement organisations, including organised labour and immigrant-rights groups, have lacked clear messages and programmes that speak directly to the vast majority of workers. We see a tremendous wave of opposition and resistance rising in this country; we must either catch that wave or lose this historic opportunity.

The Latino Question addressed the long-running theoretical debates over the ongoing nature of working-class struggle and the relationship between culture and the capitalist political economy. We have done so by offering original thoughts and research, produced alongside working-class Latinos. Our work shows that the Latino question in the United States is about power, and about the organizing it will take for working people of diverse backgrounds to democratise production relations. In this respect, the next left will require a mass movement rooted in an emancipatory ideological and political vision that surfaces organically and is employed strategically by the people who make the machine run.

Notes

INTRODUCTION

1. Ernesto Galarza (1905–84) was the most significant and prolific Mexican American social critic and public intellectual of the twentieth century. He worked as a labour organiser, researcher, college instructor, and voice of the labour movement for over four decades.

2. We agree with Galarza's assessment and reject the 'race (ethnic) relations' approach as an analytical framework. However, we posit that racism (not race nor ethnicity) represents the object of contestation and study. There are no special or distinctive social relations in the form of 'race relations' and there is no need for a distinct theory of 'race (ethnic) relations.' For recent critiques of the analytical utility of 'race', see A. Darder and R.D. Torres, *After Race* (New York: New York University Press, 2005), and Chris Kyriakides and R. D. Torres, *Race Defaced* (Stanford, CA: Stanford University Press, 2012).

3. Our use of the term *cultural political economy* is partially inspired by the seminal work of Bob Jessop and his colleagues in the Cultural Political Economy Research Centre at Lancaster University in the United Kingdom. We propose here not just to add 'culture' to politics and economics but to treat the relationship in dialectical terms—as embedded in material realities of Latino work, culture, and labour.

4. *The Latino Question*, in part, addresses labels and how they have been used to categorise working-class people with distinct backgrounds into standardised groupings. These labels include *Hispanic, Latino*, and variations of the two (Martha E. Gimenez, '"Latino/Hispanic"—Who Needs a Name? The Case Against a Standardized Terminology', in *Latinos and Education: A Critical Reader*, edited by A. Darder, R.D. Torres, and Henry Gutierrez, 225–38, New York: Routledge, 1997). In addition, labels such as *Latino* homogenise diverse experiences and obfuscate class divisions and their ideological underpinnings in US political economy (Martha E. Gimenez, 'Latino Politics—Class Struggles: Reflections on the Future of Latino Politics', in *Latino Social Movements: Historical and Theoretical Perspectives*, edited by Rodolfo D. Torres and George Katsiaficas, 163–80, New York: Routledge, 1999).

   The *Latino* label evolved as a response to the *Hispanic* label. Its proponents argued that *Hispanic* was rooted in Spanish colonisation and thus pejorative. They self-ascribed as *Latino* because it more closely aligned with their collective identity and its connection to the 'Latin' world (Suzanne Oboler, *Ethnic Labels, Latino Lives: Identity and the Politics of (Re)presentation in the United States*, Minneapolis: University of Minnesota Press,

2005). *Latino* as an identifying term also took off because of the booming Latino media market, funded by wealthy Cubans who sought to mainstream the brown experience in the United States while also helping US corporations capitalise on the growing Latino demographic as a consumer market (Arlene M. Dávila, *Latinos, Inc. The Marketing and Making of a People,* Berkeley: University of California Press, 2001). Historically speaking, it was also an attempt to de-Mexicanise this population (which remains largely Mexican), moving away from the stereotypical narrative associated with Mexicans—of being lazy, unkempt, and dirty—to one more tied to the fun, festive, and romantic discourse that is now associated with *Latino*: an essentially more marketable, albeit vague and homogenised, discourse of a faux group. Since then, it has evolved and taken on several extensions as a result from contestation by identity-politics scholars, mainly from the feminist and queer scholarly fields. Over the past twenty or so years, the *Latino* label has evolved from *Latino* (gendered masculine) and *Latina* (gendered feminine) to *Latina/o, Latinao,* and *Latin@* (gender-inclusive but binary) and the latest iteration, *Latinx* (gender-neutral, nonbinary, genderqueer, gender-nonconforming, and fluid). (See Antonio Jay Pastrana Jr., *An Examination of Latinx LGBT Populations Across the United States: Intersections of Race and Sexuality,* New York: Palgrave Macmillan, 2017.)

We define and use the labels in our book as follows:

- *Latino,* as a standardised pan-ethnic label grouping used to homogenise, in their entirety, immigrants from Latin American and second and beyond US-born generations, which includes all who apply the diverse extensions (many of which appear throughout this book) and those who are ascribed and self-ascribe the label.
- *Mexican,* as a label grouping for immigrants from Mexico.
- *Mexican American,* as a label grouping for second and beyond US-born generations of Mexican immigrant ancestry.
- *Chicano,* as a label grouping for individuals who self-identify with the 1960s Mexican American social movement that sought to improve the material conditions of Mexican Americans by reforming the political, educational, and economic systems. It is a label created by movement participants to self-ascribe a political ideology based on cultural-national traits.

5. Mike Davis. *Magical Urbanism: Latinos Reinvent the US City* (New York: Verso, 2001).
6. We discuss this transformation in detail in chapter 1, where we introduce the empire theory of migration.
7. Sandra L. Colby and Jennifer M. Ortman, 'Projections of the Size and Composition of the US Population: 2014 to 2060', March 2015, https://www.census.gov/content/dam/Census/library/publications/2015/demo/p25-1143.pdf.
8. Javier Panzar, 'It's Official: Latinos Now Outnumber Whites in California', *Los Angeles Times,* 8 July 2015, http://www.latimes.com/local/california/la-me-census-latinos-20150708-story.html.

9. Ronald Robles Sundstrom, *The Browning of America and the Evasion of Social Justice* (Albany, NY: State University of New York Press, 2008).

10. Leo Chávez, *The Latino Threat: Constructing Immigrants, Citizens and the Nation* (Palo Alto, CA: Stanford University Press, 2013), 10.

11. Daniel D. Arreola, *Hispanic Spaces, Latino Places Community and Cultural Diversity in Contemporary America* (Austin: University of Texas Press, 2004); Rodolfo O. de la Garza, Louis DeSipio, and David L. Leal eds., *Beyond the Barrio: Latinos in the 2004 Election,* (Notre Dame, IN: University of Notre Dame Press, 2010). Traditional states are Arizona, California, Texas, Illinois, and New Mexico; new destination states include Arkansas, Georgia, Nebraska, Nevada, North Carolina, Iowa, Washington, and Wisconsin.

12. We implicitly argue that the dominant population suffers from a 'false consciousness' dilemma that is created by the nature and logic of capitalism. Social relations that are in their immediate environment conceal structures of oppression.

13. Kevin Crowe and Robert Gebelhoff, 'Hispanics Now Make Up Wisconsin's Largest Minority Group', *Milwaukee Journal Sentinel,* 25 June 2014, http://archive.jsonline.com/news/wisconsin/hispanics-now-make-up-wisconsins-largest-minority-group-b99299305z1-264687531.html.

14. Barney G. Glaser, *The Discovery of Grounded Theory: Strategies for Qualitative Research* (Chicago: Aldine, 1967).

15. Clifford Geertz, *The Interpretation of Cultures: Selected Essays* (New York: Basic Books, 1973).

16. Adrian Leftwich (ed.), *What Is Politics?* (Oxford: Blackwell, 1984).

17. Elaine M. Allensworth, and Refugio I. Rochin, *The Mexicanization of Rural California: A Socio-Demographic Analysis, 1980–1997* (East Lansing, MI: Julian Samora Research Institute, Michigan State University, 1999); Ann V. Millard and Jorge Chapa, eds., *Apple Pie and Enchiladas: Latino Newcomers in the Rural Midwest* (Austin: University of Texas Press, 2004).

18. John Nichols, *The "S" Word: A Short History of an American Tradition—Socialism* (New York: Verso, 2011).

19. Not disaggregated by generation or mixed generation (i.e., immigrant group, mixed immigrant and second-generation parents, or second-plus generation).

20. Frank D. Bean and Gillian Stevens, *America's Newcomers and the Dynamics of Diversity* (New York: Russell Sage Foundation, 20).

21. Jason DeBacker et al., *Rising Inequality: Transitory or Permanent? New Evidence from a Panel of US Tax Returns.* Revised final conference draft presented at the Spring 2013 Brookings Panel on Economic Activity, 21–22 March 2013.

22. Melinda S. Jackson, 'Priming the Sleeping Giant: The Dynamics of Latino Political Identity and Vote Choice', *Political Psychology,* vol. 32, no. 4 (2011): 691–716.

23. We employ the term *Latino* with caution and in various permutations throughout this book. Its counterpart, *Hispanic,* is equally problematic. Both terms are used widely in public discourse and in most cases interchange-

ably. The terms have limited analytical utility beyond generic use to refer to all 51 million persons of Latin American origin in the United States. The authors use designation of national origin to refer to the so-called 'Latino population' in disaggregate terms—Mexican American, Puerto Rican, etc., wherever possible.

24. V.M. Rodríguez Domínguez, 'The Racialization of Mexican Americans and Puerto Ricans', *Centro Journal*, vol. 17, no. 1 (2005): 71–105.

25. In short, powerlessness in working communities is the product of a social process to 'naturalise' ability and worth justified through science and cultural acceptance of perceived differences, perpetuated by the capitalist elite class and implemented through a political system that governs society with the threat of violence (in all its forms).

26. Suzanne Oboler, *Ethnic Labels, Latino Lives: Identity and the Politics of (Re) Presentation in the United States* (Minneapolis: University of Minnesota Press, 1995).

27. Marcela Valdez, 'We're Looking at a New Divide Within the Hispanic Community', *New York Times*, 15 November 2016, https://www.nytimes.com/interactive/2016/11/20/magazine/donald-trumps-america-florida-latino-vote.html?mcubz=0&_r=0.

28. Mary Bauer, *Close to Slavery: Guest Worker Programs in the United States* (Montgomery, AL: Southern Poverty Law Center, 2007).

29. Armando Ibarra and Rodolfo Torres, *Man of Fire: Selected Writings* (Urbana-Champaign: University of Illinois Press, 2013).

30. However, more significant than an electoral constituency, Latinos have emerged as strategic actors in the major processes of socioeconomic transformation. Their (and their children's) emergence as strategic actors outside traditional electoral activities was dramatically revealed on 1 May 2006, when one of the most significant eruptions of Latino working class militancy occurred. It will be discussed in more detail in later chapters.

31. Lisa Cohen, 'How America's 'Ground-zero' for Modern Slavery Was Cleaned Up by Workers' Group', CNN, 30 May 2017, http://www.cnn.com/2017/05/30/world/ciw-fair-food-program-freedom-project/index.html.

32. Don Lee, 'L.A. County Jobs Surge Since '93, but Not Wages', *Los Angeles Times*, 26 July 1999.

33. Samantha Masunaga, 'L.A. County Has Traded High-Paying Jobs for Low-Paying Ones', *Los Angeles Times*, 22 February 2017, http://www.latimes.com/business/la-fi-county-jobs-20170221-story.html.

34. Christine Cooper, Kimberly Ritter-Martinez, and Shannon Sedgwick, *Economic Update for Los Angeles County*, Los Angeles: Institute for Applied Economics, 2016, http://laedc.org/wp-content/uploads/2016/12/2016-LAC-Economic-Update_20161129.pdf.

35. Ibid., 10.

36. Pew Research Center, 'America's Shrinking Middle Class: A Close Look at Changes Within Metropolitan Areas', Washington, DC: Pew Research Center,

2016, http://www.pewsocialtrends.org/2016/05/11/americas-shrinking-middle-class-a-close-look-at-changes-within-metropolitan-areas.

37. Jim Puzzanghera, 'Economy Has Recovered 8.7 Million Jobs Lost in Great Recession', Los Angeles Times, 6 June 2014, http://www.latimes.com/business/la-fi-jobs-20140607-story.html.

38. Gilbert G. González and Raul Fernandez, A Century of Chicano History: Empire, Nations, and Migration. New York: Routledge, 2003.

39. William Robinson, 'The Global Economy and the Latino Population in the United States', Critical Sociology, vol. 19 (1993): 29–59.

40. We offer our original theoretical work on mass labour migration, workplace democracy, and power along with case studies of workers that include migrant farmworkers, workers' cooperatives, workers organising, and workers in a 'new destination' state. We conclude with a chapter that explores Latino working-class futures and offers new lines of interrogation informed by an alternative cultural-political-economy approach.

41. Antonio Gramsci, Selections from the Prison Notebooks (New York: International Publishers, 1971), 15.

CHAPTER 1

1. US Census Bureau, 'Statistical Portrait: American Community Survey', 2012, http://www.census.gov/newsroom/releases/archives/american_community_survey_acs/cb12-228.html.

2. US Census Bureau, Decennial Censuses, 1970, 1980, 1990, and 2000; National Population Projections. Washington, DC: US Census Bureau, 2011, https://www.census.gov/newsroom/cspan/hispanic/2012.06.22_cspan_hispanics.pdf. This essay implicitly questions the analytical utility of the term Latino as used by the academy and the state to categorise diverse populations into a homogenised group. We agree with Oboler's statement that using labels such as Latino and Hispanic 'obscures rather than clarifies the varied social and political experiences in US society of more than 23 million citizens, residents, refugees, and immigrants': see Suzanne Oboler, Ethnic Labels, Latino Lives.

3. For a full discussion of American empire-building with the use of foreign economic policy, refer to R. Acuña, Occupied America: A History of Chicanos (Boston: Longman, 2011); G.G. González and R.A. Fernandez, Century of Chicano History; Juan González, Harvest of Empire: A History of Latinos in America (New York: Penguin, 2011); J.M. Hart, Empire and Revolution: The Americans in Mexico since the Civil War (Berkeley: University of California Press, 2002); and E. Krauze, Mexico: Biography of Power: A History of Modern Mexico, 1810–1996 (New York: HarperCollins, 1997).

4. Ernesto Galarza, Merchants of Labor: The Mexican Bracero Story (Santa Barbara, CA: McNally & Loftin, 1964); Ernesto Galarza, Spiders in the House and Workers in the Field (Notre Dame, IN: University of Notre Dame Press, 1970); Ernesto Galarza, Farm Workers and Agri-Business in California, 1947–1960, (Notre Dame, IN: University of Notre Dame Press, 1977); M.

Gamio, *The Mexican Immigrant: His Life-Story: Autobiographic Documents* (Chicago: University of Chicago Press, 1931); M. Gamio, *Mexican Immigration to the United States* (New York: Arno Press, 1969); M. Gamio, *The Life Story of the Mexican Immigrant: Autobiographic Documents* (New York: Dover Publications, 1971); C. McWilliams, *Factories in the Field: The Story of Migratory Farm Labor in California* (Boston: Little, Brown, 1939); C. McWilliams, *Ill Fares the Land; Migrants and Migratory Labor in the United States* (Boston: Little, Brown, 1942); C. McWilliams, *North from Mexico: The Spanish-Speaking People of the United States* (New York: Greenwood Press, 1968; P.S. Taylor, *Mexican Labor in the United States*, vols. I–III, nos. 1–10 (Berkeley: University of California Press, 1928).

5. A. Portes, 'Immigration Theory for a New Century: Some Problems and Opportunities', *International Migration Review*, vol. 31, no. 4 (1997): 799–825.

6. For more detailed descriptions and positions, and critiques of these positions, refer to F.D. Bean and S. Stevens, *America's Newcomers and the Dynamics of Diversity* (New York: Russell Sage, 2003); G.G. González and Fernandez, *Century of Chicano History*; A.A. Lopez, *The Farmworkers' Journey* (Berkeley: University of California Press, 2007); Michael Piore, 'Economics and Sociology', *Revue Économique*, vol. 53 (2002): 291–300; A. Portes, *Illegal Mexican Immigrants to the United States* (New York: Center for Migration Studies, 1978); and A. Portes and G. Rumbaut, *Immigrant America: A Portrait* (Berkeley: University of California Press, 1990).

7. Michael Ben-Gad, 'The Economic Effects of Immigration: A Dynamic Analysis', *Journal of Economic Dynamics and Control*, vol. 28 (2004): 1825–45; Piore, 'Economics and Sociology'; K. Scheve and M. Slaughter, *Globalization and the Perceptions of American Workers* (Washington, DC: Institute for International Economics, 2001).

8. George J. Borjas, 'Economic Theory and International Migration', *International Migration Review*, vol. 23 (1989): 457–85; George J. Borjas, 'The Economics of Immigration', *Journal of Economic Literature*, vol. 32 (1994): 1667–1717; George J. Borjas, *Heaven's Door: Immigration Policy and the American Economy* (Princeton, NJ: Princeton University Press, 1999); George J. Borjas, *Labor Economics* (Boston: McGraw-Hill/Irwin, 2005); George J. Borjas, *Issues in the Economics of Immigration* (Chicago: University of Chicago Press, 2008).

9. Borjas, 'Economic Theory and International Migration'.

10. Piore, 'Economics and Sociology', 292–93.

11. J. Coleman, 'The Rational Reconstruction of Society', *American Sociological Review*, vol. 58 (1993): 898–912; R.D. Putnam, 'Tuning In, Tuning Out: The Strange Disappearance of Social Capital in America', *PS: Political Science and Politics*, vol. 28, no. 4 (1995): 664.

12. Douglas S. Massey, Jorge Durand, and Nolan J. Malone, *Beyond Smoke and Mirrors: Mexican Immigration in an Era of Economic Integration* (Austin and New York: University of Texas Press and Russell Sage, 2003).

13. Massey, Durand, and Malone, *Beyond Smoke and Mirrors*, 20.

14. H.P. Anderson, *Harvest of Loneliness: An Inquiry into a Social Problem* (Berkeley, CA: Citizens for Farm Labor, 1964); Ernesto Galarza, *Strangers in Our Fields: A Report Regarding Compliance with the Contractual, Legal, and Civil Rights of Mexican Agricultural Contract Labor in the United States* (Washington, DC: US Section, Joint United States–Mexico Trade Union Committee, 1956); C. McWilliams, *North from Mexico* (Philadelphia: J. B. Lippincott, 1948).

15. O. Álvarez et al., *Integración Regional: Los Límites del Debate Económico* (El Salvador: Fundación Heinrich Böll, 2005); Gilbert G. González et al., *Labor Versus Empire: Race, Gender, and Migration* (New York: Routledge, 2004); G.G. González and Fernandez, *Century of Chicano History*; Krauze, *Mexico*; Lopez, *Farmworkers' Journey*; S. Pedraza-Bailey, *Political and Economic Migrants in America: Cubans and Mexicans* (Austin: University of Texas Press, 1985).

16. G.G. González and Fernandez, *Century of Chicano History*, 25.

17. V.I. Lenin, *Imperialism, the Highest Stage of Capitalism* (New York: International Publishers 1939 [1917]), 63.

18. Raul A. Fernandez and J.F. Ocampo, 'The Latin American Revolution: A Theory Of imperialism, Not Dependence', *Latin American Perspectives,* vol. 1 (1974): 30–61. We use the definition used by the classic writers on imperialism. Imperialism here refers to a period in the development of capitalism characterised by monopolistic corporations. The US particularly exerts economic capitalist dominance over Mexico.

19. Lenin, *Imperialism*, 85.

20. Ibid., 63.

21. Ibid., 106.

22. Antonio Gramsci, *Selections from the Prison Notebooks of Antonio Gramsci* (New York: International Publishers, 1972 [1929–35]), 13.

23. Ibid., xiv.

24. Gilbert G. González, *Culture of Empire: American Writers, Mexico, and Mexican Immigrants, 1880–1930,* (Austin: University of Texas Press, 2004), 7.

25. Gilbert G. González and Raul A. Fernandez, 'Empire and the Origins of Twentieth-Century Migration from Mexico to the United States', *Pacific Historical Review*, vol. 71, no. 1 (2002): 32.

26. A. Carlos, 'Mexico Under Siege: Drug Cartels or US Imperialism?' *Latin American Perspectives,* vol. 42 (2014): 47.

27. Michel Foucault, *Power/Knowledge: Selected Interviews and Other Writings, 1972–1977* (New York: Pantheon, 1980), 120.

28. Michel Foucault, *Discipline and Punish: The Birth of the Prison* (New York: Vintage, 1979), 194.

29. Foucault, *Power/Knowledge,* 119.

30. Edward Said, *Culture and Imperialism* (New York: Knopf, 1994), 14.

31. Ibid., xiii.

32. K.C. Dunn, *Imagining the Congo: The International Relations of Identity* (New York: Palgrave Macmillan, 2003), 6.

33. Said, *Culture and Imperialism*, 16.

34. Ibid., 36.

35. R.L. Doty, *Imperial Encounters: The Politics of Representation in North-South Relations* (Minneapolis: University of Minnesota Press, 1996), 2.

36. C. Lynch, *Beyond Appeasement: Interpreting Interwar Peace Movements in World Politics* (Ithaca, NY: Cornell University Press, 1999).

37. G.G. González, *Labor Versus Empire*, 8.

38. Doty, *Imperial Encounters*; V.M. Rodríguez, 'The Racialization of Mexicans and Puerto Ricans: 1890s–1930s', *Centro Journal*, vol. 17, no. 1 (2005): 70–105.

39. G.G. González, *Labor Versus Empire*, 6.

40. Quoted in David M. Pletcher, *Rails, Mines, and Progress: Seven American Promoters in Mexico, 1867–1911* (Ithaca, NY: Cornell University Press, 1958, 38).

41. Neoliberalism is the US political and economic doctrine of free-market policies. At the core of the doctrine is the belief that the private sector should play an integral role in external and internal governmental affairs.

42. In no way do we contend that this is a complete history of the political economy of US–Mexico relations, but it offers an insight into a larger body of literature on this subject.

43. Francisco Bulnes, 'Charges Against the Diaz Administration', in *The Whole Truth About Mexico: President Wilson's Responsibility* (New York: M. Bulnes Book Co., 1916), notes: 'The Monroe Doctrine restricts the sovereignty of all foreign nations; and later it will be seen that it restricts the sovereignty of all American nations, except the United States.'

44. Acuña, *Occupied America*.

45. Bulnes, 'Charges Against the Diaz Administration'. Officials within the Porfirian regime were known as *cientifico* and believed in applying the rational scientific method to solve problems of industrialisation, finance, and education.

46. G.G. González and Fernandez, 'Empire and the Origins of Twentieth-Century Migration'.

47. Ibid., 35.

48. K. Calavita, *Inside the State: The Bracero Program, Immigration, and the I.N.S.* (New York: Routledge, 1992).

49. Banco de México, 'Ingresos por Remesas', 2012, http://www.banxico.org.mx/SieInternet/consultarDirectorioInternetAction.do?accion=consultar Cuadro&idCuadro=CE81&sector=1&locale=es.

50. Douglas S. Massey and A. Singer, 'New Estimates of Undocumented Mexican Migration and the Probability of Apprehension', *Demography*, vol. 32, no. 2 (1995): 211.

51. 'Legally, the Maquiladora program is a creature of the Mexican Executive branch of government pursuant to the powers granted to that branch under article 89(1) of the Political Constitution of the United Mexican States'. See G. Morales, B. Aguilera, and D. Armstrong, 'An Overview of the

Maquiladora Program', Washington, DC: US Department of Labor, 1994, http://www.dol.gov/ilab/media/reports/nao/maquilad.htm#N_3_.

52. R. Feenstra and G. Hanson, 'Foreign Direct Investment and Relative Wages: Evidence from Mexico's Maquiladoras', Cambridge, MA: National Bureau of Economic Research, 1995.

53. Justin A. Chacón and Mike Davis, *No One Is Illegal: Fighting Violence and State Repression on the US-Mexico Border* (Chicago: Haymarket Books, 2006), 115.

54. G.G. González and Fernandez, *Century of Chicano History,* 55.

55. J.L. Amendariz, 'Maquiladora Overview 2012', Juarez, Mexico: Asociación de Maquiladoras, 2012, http://www.indexjuarez.org/INICIO/ARCHIVOS/Maquila%20Presentation/MAQUILA%20OVERVIEW%202012.pdf.

56. A.J. Cravey, *Women and Work in Mexico's Maquiladoras* (Lanham, MD: Rowman & Littlefield, 1998).

57. J.M. Kagan, 'Workers' Rights in the Mexican Maquiladora Sector: Collective Bargaining, Women's Rights, and General Human Rights: Law, Norms, and Practice', *Journal of Transnational Law and Policy*, vol. 15 (2005): 180.

58. J. González, *Harvest of Empire*.

59. US Census Bureau, *Statistical Portrait: American Community Survey*, 2012, http://www.census.gov/newsroom/releases/archives/american_community_survey_acs/cb12-228.html.

60. Krauze, *Mexico*, 750.

61. Bean and Stevens, *America's Newcomers*.

62. J. González, *Harvest of Empire*; V. Quintana, 'Why the Mexican Rural Sector Can't Take It Anymore'.

63. Quintana, 'Why the Mexican Rural Sector Can't Take It Anymore'.

64. G.G. González and Fernandez, *Century of Chicano History,* 54.

65. Ibid., 55.

66. G.G. González, *Culture of Empire*, 14.

67. J. González, *Harvest of Empire*.

68. Jorge G. Castañeda, 'Can NAFTA Change Mexico?' *Foreign Affairs*, vol. 72, no. 4 (1993): 66–80.

69. Sarah Anderson and John Cavanaugh, 'Happily Ever NAFTA: The Proof Is in the Paycheck', *Foreign Policy* 132 (2009): 60–62.

70. J.E. Robledo, 'Open Letter to the United States Senators and Congressional Representatives', *Colombia Report*, 2006, http://colombiareport.ss.uci.edu.

71. Anderson and Cavanaugh, 'Happily Ever NAFTA', 60.

72. A. Arroyo-Picard, 'El Mexico del TLCAN en el Contexto Latinoamericano y Caribeño', *Deslinde*, vol. 45 (2005): 1–22.

73. *Trading Economics*, '2013a Mexico Inflation Rate; 2013b Mexico GDP Growth Rate', 2013, http://www.tradingeconomics.com/mexico/inflation-cpi.

74. Arroyo-Picard, 'El Mexico del TLCAN'.

75. G.G. González and R. Fernandez, *Century of Chicano History,* 57.

76. Ibid., 54.

77. Quintana, 'Why the Mexican Rural Sector Can't Take It Anymore', 251.

78. Raul A. Fernandez and D. Whitesell, 'Doublespeak, Deadly Silence, and Deception', *Colombia Report*, 2008, http://colombiareport.ss.uci.edu.
79. Quintana, 'Why the Mexican Rural Sector Can't Take It Anymore', 256.
80. Office of the US Trade Representative, 'Trade Facts: NAFTA: A Strong Record of Success', 2006, http://www.ustr.gov/trade-agreements/free-trade-agreements/north-american-free-trade-agreement-nafta.
81. Quintana, 'Why the Mexican Rural Sector Can't Take It Anymore', 256.
82. Peter S. Goodman, 'In Mexico, "People Do Really Want to Stay"', *Washington Post*, 7 January 2007, http://www.washingtonpost.com/wp-dyn/content/article/2007/01/06/AR2007010601265.html.
83. Quintana, 'Why the Mexican Rural Sector Can't Take It Anymore', 256.
84. G.G. González and Fernandez, *Century of Chicano History*, 57.
85. Quintana, 'Why the Mexican Rural Sector Can't Take It Anymore', 257.
86. Marla Dickerson, 'Placing Blame for Mexico's Ills', *Los Angeles Times*, 1 July 2006; World Bank, 'Mexico 2013: Development Indicators', 2013, http://data.worldbank.org/country/mexico.
87. Quintana, 'Why the Mexican Rural Sector Can't Take It Anymore', 258.
88. Goodman, 'In Mexico, "People Do Really Want to Stay"'.
89. J.S. Passel, 'The Size and Characteristics of the Unauthorized Migrant Population in the US: Estimates Based on the March 2005 Current Population Survey', Pew Hispanic Center, 2006, http://pewhispanic.org/files/reports/61.pdf.
90. M. Weisbrot, D. Rosnick, and D. Baker, 'Getting Mexico to Grow with NAFTA: The World Bank's Analysis', issue brief, Washington, DC: Center for Economic Policy Research, 2004, http://www.cepr.net/documents/publications/nafta_2004_10.pdf.
91. Ibarra and Torres, *Man of Fire*.
92. US Department of Homeland Security, 'Deferred Action for Childhood Arrivals', 2014, https://www.dhs.gov/deferred-action-childhood-arrivals.
93. US Department of Homeland Security, 'Memorandum on Rescission of Deferred Action for Childhood Arrivals (DACA)', 5 September 2017, https://www.dhs.gov/news/2017/09/05/memorandum-rescission-daca.
94. Eyder Peralta, 'National Council of La Raza Dubs Obama "Deporter-in-Chief"', National Public Radio, 4 March 2014, www.npr.org/blogs/thetwo-way/2014/03/04/285907255/national-council-of-la-raza-dubs-obama-deporter-in-chief.
95. As we write this, thousands of immigrant children and their parents seeking refuge in the US have been violently separated from one another by Border Patrol agents. The current administration has employed a 'zero tolerance' policy approach toward immigrants and has placed children as young as 18 months of age in detention centres alone, under conditions no child or human should experience, while they await deportation proceedings that would have them return to the war-torn and economically devastated countries which they escaped. Many of these centres are part of the for-profit prison-industrial complex.

CHAPTER 2

1. Heather Stewart, 'IMF Says US Crisis Is "Largest Financial Shock Since Great Depression"', *Guardian*, 9 April 2008, https://www.theguardian.com/business/2008/apr/09/useconomy.subprimecrisis.

2. H.M. Schwartz, *Subprime Nation: American Power, Global Capital, and the Housing Bubble* (Ithaca, NY: Cornell University Press, 2009).

3. Ibid., xiii.

4. Wells Fargo: $25 billion; Bank of America: $15 billion; JPMorgan Chase: $25 billion; Citigroup: $25 billion; Goldman Sachs: $10 billion. See CNN Money, "Bailed Out Banks," 2009, http://money.cnn.com/news/specials/storysupplement/bankbailout/.

5. Andrea Orr, 'Income Inequality: It Wasn't Always This Way', Economic Policy Institute, 9 February 2011, http://www.epi.org/publication/income_inequality_it_wasnt_always_this_way.

6. Lawrence Mishel and Alyssa Davis, 'Top CEOs Make 300 Times More than Typical Workers', Economic Policy Institute, 21 June 2015, http://www.epi.org/publication/top-ceos-make-300-times-more-than-workers-pay-growth-surpasses-market-gains-and-the-rest-of-the-0-1-percent/.

7. Ross Eisenbrey, 'The Economy in Numbers', Economic Policy Institute, 2008.

8. Mark Maremont, John Hechinger, and Maurice Tamman, 'Before the Bust, These CEOs Took Money Off the Table', *Wall Street Journal*, 20 November 2008, https://www.wsj.com/articles/SB122713829045342487.

9. Edmund L. Andrews and Peter Baker, 'A.I.G. Planning Huge Bonuses after $170 Billion Bailout', *New York Times*, 14 March 2009, http://www.nytimes.com/2009/03/15/business/15AIG.html; Associated Press, 'Bailed-Out AIG Considers Joining Lawsuit Against U.S.', CBS News, 8 January 2013, http://www.cbsnews.com/8301-34227_162-57562889/bailed-out-aig-considers-joining-lawsuit-against-u.s/.

10. Steve Hargreaves, 'Exxon Reports Record Profit Nearly $16 Billion', *CNN Money*, 26 July 2012, http://money.cnn.com/2012/07/26/news/companies/exxon-profit/index.htm.

11. Pat Garofalo, 'Corporate Profits Hit Record High While Worker Wages Hit Record Low', *ThinkProgress*, 3 December 2012, https://thinkprogress.org/corporate-profits-hit-record-high-while-worker-wages-hit-record-low-7f5f0626f239.

12. Elise Gould and Heidi Shierholz, 'A Lost Decade: Poverty and Income Trends Paint a Bleak Picture for Working Families', Economic Policy Institute, 2010.

13. Heidi Shierholz, 'Alt-Underemployment', Economic Policy Institute, 24 October 2013, http://www.epi.org/blog/alt-underemployment.

14. Heidi Shierholz, 'Job Openings and Hiring Have Not Improved Since Early 2012', Economic Policy Institute, 10 January 2013.

15. Alternatively called 'marginally attached workers'. See J. Bivens, 'Job Growth Is Picking Up. But What About All the Sidelined Workers?' *Wall Street Journal*, 7 November 2014.

16. *Underemployed* is defined as the inability to secure full-time work and refers to: 1) 'involuntary part-timers' who are working one or multiple jobs part time at part time pay, but want and are available for full time work; or 2) 'marginally attached' workers who want a job and are available for work but have become tired of searching and given up actively seeking work. Neither is included in unemployment figures.

17. Economic Policy Institute, 'Unemployment and Underemployment', *State of Working America*, January 2013, http://stateofworkingamerica.org/great-recession/unemployment-and-underemployment.

18. Shierholz, 'Alt-Underemployment'.

19. John Irons, 'Economic Scarring: The Long-Term Impacts of the Recession', Economic Policy Institute, 2009.

20. Amy Novotny, 'The Recession's Toll on Children', *Monitor on Psychology* 41, no. 8 (2010).

21. Ibid.; Richard Rothstein, *Class and Schools: Using Social, Economic, and Educational Reform to Close the Black-White Achievement Gap* (Washington, D.C.: Economic Policy Institute and Teachers College, 2004); Jeanne Brooks-Gunn and Greg Duncan, 'The Effects of Poverty on Children', *Children and Poverty* 7, no. 2 (Summer/Fall 1997).

22. Labor Council for Latin American Advancement, *Trabajadoras: Challenges and Conditions of Latina Workers in the United States*, Washington, DC: Labor Council for Latin American Advancement, 2012, http://files.cwa-union.org/teletech/Trabajadoras_Report.pdf.

23. Karl Marx, *Capital*, vol. 1 (New York: International Publishers, 1967 [1867]).

24. Ibid.; Marx thoroughly describes and documents this process in Part 8, 'So-Called Primitive Accumulation'.

25. Paul Thompson, *The Nature of Work* (London: Macmillan, 1983), 2.

26. Marx, *Capital*, 166.

27. Karl Marx, *The Economic & Philosophic Manuscripts of 1844* (New York: International Publishers, 1964 [1844]), 106.

28. Ibid., emphasis added.

29. Marx, *Capital*, 689.

30. Ibid., 343.

31. Raul A. Fernandez, 'On Marx and Human Nature, Class Domination, Social Inequality and Social Change', 2009, emphasis added. Speech delivered 5 February 2009 at the University of California at Irvine.

32. Gramsci, *Prison Notebooks*, 133.

33. G. Baldacchino, 'A War of Position: Ideas on a Strategy for Worker Cooperative Development', *Economic and Industrial Democracy*, vol. 11 (1990): 463–82.

34. G. Williams, 'Gramsci's Concept of Egemonia', *Journal of the History of Ideas*, vol. 21, no. 4 (1960): 586–98.

35. Baldacchino, 'War of Position'.

36. Antonio Gramsci, *The Antonio Gramsci Reader: Selected Writings 1916–1935*, edited by D. Forgacs (New York: New York University Press, 2000), 300.

37. Mike Donaldson, ' Gramsci and Class', paper presented at International Gramsci Society, Sardinia, Italy, 3–6 May 2007, http://ro.uow.edu.au/artspapers/138.
38. Gramsci, *Gramsci Reader,* 300.
39. Gramsci, *Prison Notebooks*, 12.
40. Karl Marx and Friedrich Engels, *The German Ideology* (New York: International Publishers, 1970 [1845]).
41. J. Pocock, *Virtue, Commerce and History* (New York: Cambridge University Press, 1985), 19.
42. Baldacchino, 'War of Position'.
43. Stanley Aronowitz, William DiFazio, Harriet Fraad, Michael Pelias, and Richard Wolff, 'Manifesto for a Left Turn: An Open Letter to U.S. Radicals', New York: Fifteenth Street Manifesto Group, 2008.
44. Gramsci, *Prison Notebooks*, 15.
45. Ibid., 10.
46. Ibid., 133.
47. Baldacchino, 'War of Position'.
48. Gramsci, *Gramsci Reader,* 224.
49. Ibid., 226.
50. Baldacchino, 'War of Position'.
51. Gramsci, *Gramsci Reader,* 223.
52. The first being the stage of primitive accumulation outlined in Part 8 of Marx, *Capital.*
53. Gramsci, *Gramsci Reader,* 198.
54. A.O. Hirschman, *The Passions and the Interests: Political Arguments for Capitalism before Its Triumph* (Princeton, NJ: Princeton University Press, 1977), 59.
55. Baldacchino, 'War of Position'.
56. Zaragosa Vargas, *Crucible of Struggle*, 2nd ed. (Oxford: Oxford University Press, 2016).
57. Ibid.
58. Ibid.
59. Ibid.
60. Ibid.
61. *Labour* spelt with a capital L denotes Big Labour, as in big, organised union labour under the umbrella of the AFL-CIO. This is different than *labour* as representing how laborers themselves organise at the point of production, on the shop floor.
62. Sharon Smith, *Subterranean Fire: A History of Working-Class Radicalism in the United States* (Chicago: Haymarket Books, 2006).
63. Ibid., 174.
64. B. Drake, 'Opinion of Unions Is Up, Membership Down', Pew Research Center, 2 September 2013, http://www.pewresearch.org/fact-tank/2013/09/02/opinion-of-unions-is-up-membership-down.
65. Smith, *Subterranean Fire.*

66. F. Fletcher and F. Gapasin, *Solidarity Divided: The Crisis in Organized Labor and a New Path Toward Social Justice* (Berkeley: University of California Press, 2008), ix.

67. Jillian Berman, 'Leaked PowerPoint Reveals Walmart's Anti-Union Strategy', *Huffington Post*, 15 January 2014, http://www.huffingtonpost.com/2014/01/15/walmart-anti-union_n_4603253.html; Fiona Ortiz, 'Police Arrest Los Angeles Walmart Workers During Protest', Reuters, 14 November 2014, http://www.reuters.com/article/us-usa-california-wage/police-arrest-los-angeles-walmart-workers-during-protests-idUSKCN0IY1O920141114.

68. John Nichols, 'The State Where Even Republicans Have a Problem with Busting Unions', *Nation*, 16 February 2015, https://www.thenation.com/article/state-where-even-republicans-have-problem-busting-unions.

69. Smith, *Subterranean Fire*.

70. Ibid.

71. Immanuel Ness and Dario Azzellini, *Ours to Master and to Own: Workers' Control from the Commune to the Present* (Chicago: Haymarket Books, 2011).

72. L.B. Cohen, Workers and Decision-Making on Production', *After Capitalism: From Managerialism to Workplace Democracy*, edited by S. Melman (New York: Alfred A. Knopf, 2001 [1954]), i, emphasis added.

73. M. Carnoy and D. Shearer, *Economic Democracy: The Challenge of the 1980s* (Armonk, NY: M.E. Sharpe, 1980), 29–30.

74. Ibid., 30, emphasis added.

75. Ibid.

76. T. Schuller, *Democracy at Work* (Oxford: Oxford University Press, 1985), 25.

77. W. Brown, *States of Injury: Power and Freedom in Late Modernity* (Princeton, NJ: Princeton University Press, 1995), 10, 15.

78. Abraham Lincoln, 'First Annual Message', speech delivered 3 December 1861, Washington, DC.

79. Mark Dworkin and Melissa Young (dir.), *Shift Change: Putting Democracy to Work*, Moving Images, 2012.

80. Gramsci, *Prison Notebooks*, 210.

81. S.S. Wolin, 'Fugitive Democracy', *Constellations*, vol. 1, no. 1 (1994): 11.

82. Ibid., 18, 22.

83. Ibid., 19, 23.

CHAPTER 3

1. An *implicit* theme of this work is that current capitalist socio-economic and cultural arrangements are implicated in the lives of workers, in and out of the fields—in the camps, fields, schools, and wider community. It is our intention in future writings and research to articulate these relations explicitly as they apply to the changing nature of work and labour in contemporary capitalism.

2. All heads of families are legal immigrants or US citizens.

3. 'HCD's Office of Migrant Services operates more than 2,000 rental units for migrant families in twenty-six centres that are open six months a year. HCD also makes loans and grants to local agencies to build or renovate housing for farmworkers, and had $46 million for construction and rehabilitation of farmworker housing in 2000–01, ten times the usual $2 to $4 million' (P.L. Martin, 'AgJOBS: New Solution or New Problem?', *University of California–Davis Law Review,* vol. 38 (2005): 973–91).

4. The terms *camp, community,* and *centre* are used interchangeably.

5. Office of Migrant Services (OMS), 'Office of Migrant Services Background and History', California Department of Housing and Community Development, 1998, http://www.hcd.ca.gov/grants-funding/active-no-funding/oms.shtml.

6. OMS, 'Background and History'.

7. Ernesto Galarza, *Spiders in the House and Workers in the Field* (Notre Dame, IN: University of Notre Dame Press, 1970); Ernesto Galarza, *Merchants of Labor: The Mexican Bracero Story* (Santa Barbara: McNally and Loftin, 1964); Gilbert G. González, *Labor and Community: Mexican Citrus Worker Villages in a Southern California County, 1900–1950* (Urbana-Champaign: University of Illinois Press, 1994); Martha Menchaca, *The Mexican Outsiders: A Community History of Marginalization and Discrimination in California* (Austin: University of Texas Press, 1995); Elaine Allensworth and Refugio I. Rochín, *The Mexicanization of Rural California: A Socio-Demographic Analysis, 1980–1997,* Ann Arbor, MI: Julian Samora Research Institute, 1998.

8. *Pooled labour* is used in two ways in this chapter. In this citation it refers to families working as collective units. Later in the chapter, we use this term to mean an industry employment system that purposely recruits more labourers than there are jobs available.

9. Daniel Rothenberg, *With These Hands: The Hidden World of Migrant Farmworkers Today* (New York: Harcourt Brace, 1998); Ann Aurelia López, *The Farmworkers' Journey* (Berkeley: University of California Press, 2007).

10. C. McWilliams, *Factories in the Field: The Story of Migratory Farm Labor in California* (Boston: Little, Brown, 1939).

11. Tomás Almaguer, *Racial Fault Lines: The Historical Origins of White Supremacy in California* (Berkeley: University of California, 1994); G.G. González, *Labor and Community.*

12. Alice C. Larson, 'Migrant and Seasonal Farmworker Enumeration Profiles Study California', Vashon Island, WA: Larson Assistance Services, 2000, http://lib.ncfh.org/pdfs/5453.pdf.

13. Aguirre International, 'Findings from the National Agricultural Workers Survey (NAWS) 2001–2002: A Demographic and Employment Profile of United States Farm Worker', report to the US Department of Labor, Research Report # 9, March 2005. This report was produced through a collaboration of the U.S. Department of Labor, Office of the Assistant Secretary for Policy, and Aguirre International, Burlingame, California.

14. Armando Ibarra, interview of Arturo Rodriguez, Office of Migrant Services director, California Department of Housing and Community Development, 2009.
15. Elliott Robert Barkan, *Immigration, Incorporation and Transnationalism* (New Brunswick, NJ: Transaction Publishers, 2007).
16. Manuel Pastor Jr. and Chris Benner, *This Could Be the Start of Something Big: How Social Movements for Regional Equity Are Reshaping Metropolitan America* (Ithaca, NY: Cornell University Press, 2009).
17. H.R. Rosenberg, S.M. Gabbard, E. Alderete, and R. Mines, 'California Findings for the National Agricultural Workers Survey', Washington, DC: US Department of Labor, Office of the Assistant Secretary for Policy, Office of Program Economics, Research Report No. 3, 1993.
18. Aguirre International, March 2005.
19. Rosenberg, Gabbard, Alderete, and Mines, 'California Findings'.
20. Ibid.
21. Galarza, *Merchants of Labor*; G.G. González and Fernandez, *Century of Chicano History*; G.G. González, *Culture of Empire*.
22. Gilbert G. González, *Guest Workers or Colonized Labor? Mexican Labor Migration to the United States* (Boulder, CO: Paradigm Publishers, 2006); G.G. González, *Culture of Empire*; G.G. González, *Labor and Community*.
23. Isabel Valle, *Fields of Toil: A Migrant Family's Journey* (Pullman: Washington State University Press, 1994).
24. W.H. Friedland and D. Nelkin, *Migrant Agricultural Workers in America's Northeast* (New York: Holt, Rinehart and Winston, 1971).
25. Ana Elizabeth Rosas, *Flexible Families: Bracero Families' Lives across Cultures, Communities, and Countries, 1942-1964*, Ph.D. dissertation, Los Angeles: University of Southern California, 2006.
26. Quintana, 'Why the Mexican Rural Sector Can't Take It Anymore'.
27. Ibarra, OMS director interview.
28. Massey, Durand, and Malone, *Beyond Smoke and Mirrors*.
29. Kelly Lytle Hernandez, *Migra! A History of the U.S. Border Patrol* (Berkeley: University of California Press, 2010).
30. Safe communities were made up of farmworker families (authorised and unauthorised) who made minimal contact with outsiders and public officials. This meant less risk for the families working illegally in the United States.
31. Quintana, 'Why the Mexican Rural Sector Can't Take It Anymore'.
32. Pranab K. Bardhan, *The Economic Theory of Agrarian Institutions* (Oxford: Clarendon Press, 2004).
33. US Department of Labor, 'Child Labor Requirements in Agricultural Occupations under the Fair Labor Standards Act', 2007, https://www.dol.gov/whd/regs/compliance/childlabor102.pdf.
34. Ibarra, OMS director interview.
35. Council of Fresno City Governments, 'Farmworker Housing Needs', 2001, http://www2.co.fresno.ca.us/4510/4360/General_Plan/GP_REVISED_Final_Housing_Element/pdf/AppenL.pdf.

36. Valle, *Fields of Toil*.
37. Paul Pierson, *Politics in Time: History, Institutions, and Social Analysis* (Princeton, NJ: Princeton University Press, 2004).
38. Friedland and Nelkin, *Migrant Agricultural Workers in America's Northeast*; R. L. Goldfarb, Goldfarb, *Migrant Farm Workers: A Caste of Despair*, Ames: Iowa State University Press, 1981.
39. Roberto P. Rodriguez-Morazzani, 'Beyond the Rainbow: Mapping the Discourse on Puerto Ricans and "Race"', in Darder and Torres, *Latino Studies Reader*.
40. Lamar B. Jones, 'Labor and Management in California Agriculture, 1864–1964', *Labor History*, vol. 11, no. 1 (1970): 23–40.
41. Don T. Nakanishi and James S. Lai, *Asian American Politics: Law, Participation, and Policy* (Lanham, MD: Rowman and Littlefield, 2003).
42. Estimates place the unauthorised population in the United States at approximately 11.5 to 12 million. Of this total, 78 percent are from Latin America, of which 56 percent are from Mexico. See Jeffrey S. Passel, 'The Size and Characteristics of the Unauthorized Migrant Population in the U.S. Estimates Based on the March 2005 Current Population Survey', Washington, DC: Pew Hispanic Center, 2006.
43. L. DeSipio, *Counting on the Latino Vote: Latinos as a New Electorate* (Charlottesville: University of Virginia Press, 1996).
44. At the Watsonville OMS labour camp, it is mandatory for a member of each family to attend monthly community meetings. If they do not attend, they are penalised ten dollars. The *comite directiva* calls the meeting to order, followed by a roll call of family representatives and continuing with concerns and announcements by tenants, outside organisations, and the housing authority.
45. No identifiable personal information about the interview subjects is provided.
46. Housing administrators shared a sense of justice toward mixed-status families. Their first responsibility was to provide housing to 'qualified' applicants. As long as the person applying on behalf of the family has legal documents, they will provide service to the family. This attitude was present at all levels of bureaucracy.

CHAPTER 4

1. Carlos, participant observation, 2013.
2. Richard Wolff, *Democracy at Work: A Cure for Capitalism* (Chicago: Haymarket Books, 2012); Democracy Collaborative, *Vision and Mission*, accessed September 21, 2013, http://community-wealth.org/about/vision-mission.html; Gar Alperovitz, Thad Williamson, and Ted Howard, 'The Cleveland Model', *Nation*, 1 March 2010; Gar Alperovitz, *America Beyond Capitalism: Reclaiming Our Wealth, Our Liberty, and Our Democracy* (Takoma Park, MD: Democracy Collaborative Press, 2011).

3. Ron Schmidt, 'Race and Politics', in *Handbook of Intepretive Political Science*, edited by Mark Bevir and R.A.W. Rhodes (New York: Routledge, 2015), 326.

4. Richard Delgado and Jean Stefancic, *Critical Race Theory: An Introduction* (New York: New York University Press, 2001).

5. Ibid., 6.

6. Michael Omi and Howard Winant, *Racial Formation in the United States* (New York: Routledge, 2014), 82.

7. Delgado and Stefancic, *Critical Race Theory*, 66.

8. Ibid., 67.

9. Ibid., 55.

10. Quoted in Denise Lynn, 'Black Nationalism and Triple Oppression: Claudia Jones and African American Women in American Communism', paper presented at Association for the Study of African American Life and History, Cincinnati, OH, 2009.

11. Lynn, 'Black Nationalism and Triple Oppression'.

12. Kimberlé Crenshaw, 'Mapping the Margins: Intersectionality, Identity Politics, and Violence Against Women of Color', *Stanford Law Review*, vol. 43, no. 6 (July 1991): 1242.

13. Patricia Hill Collins, *Black Feminist Thought: Knowledge, Consciousness and the Politics of Empowerment* (New York: Routledge, 2000).

14. Peggy McIntosh, 'White Privilege and Male Privilege: A Personal Accounting of Coming to See Correspondences through Work in Women's Studies', Wellesley, MA: Wellesley Center for Research on Women, 1988, http://www.collegeart.org/pdf/diversity/white-privilege-and-male-privilege.pdf.

15. Samantha, interview by Alfredo Carlos, 7 July 2013.

16. Osvaldo, interview by Alfredo Carlos, 24 July 2013.

17. 'Coalition' here refers to the Coalition of Immokalee Workers (CIW), which is a worker-based human rights organisation internationally recognised for its achievements in the fields of social responsibility, human trafficking, and gender-based violence at work. Built on a foundation of farmworker community organising starting in 1993 and reinforced with the creation of a national consumer network since 2000, CIW's work has steadily grown over more than twenty years: http://ciw-online.org.

18. Osvaldo, interview, 24 July 2013.

19. McIntosh, 'White Privilege and Male Privilege'.

20. Worker cooperative developers are people who work for nonprofit organisations whose mission it is to promote, expand, and develop worker cooperatives.

21. Gabriela, interview by Alfredo Carlos, 17 July 2013.

22. Mike Davis, *City of Quartz*, New York: Verso, 1990.

23. Gabriela, interview, 17 July 2013.

24. National Coalition Against Domestic Violence, 'About Us', 2015, https://ncadv.org/about-us.

25. Vera E. Mouradian, 'Abuse in Intimate Relationships: Defining the Multiple Dimensions and Terms', National Violence Against Women Prevention Research Center, 2000.

26. Antonia Darder and Rodolfo D. Torres, *After Race: Racism after Multiculturalism,* New York: New York University Press, 2004.

27. Osvaldo, 24 July 2013.

28. Darder and Torres, *After Race*, 99.

29. Ibid., 105.

30. Ellen M. Wood, *Democracy against Capitalism: Renewing Historical Materialism,* New York: Cambridge University Press, 1995, 242.

31. Wood, *Democracy against Capitalism*, 246.

32. Darder and Torres, *After Race*, 114.

33. Ibid., 101, emphasis added.

34. Wood, *Democracy against Capitalism*, 246.

35. Darder and Torres, *After Race*.

36. Mark Dworkin and Melissa Young (dir.), *Shift Change: Putting Democracy to Work*, Moving Images, 2012.

37. Ibid., *Shift Change*.

38. Tim Huet, interview by Alfredo Carlos, 19 July 2013.

39. Labor Council for Latin American Advancement, *Trabajadoras: Challenges and Conditions of Latina Workers in the United States*, Washington, DC: Labor Council for Latin American Advancement, 2012, http://files.cwa-union.org/teletech/Trabajadoras_Report.pdf.

40. Ibid.

41. W.A.G.E.S. 'The Role of Non-Profits in Developing Worker Cooperatives.' Powerpoint presentation, 23 January 2013.

42. Samantha, interview, 7 July 2013.

43. Huet, interview, 19 July 2013.

44. Maria Teresa V. Taningco, Ann Bessie Mathew, and Harry P. Pachon, *STEM Professions: Opportunities and Challenges for Latinos in Science, Technology, Engineering, and Mathematics* (Los Angeles: University of Southern California, Tomas Rivera Policy Institute, 2008).

45. Valerie Wilson, 'The Impact of Full Employment on African American Employment and Wages', Economic Policy Institute, 30 March 2015, http://www.epi.org/publication/the-impact-of-full-employment-on-african-american-employment-and-wages. Note that the unemployment figures do not account for underemployed and marginally attached workers.

46. Osvaldo, interview, 24 July 2013.

47. Ibid.

48. Jessica Gordon Nembhard, *Collective Courage: A History of African American Cooperative Economic Thought and Practice* (State College: Penn State University Press, 2014), 18.

49. Gramsci, *Gramsci Reader*, 190.

50. Quoted in Howard Zinn, *A People's History of the United States* (New York: HarperCollins, 2005), 249.

51. Sheldon S. Wolin, 'Fugitive Democracy', *Constellations* 1, no. 1 (1994): 11.

52. Ibid.

53. C. Douglas Lummis, *Radical Democracy* (Ithaca, NY: Cornell University Press, 1996).

54. Ernesto Laclau and Chantal Mouffe. *Hegemony and Socialist Strategy: Towards a Radical Democratic Politics* (London: Verso, 2001).

55. Marx, *Capital*, vol. 1.

56. Maurice Dobb, *Studies in the Development of Capitalism* (London: Routledge & Kegan Paul, 1946), 11.

57. Ibid., 59.

58. Seymour Melman, *After Capitalism: From Managerialism to Workplace Democracy* (New York: Alfred A. Knopf, 2001), 60.

59. Phil LeBeau, 'Hyperloop Moves Closer to Becoming Reality', CNBC, 26 February 2015, https://www.cnbc.com/2015/02/26/oves-closer-to-becoming-reality.html; Philip Oltermann, 'World's First Solar Cycle Lane Opening in the Netherlands', *Guardian*, 5 November 2014; Jessica Prois, 'Billboard In Lima, Peru Creates Drinking Water Out Of Thin Air', *Huffington Post*, 18 March 2013.

60. David Harvey, *A Brief History of Neoliberalism* (New York: Oxford University Press, 2005), 2.

61. Ibid.

62. Betsy Stark, 'Gas Industry Accused of Price Gouging', ABC News, 21 February 2015.

63. Bureau of Labor Statistics. *Employment by Major Industry Sector* (Washington, DC: US Department of Labor, 2013); Catherine Rampell, 'Majority of New Jobs Pay Low Wages, Study Finds', *New York Times*, 30 August 2012.

64. Christian E. Weller and Jaryn Fields, 'The Black and White Labor Gap in America: Why African Americans Struggle to Find Jobs and Remain Employed Compared to Whites', issue brief (Washington, DC: Center for American Progress, 2011).

65. Leland Ware, 'Racial Segregation and the Baltimore Riots', *Huffington Post*, 11 May 2015.

66. Robert Pollin, *Contours of Descent: U.S. Economic Fractures and the Landscape of Global Austerity* (New York: Verso, 2005), 3.

67. Allan Engler, *Economic Democracy: The Working Class Alternative to Capitalism* (Winnipeg: Fernwood Publishing, 2010), 37.

68. Brendan Martin, *In the Public Interest? Privatization and Public Sector Reform* (London: Zed Books, 1993), 200.

69. Robert Reich, 'Why the Trans-Pacific Partnership Agreement Is a Pending Disaster', *Huffington Post*, 5 January 2015.

70. Wendy Brown, *States of Injury: Power and Freedom in Late Modernity* (Princeton, NJ: Princeton University Press, 1995), 10, 15.

71. E.P. Thompson, *The Poverty of Theory and Other Essays* (New York: Monthly Review Press, 2008), 141.

72. Ibid., 164.

73. Joseph Blasi, Richard B. Freemen, and Douglas L. Kruse, *The Citizen's Share: Reducing Inequality in the 21st Century* (New Haven, CT: Yale University Press, 2014); Edward J. Carberry, *Employee Ownership and Shared Capitalism: New Directions in Research* (Ithaca, NY: ILR Press, 2011).

74. Sustainable Economies Legal Center, 'CA Worker Cooperative Act', 2015, http://www.theselc.org/ca-worker-cooperative-act.

75. Jacques Rancière, *Disagreement: Politics and Philosophy* (Minneapolis: University of Minnesota Press, 2004).

76. Michel Foucault, *The Foucault Reader,* edited by Paul Rabinow (New York: Pantheon Books, 1984), 196.

77. Subcomandante Marcos, 'The Fourth World War Has Begun', in *The Zapatista Reader* (New York: Thunder's Mouth Press, 2002).

78. Ibid., 279.

79. Gustavo Esteva and Madhu Suri Prakash, *Grassroots Post-Modernism* (London: Zed Books, 1998); Marcos, 'Fourth World War'.

80. E.P. Thompson, *The Poverty of Theory and Other Essays* (New York: Monthly Review Press, 2008).

81. Melman, *After Capitalism.*

82. Erich Fromm, *The Heart of Man* (New York: HarperCollins, 1966), 52–53.

83. Paulo Freire, *Pedagogy of the Oppressed* (New York: Continuum International Publishing, 1970), 48.

84. Carnoy and Shearer, *Economic Democracy*, 403.

CHAPTER 5

1. P. Reason and H. Bradbury, 'Inquiry and Participation in Search of a World Worthy of Human Aspiration', in *Handbook of Action Research: Participative Inquiry and Practice* (London: Sage, 2001), 10–11.

2. Ernesto Galarza, *The Burning Light: Action and Organizing in the Mexican Community in California* (Berkeley: Regional Oral History Office, Bancroft Library, University of California, 1982), 41.

3. Laura Dresser, Joel Rogers, and Edo Navot, *The State of Working Wisconsin*, Madison: Center on Wisconsin Strategy, 2010, https://www.cows.org/_data/documents/1112.pdf.

4. Jill Harrison, Sarah Lloyd, and Trish O'Kanel, *Overview of Immigrant Workers on Wisconsin Dairy Farms* (Madison: Program on Agricultural Technology Studies, University of Wisconsin, 2009), http://www.pats.wisc.edu/pubs/98.

5. Orin M. Levin-Waldman, *The Political Economy of the Living Wage* (Armonk, NY: M.E. Sharp, 2005).

6. A wage of $11.19 an hour at forty hours per week for four weeks totals $1,790.40 in monthly wages. See Center on Wisconsin Strategy, *Raise the Floor Milwaukee: Better Wages and Labor Standards for Low-Wage Workers*, Madison: University of Wisconsin, 2013.

7. John Pawasarat, 'The Employer Perspective: Jobs Held by the Milwaukee County AFDC Single Parent Population (January 1996–March 1997)', Milwaukee: University of Madison School of Continuing Education, Employment and Training Institute, 1997, http://www4.uwm.edu/eti/employer.htm.

8. Center on Wisconsin Strategy, *Raise the Floor Milwaukee*.

9. A life expectancy of 78.64 divided by twelve projected moves in a lifetime equals a move every 6.55 years. Based on US Census Bureau, 'Current Population Survey Data on Geographical Mobility/Migration', 2013, https://www.census.gov/topics/population/migration/guidance/calculating-migration-expectancy.html.

10. At a $7.25 hourly rate (minimum wage), it takes working seventy-nine hours per week to afford a two-bedroom rental in Wisconsin. National Low-Income Housing Coalition, *Out of Reach*, 2012, http://nlihc.org/oor/2012.

11. US Census Bureau, 'State and County QuickFacts'. Data derived from Population Estimates, American Community Survey, Census of Population and Housing, County Business Patterns, Economic Census, Survey of Business Owners, Building Permits, Census of Governments, 27 June 2013.

12. We recognise that Latinos are not the only ethnic and racial immigrant group, but because of time and resource restrictions we focused on this group to gauge attitudes toward immigrant labour and immigration reform.

13. US Census Bureau, '2007–2011 American Community Survey 5-Year Estimates', https://www.census.gov/newsroom/releases/archives/news_conferences/20121203_acs5yr.html.

14. We use *unauthorised* and *undocumented* interchangeably.

15. 'E-Verify is an Internet-based system that compares information from an employee's Form I-9, Employment Eligibility Verification, to data from US Department of Homeland Security and Social Security Administration records to confirm employment eligibility' (US Citizenship and Immigration Services, 'What Is E-Verify?' 2017, https://www.uscis.gov/e-verify/what-e-verify).

16. *The Nation*, 'Most Valuable Grassroots Group: Voces de la Frontera', January 2013, https://www.thenation.com/article/progressive-honor-roll-2012/#.

17. Unauthorised immigrants, who make up a large portion of the working-but-poor workforce, do not qualify for public benefits and live in extreme poverty. For them, health and wellness are based on the hope of not getting sick. In instances of severe illness or when medical attention is needed, they use emergency rooms and public clinics.

18. State of Wisconsin, *Access: Your Connection to Programs for Health, Nutrition and Childcare*, n.d., https://access.wisconsin.gov.

19. Joel A. Devine and James D. Wright, *The Greatest of Evils: Urban Poverty and the American Underclass* (New York: A. de Gruyter, 1993).

20. The American Immigration Council estimated in 2012 that 1.4 unauthorised immigrants in the country were eligible for DACA: American Immigration Council, 'Who and Where the DREAMers Are, Revised Estimates', 16 October 2012, http://www.immigrationpolicy.org/just-facts/who-and-where-dreamers-are-revised-estimates.

21. Al Jazeera, 'What Is DACA and Who Are the US "Dreamers"?' 10 October 2017,

CHAPTER 6

1. The 'big Other,' as opposed to the 'small other,' is commonly used in psychoanalysis to refer to a fundamental modality of otherness wherein language, or the symbolic order, always functions as a wall that prevents a self-same understanding of others. As Jacques Lacan claims, 'Language is as much there to found us in the Other as to drastically prevent us from understanding him [or her]'. Thus, in this chapter we recurrently utilise the 'big Other' to emphasise the symbolic density of multicultural discourses that paradoxically prevent an understanding of ethnic and minority others even though the intention of such discourses is to know, to understand, an 'exoticised' Other. See Ellie Ragland-Sullivan and Mark Bracher, eds., *Lacan And the Subject of Language* (New York: Routledge, 1991), 244.
2. This concept is utilised by Sharon Zukin in *Landscapes of Power* (Berkeley: University of California Press, 1991) to refer to a broad spectrum of knowledge workers and cultural service workers typically identified with the cultivation of urban taste. Knowledge service workers might include artists and performers, whereas chefs and museum curators might constitute cultural service workers.
3. Pierre Bourdieu, *Outline of a Theory of Practice* (Cambridge: Cambridge University Press, 1977), 243.
4. Mike Davis, *Magical Urbanism: Latinos Reinvent the U.S. City* (London: Verso, 2000), 9.
5. Homi K. Bhabha, *The Location of Culture* (London: Verso, 109).
6. Fredric Jameson, *The Political Unconscious: Narrative as a Socially Symbolic Act* (Ithaca, NY: Cornell University Press, 1981), 82.
7. Sharon Zukin, *The Culture of Cities* (Cambridge: Blackwell, 1995), 180.
8. Rey Chow, *Ethics after Idealism: Theory, Culture, Ethnicity, Reading* (Bloomington: Indiana University Press, 1998), xxi.
9. Herbert Marcuse, *One-Dimensional Man: Studies in the Ideology of Advanced Industrial Society* (Boston: Beacon Press, 1991), 31.
10. Zukin, *Culture of Cities,* 7.
11. Ibid., 159.
12. Ibid., 173.
13. Maria L. LaGanga, 'At a Career Crossroads? Try the Kitchen', *Los Angeles Times*, 2 March 1997.
14. Josh Meyer, 'County Crackdown on Dirty Restaurants OK'd', *Los Angeles Times*, 26 November 1997.
15. Michael Dear, ed., *Atlas of Southern California*, prepared for the USC Roundtable, 12 November 1996, Los Angeles: University of Southern California, Southern California Studies Center, 13; John G. Watson, 'Busboys' Night Out: Top Latino Restaurant Workers to Be Feted at Ceremony Jan. 17', *Los Angeles Times*, 5 November 1992, http://articles.latimes.com/1992-11-05/news/ti-1207_1_restaurant-management.

16. Charles Fletcher Lummis, *Letters from the Southwest, September 20, 1884, to March 14, 1885*, edited by James W. Byrkit (Tucson: University of Arizona Press, 1989), xxxvi.

17. Charles Fletcher Lummis, *1859–1928: A Tramp Across the Continent* (New York: C. Scribner's Sons, 1892).

18. Chon Noriega, 'Birth of the Southwest: Social Protest, Tourism, and D. W. Griffith's *Ramona*', in *The Birth of Whiteness: Race and the Emergence of U.S. Cinema*, edited by Daniel Bernardi (New Brunswick, NJ: Rutgers University Press, 1996), 206.

19. Oboler, *Ethnic Labels, Latino Lives*, xii; emphasis in original.

20. Peter McLaren writes that liberal multiculturalists believe that there is a certain 'intellectual "sameness" among the races, on their cognitive equivalence or the rationality immanent in all races that permits them to compete equally in a capitalist society'. He admits that this view 'often collapses into an ethnocentric and oppressively universalistic humanism in which the legitimating norms which govern the substance of citizenship are identified most strongly with Anglo-American cultural-political communities'. See Peter McLaren, 'White Terror and Oppositional Agency: Towards a Critical Multiculturalism', in *Multiculturalism: A Critical Reader*, edited by David Theo Goldberg (Cambridge: Blackwell, 1995), 51.

21. David Rieff, *Los Angeles: Capital of the Third World* (New York: Simon and Schuster, 1991), 230.

22. Lisa Lowe, *Immigrant Acts: On Asian American Cultural Politics* (Durham, NC: Duke University Press, 1996), 89.

23. Leela Gandhi, *Postcolonial Theory: A Critical Introduction* (New York: Columbia University Press, 1998), 5.

24. Bhabha, *Location of Culture*, 110.

25. Jameson, *Political Unconscious*, 53.

CHAPTER 7

1. Our use of the term *cultural political economy* is especially indebted to the work of Bob Jessop and his colleagues in the Cultural Political Economy Research Centre (CPERC) at Lancaster University in the United Kingdom. CPERC promotes cultural political economy as a principal theoretical orientation, a method of analysis, and valuable adjunct to other theories that examines the relations among semiosis, imaginaries, political economy broadly conceived, and issues of governance, government, and governmentality.

2. Ramon Ribera-Fumaz, 'From Urban Political Economy to Cultural Political Economy: Rethinking Culture and the Economy In and Beyond the Urban', *Progress in Human Geography*, vol. 33, no. 4 (2009): 447–65; Bob Jessop and Stijn Oosterlynck, 'Cultural Political Economy: On Making the Cultural Turn without Falling into Soft Economic Sociology', *Geoforum*, vol. 39 (2008): 1155–69.

3. Victor M. Valle and Rodolfo D. Torres, *Latino Metropolis* (Minneapolis: University of Minnesota Press, 2000).
4. Marx, *Capital*, vol. 1, 163.
5. Slavoj Žižek, 'Why Populism Is (Sometimes) Good Enough in Practice, but Not in Theory', in *In Defense of Lost Causes* (London: Verso, 2009), 301–302.
6. Henri Lefebvre, *Everyday Life in the Modern World* (New Brunswick, NJ: Transaction Publishers, 2007), 32.
7. Michel Foucault, 'Governmentality', in *The Foucault Effect: Studies in Governmentality,* edited by Graham Burcell, Colin Gordon, and Peter Miller (Chicago: University of Chicago Press, 1991 [1978]), 102–103.
8. Gerald E. Frug, *Citymaking: Building Communities without Building Walls* (Princeton, NJ: Princeton University Press, 1999), 31.
9. Foucault, 'Governmentality', 102.
10. Victor M. Valle, *City of Industry: Genealogies of Power in Southern California* (New Brunswick, NJ: Rutgers University Press, 2009).
11. Mao Tse-tung, 'To Be Attacked by the Enemy Is Not a Bad Thing but a Good Thing', speech, 26 May 1939, www.marxists.org/reference/archive/mao/selected-works/volume-6/mswv6_32.htm.
12. Ian Hart, ed., 'Paying with Our Health: The Real Cost of Freight Transportation in California', Oakland, CA: Pacific Institute, 2006, 28.
13. Dave Jamieson, 'The New Blue Collar: Temporary Work, Lasting Poverty and the American Warehouse', *Huffington Post,* 12 December 2011, http://www.huffingtonpost.com/2011/12/20/new-blue-collar-temp-warehouses_n_1158490.html.
14. 'In a 2005 effort to reinvigorate new-member organizing efforts, seven unions split from the American Federation of Labor and Congress of Industrial Organizations (AFL-CIO) to form a new union federation, Change to Win': R. Aleks, 'Estimating the Effect of "Change to Win" on Union Organizing', *Industrial and Labor Relations Review*, vol. 68, no. 3 (2015): 584–605.
15. Spencer Woodman, 'Labor Takes Aim at Walmart—Again', *Nation,* 4 January 2012, http://www.thenation.com/article/165437/labor-takes-aim-walmart-again?page=0,0.
16. Marc Lifsher, 'State Fines Warehouse Companies for Safety Violations', *Los Angeles Times,* 18 January 2012, http://www.latimes.com/business/money/la-state-fines-warehouse-companies-for-safety-violations-20120118,0,5322746.story; Kari Lydersen, 'California Workers Take Walmart's Warehouses to Court', *In These Times*, 21 October 2011, http://inthesetimes.com/working/entry/12159/california_walmart_warehouses_feel_the_heat.
17. Jesse Diaz and Javier Rodriguez, 'Undocumented in America', *New Left Review*, vol. 47 (2007): 99–101.
18. Michael Soldatenko, *Chicano Studies: The Genesis of a Discipline* (Tucson: University of Arizona Press, 2009).

19. Ignacio López-Calvo, *Latino Los Angeles in Film and Fiction: The Cultural Production of Social Anxiety* (Tucson: University of Arizona Press, 2011), xii, 3.

20. Ernesto Galarza, 'The Burning Light: Action and Organizing in the Mexican Community in California', interviews by Gabrielle Morris and Timothy Beard, 1977, 1978, and 1981, transcript, Regional Oral History Office, Bancroft Library, University of California, 1982, www.archive.org/stream/burninglightactioogalarich/burninglightactioogalarich_djvu.txt.

21. 'Bert Corona, a sometimes fiery labor organizer, community activist and educator who championed the rights of undocumented workers, Mexicans and other Latinos in the United States for more than seven decades, has died from complications of kidney failure': George Ramos, 'Bert Corona; Labor Activist Backed Rights for Undocumented Workers', *Los Angeles Times*, 17 January 2001, http://articles.latimes.com/2001/jan/17/local/me-13397.

22. Laura Pulido, *Black, Brown, Yellow, and Left: Radical Activism in Los Angeles* (Berkeley: University of California Press, 2006), 221.

23. Sergio Munoz, 'Guided by a Vision: How Bert Corona Met the Challenges of Latino Leadership: *Memories of Chicano History: The Life and Narrative of Bert Corona*, by Mario T. Garcia', *Los Angeles Times*, 9 October 1994, 4.

24. Quoted in Laura Lomas, *Translating Empire: José Martí, Migrant Latino Subjects, and American Modernities* (Durham, NC: Duke University Press, 2008), 252–53.

CONCLUSION

1. Doreen Massey, 'Exhilarating Times', *Soundings*, no. 61 (Winter 2015).

2. Martin Carnoy and Derek Shearer, *Economic Democracy: The Challenge of the 1980s* (Armonk, NY: M.E. Sharpe, 1980), 403.

3. Karl Marx, *Wage-Labor and Capital* (Chicago: C.H. Kerr, 1935).

4. Eugene V. Debs, *Debs: His Life, Writings and Speeches, with a Department of Appreciations* (Girard, KS: Appeal to Reason, 1908), 361.

5. Leigh Ann Caldwell and Benjy Sarlin, 'How Trump Won: His Populist Message Proved Everyone Wrong', NBC News, 14 December 2016, https://www.nbcnews.com/specials/donald-trump-republican-party/presidency.

6. Ellen Meiksins Wood, *Democracy Against Capitalism: Renewing Historical Materialism* (Cambridge: Cambridge University Press, 1995).

7. Thompson, *Making of the English Working Class*, 11.

8. Another important dimension of class analysis that is beyond the scope of our current critique is the moral aspect of class analysis. Here we are inspired by the work of another Lancaster University 'postdisciplinary' colleague of Bob Jessop, Andrew Sayer, in his magnificent book *The Moral Significance of Class* (Cambridge: Cambridge University Press, 2005). Sayer posits that class is not only about materiality but also defines what a person will become.

9. Rosalinda González, 'Distictions in Western Women's Experience: Ethnicity, Class, and Social Change', in *The Women's West*, edited by Susan Aritafe (Norman: University of Oklahoma Press, 1987); Maria Linda Apodoca, 'The

Chicana Woman: A Historical Materialist Perspective', in *Latino/a Thought: Culture, Politics, and Society*, edited by Francisco Vazquez and Rodolfo D. Torres (Lanham, MD: Rowman & Littlefield, 2003).

10. Resistance, in our estimation, is limiting, reactionary, and ultimately conservative. One who resists is one who is always stuck in a defensive position, never advocating or moving toward a vision of the world they want to build. If Latino workers are to overcome the onslaught of capital, they must not only resist but also begin to build the society they wish to see.

Index

AB 816. *See* California Worker Cooperative Act (AB 816)

Acuña, Rudy, 175

African Americans: Black feminism, 86–7; Black Lives Matter protests, 118; civil rights movement, 121; as cooperative worker-owners, 104, 112–13; as farmworkers, 63, 78; in Milwaukee, 134–6; and slavery, 45, 112; solidarity with undocumented immigrants, xiv, 138; unemployment and underemployment, 40, 105, 139

agriculture: agrarian reform, 29; California farmworkers, 59–83; child labour, 73–4, 120; dependence on labour, 52, 82–3; effect of NAFTA on, 31–4; in Mexico, 23–4, 28–9, 31–4; migration patterns, 72–8, 80; political economy of production, 17

American Recovery and Reinvestment Act of 2009, 40

anarcho-syndicalism, 56

Apodoca, Linda, 180

Argentina, 172

Arizona, 77, 163–4, 167

Artesi II labour camp, 66–7

Asian Americans, 10, 78. *See also* Chinese Americans; Filipino Americans; Japanese Americans

assimilation, 17, 144, 170

auto industry, 10

Ayala family, 68–70

Baltimore, Maryland, 118

Barrera, Mario, 175

Bay View massacre, 51

Bhabha, Homi, 143, 154

Bloods gang, 93

Borjas, George, 18

Bourdieu, Pierre, 142

boycotts, 53, 78. *See also* immigrant rights movement

Bracero Program: attempts to re-establish, 9; backlash against, 34; gender aspects, 25, 35; labour networks rooted in, 25–6, 63, 66–8, 176

California: colonisation, 148, 154; cuisine, 150–3; demographic shifts, 2–3, 62–3; Department of Housing and Community, 60–2, 198n3; effects of recessions on, 10; logistics industry, 165–6; migrant workers in, 59–83; Office of Migrant Services (OMS), 59–70, 73–5, 198n3. *See also* Los Angeles; San Francisco

California Council for Social Studies, 6

California Worker Cooperative Act (AB 816), 122–3

Callinicos, Alex, 3–4

Canada, 29, 70

capitalism: alternatives to, 120–7, 162, 210n10; commodity fetishism, 158; decentralisation, 117–19; deregulation, 117; early stages, 41–9; hegemony of, 43–9, 57, 115–16, 182, 188n25; and identity, 99–102, 175–6, 178–9; normalisation of, 51; privatisation, 117; second period of development, 49–55; and worker-owned cooperatives, 112–15; and the working class, 3–5, 13, 15, 44, 49,

Open Places Milwaukee (OPM)
 coalition, 130
Operation Gatekeeper, 29
Operation 'Wetback,' 52
Oregon, 77
Orozco family, 76–8
Ortega, Fabio Francisco, xiv
Osvaldo (bakery worker-owner),
 88–91, 94, 98–9, 106, 109–10, 120,
 124–7
Owen, Robert, 56

Palermo's Pizza, 141
Parlier, California, 59–83
Parsons, Lucy Gonzales, 173–4
PEMEX, 28, 34. *See also* Mexico (oil
 reserves)
Peña Nieto, Enrique, 34
Perez, Donato, 66–7
Perez, Emma, 180
Perez, Manuel, 66–7
Personal Responsibility and Work
 Opportunity Reconciliation Act of
 1996, 81
Polish Americans, 4
prisons. *See* incarceration
Puerto Ricans, 5, 16, 78, 150, 188n23
Pulido, Laura, 170–1

racial formation theory, 85–6
Racine, Wisconsin, 4
racism: alternatives to, 120–1; and
 capitalism, 99–102; in cooperative
 workplaces, 85–91, 102, 107; and
 election of Trump, 178–9;
 employment discrimination,
 133–4; and paternalism, 91–7;
 racial profiling, xii; scholarship on,
 85–6, 175, 185n2. *See also* African
 Americans; white supremacy
railroad industry, 17, 24, 26, 45
Raise the Minimum Wage campaign,
 141
Ranciere, Jacques, 123
Reagan, Ronald, 119
Reed, Adolph, 183

Republican Party, 5, 54, 163–4, 177–9
restaurant industry, 14, 142–55, 165.
 See also service industry
retirement, 176–7
Rivera, Ruben, 31–2
Robinson, William, 11
Rodriguez, Arturo, 63
Rodriguez, Javier, 167
Rosecrans, William S., 21, 23
Ruiz, Vicki, 175

Said, Edward, 22
Salazar, Yesenia and Mario, 80–1
Salvadoran Americans, 5
Samantha (bakery worker-owner),
 87–8, 94, 97–9
San Antonio, Texas, 51
San Francisco, 1, 84–107
Sanders, Bernie, 8–9
Sensenbrenner, Jim, xiii, 78–9. *See
 also* HR 4437: Border Protection,
 Anti-Terrorism, and Illegal
 Immigration Control Act
Serra, Jaime, 30
service industry, 10, 129–30, 132,
 142–57, 207n2
Shift Change (film), 102
Silver, Nate, 7
smelting industry, 17, 24
social capital theory of migration,
 18–19, 36
socialists, 8, 47, 53, 56, 172, 180
Soldatenko, Michael, 168
Southern Poverty Law Center, 9
Spanish-language media, 79, 149,
 166–7, 173
Spence, Thomas, 56
strikes, xii–xiv, 51, 53–4, 57, 166. *See
 also* Taft-Hartley (Labor-
 Management Relations Act);
 unions
subprime mortgage crisis, 38–9
symbolic production, 142–54, 206n1

Taft-Hartley (Labor-Management
 Relations Act), 52–4

The Pluto Press Newsletter

Hello friend of Pluto!

Want to stay on top of the best radical books we publish?

Then sign up to be the first to hear about our new books, as well as special events, podcasts and videos.

You'll also get 50% off your first order with us when you sign up.

Come and join us!

Go to bit.ly/PlutoNewsletter